BETWEEN FEMINISM AND ISLAM

Social Movements, Protest, and Contention

Series Editor   Bert Klandermans, Free University, Amsterdam

Associate Editors   Ron R. Aminzade, University of Minnesota
                     David S. Meyer, University of California, Irvine
                     Verta A. Taylor, University of California, Santa Barbara

(continued on page 197)

BETWEEN FEMINISM AND ISLAM

Human Rights and Sharia Law in Morocco

Zakia Salime

Social Movements, Protest, and Contention
Volume 36

University of Minnesota Press
Minneapolis • London

Chapter 5 was previously published as "The 'War on Terrorism': Appropriation and Subversion by Moroccan Women," *Signs: Journal of Women in Culture and Society* 33, no. 1 (Autumn 2007): 1–24.

Published by the University of Minnesota Press
111 Third Avenue South, Suite 290
Minneapolis, MN 55401-2520
http://www.upress.umn.edu

Library of Congress Cataloging-in-Publication Data

Salime, Zakia.
Between feminism and Islam : human rights and Sharia law in Morocco / Zakia Salime.
p. cm. — (Social movements, protest, and contention ; 36)
Includes bibliographical references and index.
ISBN 978-0-8166-5133-7 (hc : alk. paper) —
ISBN 978-0-8166-5134-4 (pb : alk. paper)
1. Feminism—Morocco. 2. Muslim women—Political activity—Morocco.
3. Women in Islam—Morocco. 4. Human rights—Morocco. I. Title.
HQ1236.5.M8S25 2011
305.420964—dc22
2011003817

Printed in the United States of America on acid-free paper

The University of Minnesota is an equal-opportunity educator and employer.

17 16 15 14 13 12 11   10 9 8 7 6 5 4 3 2 1

To the people who are remaking the Middle East

and

to my mother, father, and Yasmine

Contents

Acknowledgments

This book owes a great deal to the support and commitment of many women. I am grateful to Nadia Yassin, Mona Khalifi, Leila Rhiwi, Khadija Mufid, Bouchra Abdou, Ghizlane el Bahraoui, Naima Benyaich, Oufae Benabdelkader, Najia Zirari, Najat Razi, Rabea Naciri, Rachida Tahiri, Halima Banaoui, Soumaya Benkhaldoun, Saadia Wadah, Khadija Rougani, Fatema Bouslama, Khadija Zaki, Fatouma Benabdenbi, Sabah Shraibi, Samira El-Adnani, Fatema Mghanaoui, Souad Al-Amari, and many others, who tolerated my intrusive questioning, hosted me in their homes, and introduced me to others.

I am most grateful to my mentors and friends Manisha Desai and Michael Goldman for providing intellectual leadership and professional support during the research and writing of this book. My most sincere gratitude goes to Fatema Mernissi, Rachel Schurman, Paul Zeleza, Assata Zerai, Jan Nederveen Pieterse, Winnifred Rebecca Poster, and Rebecca Saunders for providing various kinds of support to this research. I am thankful to Suad Joseph for reading the earlier drafts of this book, and to Sean Brotherton and Xuefei Ren for their significant feedback as I was crafting the first chapters. Ronald Aminzade and Shana Cohen's productive and positive critiques put the manuscript on the path for publication. My colleagues and friends Arlene Stein and Judith Gerson were a major source of support as I was going through the final stages of this book. My graduate students at Michigan State University and at Rutgers University inspired this book in too many ways, as did my research assistants Lori Barat and Megan Kennedy. I thank the editorial team of the University of Minnesota Press, notably Jason Weidemann, for supervising its publication.

The research for this book was supported by numerous fellowships and awards from the University of Illinois at Urbana–Champaign, notably the 2004–2005 Rita and Arnold Goodman Fellowship, the 2000 Kathleen Cloud International Research Fund, a 2004 Dissertation Completion Fellowship, and a 2002 Dissertation Travel Grant. Complementary research was provided by a 2007 Intramural Research Grant Proposal from Michigan State University. I am grateful to the Women and Gender in Global Perspectives Program at UIUC for fully supporting the research and the writing of this book. Many papers emerged from this project and were presented at conferences thanks to the support of the Social Science Research Center, the Women's Studies and African Studies programs at the UIUC, and the African Studies program at Michigan State University.

The intellectual journey of writing this book has been profoundly marked by the struggle for gender equality in Morocco. To all the women and men who committed themselves to this goal, I dedicate this book. My personal involvement in this movement increased my awareness of how much of my own upbringing put me on this path. I had seen my mother, Fatema, open books she could not read and scan all the pages as she simulated reading. My father, Abderrahman, a self-educated craftsman and nationalist resistant, believed that education is the most important asset for a woman. For both, I keep the deepest gratitude, love, and respect. Finally, my sisters, Hasna, Hassania, Saida, Leila, and Fatema Zohra, deserve the deepest expression of gratitude for always being there.

Introduction

Struggles over Political Power: Entangled Feminist and Islamist Movements

"The feminist movement is the locomotive; if it breaks down, it will take with it all democratic forces in this country." With these words, Samira explained why she had traveled all the way north from the southern city of Marrakech to join the feminist rally in Rabat in March 2000. The trains were packed, she added. The socialist mayor of Fez, another major city, offered six buses to shuttle in participants. Upon the buses, men and women were writing slogans: "Yes for the New Morocco, No to Reactionaries." A man in his sixties was on one of these buses. His daughter, trapped in a bad marriage, had been trying unsuccessfully to obtain a divorce. "Her husband has the last word," he said angrily. Once in Rabat, participants rushed to their meeting points with friends and relatives. People were coming from everywhere. They gathered first in the neighborhood of the major labor unions before starting to march under the slogan "We share the earth, let's share its resources," attracting more of the people gathered on both sides of the street. Others applauded from balconies.

In this celebratory atmosphere, feminist groups and their supporters marched in Rabat to request the implementation of a governmental project to reform the sharia-based family law, *mudawwana*. This is the code regulating men's and women's relationship within the family, giving men the upper hand in marriage, divorce, and child custody, among other matters, and justifying these inequalities through highly patriarchal interpretations of the Islamic sharia, or legal code (see Moulay R'chid 1991). Since the early 1980s, demands for reforming this code have become the benchmark of the feminist movement, represented by hundreds of women's rights organizations and research advocacy centers. The dream of feminist reform only materialized in 1999, when the government proposed the National Plan of Action for Integrating Women into Development (NPA), promising to remove the conditions of gender inequalities from family law. The NPA was the outcome of yearlong teamwork between feminist groups and the newly elected socialist government. It drew heavily upon the United Nations' conventions on women's rights, notably the Convention on the Elimination of All Forms of Discrimination against Women (CEDAW), and the Beijing Platform for Action (1995), all the while ignoring the Islamic sharia as a source of inspiration. Not surprisingly, the project met with virulent opposition by Islamists and conservatives, polarizing Moroccan society and the women's movement alike, with "secular" feminists supporting the reform and "pro-sharia" Islamists opposing it, driving all of these forces to street demonstrations on March 12, 2000.

In Rabat, women and men of all ages and social backgrounds marched together. Veiled and unveiled, in blue jeans and T-shirts, men and women rallied to support the governmental reform. Within the crowds were also representatives of international funding programs and international feminist groups, as well as several parliamentary deputies and members of the government. The number of participants was heavily disputed, with estimates ranging from four hundred thousand, a *New York Times* estimate, to half a million, as the organizers and their supporting press claimed.[1] The event was organized by a network of sixty women's rights organizations and women's sections of political parties and labor unions, all present at the march.

The rally was only one aspect of the feminist mobilization. For a few days, the capital city of Rabat lived under the rhythm of women's voices through meetings, conferences, and artistic events. The purpose of these events was to reflect the "discrepancies between women's subordination in the codification of family law, and their numerous contributions to the country," stated Fatima Maghnaoui, from the Union de l'Action Feminine (UAF; Union of Women's Action), a leading feminist organization. Her group was also the focal point in North Africa for the World Women's March of 2000, a transnational feminist mobilization, launched one year earlier by the Québec Women's Federation. The World Women's March was an expression of transnational solidarities among women to eradicate poverty and end violence in women's lives worldwide. This event gained more meaning for a domestic audience in the face of sustained opposition to the NPA by the Islamists. The latter were also marching.

Forty miles away from Rabat, in metropolitan Casablanca, Islamists and conservatives took to the streets in a powerful display of public dissent. Their rally was spectacular. It was composed of overwhelming numbers of veiled women, most wearing the Moroccan djellaba—a long, loose women's dress—in what seemed to be a statement of national identity. Qur'an in one hand, women alternated religious citations from the Qur'an and *hadīth* (prophet's sayings) with political slogans: "Men and women are equal before God," and "No to the international conventions on women's rights." They came from all over Morocco to take part in what the Islamist press called "the march of the twentieth century," claiming that one million people marched that day in Casablanca.

Unlike the feminist rally, the gendered division of space was strict. Men and women marched in separate columns, while some of the men held hands to form lines that circled their columns, separating them from women and the cheering public. The atmosphere was described as militaristic by many commentators and feminist leaders (see A. Freeman 2004), due to the strict division of geographical space and the rigorous discipline displayed by the marchers. Here too, prominent figures in the government and the Parliament marched to mark another split among decision makers. The 'ulama (religious orthodoxy) and religious professional associations came out as a unified front, delegitimizing the NPA and providing the march with significant symbolic capital.

Women's mobilization for the Islamist rally was organized by large networks of women active within the two major Islamist organizations: Jamā'at al-'adl wa-l-ihsāne (Justice and Spirituality) and Harakat al-tawhīd wa-l-islāh (Movement of Unification and Reform).[2] The Casablanca Islamist rally took women to the forefront of the forces opposing the project of reform, providing it with significant social capital as well, due to the abilities of its leaders to organize thousands of women from different social and economic backgrounds. After the march, the Islamist press declared the NPA dead and the government declared it withdrawn, but only to launch a new "cycle" (Tarrow 1989) of feminist mobilization to keep alive the debate on the secularization of family law.

Following the rallies, intense controversies swept the entire political spectrum and social body over the massive mobilization of women for the Islamist march. The spectacle of veiled women filling the streets of a major Moroccan city was followed by international media outlets and debated by a transnational Arabic public on al-Jazeera talk shows.[3] The struggle over women's rights in Morocco became the site for "feminist reverberations" (Scott 2002) and debates by activists, religious authorities, and decision makers across the region. It also became the platform for discussing the limits of the democratization projects launched in North Africa and the Middle East since the middle of the 1980s (see Brand 1998; Waltz 1995).

It is worth noting, however, that some of the polemics launched by the women's rallies were not entirely new. They were reminiscent of old nationalist struggles, which took women as symbols of both cultural authenticity and the project of postcolonial capitalist modernity. Thus, the 2000 rallies testified to how the meanings of "citizenship" and "national identity" in postcolonial Morocco have been produced, contested, and negotiated during moments of amplified interactions among the feminist and the Islamist women's movements.

While public opinion was sharply divided about the issues at stake, scholars questioned the ability of the feminist movement to translate its claims into so-called common sense, and to counter the hegemony of the Islamist discourse of identity (Alami 2002; Zeghal 2005). To them, the upsurge of women's voices in the Islamist press, the scope of international media coverage of their march, and the withdrawal of the NPA all denoted the ability of these activists to shape together the state's "gender policy" (Charrad 1997) and the public debate on feminism and women's rights. It would seem that this mobilization was animated exclusively by Islamist women's opposition to feminism and to women's rights. To most analysts, the story of these two women's movements, Islamist and feminist, starts and ends around their polarization.

This study complicates this story. It began with my own involvement in the feminist movement during the 1990s and my interest to write a book on Moroccan feminism, noticing the scarcity of studies on this movement in the United States despite its deep impact on feminism in North Africa and the Middle East, and the major breakthroughs it had made at the level of the state gender policy. I wanted to explore what went "wrong" in feminist organizing that enabled the government to withdraw the NPA.

But answering this question, I came to realize, entailed revisiting not only feminist groups' relationship with the state, but also the trajectory of feminism in light of the growing impact of Islamist women's activism on public representations of feminism and alternative definitions of women's rights. Thus, to explore feminist politics requires, on the one hand, an examination of how the feminist movement has been both enabled and circumscribed by Islamist women's activism over the past two decades. On the other hand, it entails the identification of the various ways in which the feminist movement has shaped the politics of protest among Islamist women.

Focusing on these movements' polarization, characteristic of most analyses of the event, is disabling, I argue, as a place to understand the "interdependent" trajectories (see Abbott 2001; Aminzade 1992; Pierson 2004) of these movements, and two decades of interactions among them. Studying these movements relationally rather than comparatively, or as isolated case studies, is the main contribution of this ethnography. Through participant observation, in-depth interviews, archival research, and discourse analysis, the unfolding chapters of this study explore how these interactions have also shaped the public debate on women's rights, affected state gender policies, and transformed the movements themselves. I describe these changes in terms of *feminization* of Islamist women and *Islamization* of the feminist movement.

Polarized Movements?

The social movement literature has looked at forms of collective mobilization against feminist activism, in Western contexts, in terms of movements and countermovements, and feminist and antifeminist struggles (Chafetz and Dworkin 1987; Gale 1986; Klatch 1987, 1999; Lo 1982; Mottl 1980). These binaries are reproduced through the semiotic categories of feminism and "fundamentalism," a lens used to understand women's mobilization at the encounter of feminism and political Islam in the Middle East (Badran 1994; Deeb 2006; El-Guindi 1999; Moallem 2005; Moghissi 1999). Arguably, the rallies of 2000 are the best place to illustrate the women's split along secular and religious lines.

On the one hand, we have women's rights groups who mobilize the United Nations' regime of rights and the liberal discourse of equality and individual rights to request the secularization of the *mudawwana*.[4] Empowered by the United Nations' Decade for Women (1976–85) and sponsored through transnational funds, these groups perceived the legal system as an engine of social change and therefore targeted the *mudawwana* as a means to remove the conditions of gender inequalities from this state-controlled and religious-based codification of women's rights. In 1992 these groups started their collective mobilization against the sharia-based family law by launching a mass petition campaign, collecting one million signatures against the *mudawwana*. Most leaders of this campaign had been active in leftist political parties and unions since the 1970s before forming their independent organizations in the early 1980s.

Feminist groups did not operate in vacuum, however. During the 1980s, another mass movement was on the rise. It was composed of women working within the agenda of political Islam (or Islamism). To these groups, the Islamic sharia—the body of interpretations of the Qur'an and the sunna (prophet teaching) by Muslim scholars—provides codes of ethical conduct for both individuals and the state and therefore stands as the uniquely legitimate place to rethink social change. Like their male counterparts, Islamist women have been involved in the project of Islamization of everyday life, or that of "the sociocultural landscape" (Mahmood 2005, 3) as a path for Islamizing the state. This entails the reinscription of individual and social practices within the interpretive framework of the sharia, and public expressions of piety in which the veil remains a potent symbol.

Islamist women's "collective identities" (Melucci 1995) have been shaped by a movement of interpretation of the sharia that was taking place in informal women's circles. This movement competed with feminist formal groups and countered their reliance on foreign funds and North–South alliances with locally funded activities and alternative discourse of rights and transnational solidarities. Family law is central to this Islamization project. It is the only state code that claims adherence to the Islamic sharia, and thus preserving it became a major goal of Islamist organizing since the feminist mass petition campaign in 1992.

To the feminist rhetoric of women's rights as universal, Islamist women propose their "Islamic alternatives" articulated in a nationalist discourse of state sovereignty and Islamic identity. This discourse resonated beyond proper Islamist circles as images of the first Gulf War, the Palestinian intifadah, and the anti-Soviet war in Afghanistan grew intertwined with International Monetary Fund and World Bank policies of economic restructuring and their impact on education, health, and employment for thousands of young men and women during the 1980s and 1990s. This constituency formed the backdrop of the Islamist mobilization during the controversy over the NPA.

Unlike feminist groups who targeted the legal system, Islamist women's activism is informed by a Gramscian understanding of culture as the field of struggle. Thus, instead of focusing on the state, these activists have sought to reverse what they call "a culture of denigration of women" through educating the masses in the "true ethics" of Islam. Nevertheless, their marginalization of questions of gender inequalities and their mobilization to preserve the "sacred" foundations of the *mudawwana* set them apart from feminist groups.

Despite these seemingly divergent trajectories and contradictory societal projects, the rallies of 2000 highlighted the web of exchanges among these movements. As we will see, these exchanges take on fuller meaning when linked to particular time-events, such as the feminist petition campaign of 1992, the Islamist rally of 2000, and the Casablanca attack by a group of radical Islamists in 2003. This attack legitimized the Moroccan state's contribution to the controversial war on terror and pushed both movements to reposition their discourse and activism in this new international conjuncture. It is also the purpose of this study to show how these conjunctures have been shaped and redefined by interacting feminist and Islamist movements.

To depict significant time-events as starting points of my analysis is also to determine a lens through which the intersections between feminism and Islamism become more accessible to sociological inquiry. I illustrate these intersections with the concept of *movement moment*. This concept enables me to link women's mobilization (movement) to the historical conjunctures (moment) in which this mobilization is taking place. A movement moment first refers to the disruptive effect of this mobilization, paving the way to analyses of the tensions, contradictions, and negotiations that take place among various players. Hence, if the interactions among competing movements have been described along an action/reaction continuum, a movement moment better describes the disruption of this continuum, reversing its most likely outcomes.

Second, to organize this study around movement moments means placing women's mobilization at the heart of sociological analyses of historical contingencies. The movement moment denotes, therefore, a nonlinear mode of thinking about the interactions among social movements. The proceeding chapters of this study illustrate this argument.

Movement Moment

When I asked Nadia Yassine, spokesperson for al-'Adl wa-l-ihsāne and president of its Women's Section, if she was against women's rights, her answer pointed in a completely different direction. She suggested that I should rather question the conjuncture, moment, or combination of critical events in which this rally took place and their contradictory meanings for women's movements. Yassine called the Casablanca rally "a show of force" denying that her participation had something to do with opposing women's rights. It is worth noting that Nadia Yassine played a prominent role in the Islamist rally and was perceived by feminist groups and their supporting press as one of the main opponents of feminism in Morocco. Describing the rally, Nadia Yassine gave a different account. To her, the Islamist march was meant to "show that the true mobilization power of the country is that of the Islamists." Adding to my confusion, Yassine pointed to the contradictions of that moment, when she said that she "walked in Casablanca with her heart turned to the women marching in Rabat."

Why should the Islamist march be a show of force? What did this mobilization say about the contradictory nature of this conjuncture? The Islamist mobilization against the NPA started a year earlier, as soon as the prime minister, Abderahman al-Youssoufi, unveiled his strategy for promoting women's rights. Al-Youssoufi is a socialist and former political dissident. His government illustrated the state's desire to enter a new phase of liberalization (see

Brand 1998) known as political alternance. This alternance is shaped by new political arrangements initiated with the first ever transparent election in the postindependent Morocco, which took place in 1997 (Daoud and Ouchleh 1997), bringing the former opposition into the government and one Islamist party to the Parliament, al-'Adāla wa-l-tanmia.

These new arrangements brought big anxieties but also great hopes for feminist groups. At the end of the twentieth century, as the state started embracing the goals of "democratization" and free market economy, the feminist discourse of equality and full citizenship for women started making more sense to its bureaucrats (see Eisenstein 2005). As its name indicates, the NPA narrated these ambitions of the state in a development discourse and a liberal feminist rhetoric, Women in Development (WID), acknowledging the importance of gender to this conjuncture, and ignoring the Islamists' reservations. Not only its name, but also the way the NPA was unveiled by the prime minister—from a five-star hotel and before a selected audience of international media, feminist groups and human rights activists on International Women's Day—were indicators of the importance of feminism and gender to the state's economic and political liberalization.

As foreign investors kept a vigilant eye on Morocco's reforms, and the Moroccan government an envious eye on feminist groups' ability to attract funds and enhance the image of the country in international forums, the Women in Development discourse and the United Nations' regime of rights became intertwined. It was in this context that feminist groups managed to infiltrate state institutions and work out the reform of the *mudawwana* from within these institutions.[5] The NPA was the outcome of this effort. However, the access of the Islamists to the Parliament brought major anxieties to these groups, increasing their fear of seeing such forces undermine their process.

To the Islamists, the NPA was simply a nightmare. Not only did it testify to speedy secularization of the state under a feminist-friendly government, but it also illustrated the growing legitimacy of liberal feminism in the context of neoliberal transitions (see Eisenstein 2005). More disturbing was the range of international players involved in the NPA. This was indeed the first time that both domestic and global players had openly collaborated in the reform of a sharia-based code. Feminist groups worked with state bureaucrats who commissioned them and gained support from a wide range of international players, notably the United Nations' programs, the European Union and the very controversial World Bank. All seemingly offensive factors combined; the project was hard to sell to the Islamists and conservatives, who viewed it as symptomatic of foreign interventions in the country and dubbed it an illegitimate product of secular and Western(ized) feminists. How do women negotiate rights through specific forms of mobilization within these conflicting agendas? What kind of disruptive effect does women's mobilization have on these conjunctures?

To answer these questions I organize this study around the three movement moments noted before: the first is the feminist petition campaign of 1992; the second is the Islamist rally of 2000; and the third is the attack in Casablanca by a group of young Islamist radicals in 2003. Each of these moments is grounded in global power arrangements and defined through the lens of women's mobilization. These movement moments show how women's movements exist at the intersection of domestic and global regulatory regimes, and how the latter are mediated through women's agency and movements.

As we will see, these movement moments also constitute "turning points" in the trajectory of the Islamist and feminist movements. Turning points involve, Abbott contends, "the separation of relatively smooth and directional tracks by relatively abrupt and diversionary moments" (Abbott 2001, 247). Nevertheless, my concept of movement moment stresses not only a chronological separation of prevailing "tracks" but also the subversion of these "tracks."

My definition of movement moments is informed by two bodies of literature: historical sociology analyses of trajectories and turning points, and Gramscian definitions of conjunctures (Grossberg 2006; Hall 1996). Both literatures are interrelated. The conjuncture denotes the "intersection of contradictory trajectories" (Pierson 2004, 55) that constitute the historical, cultural, and political moment of a given event (Grossberg 2006). It has been also argued that while the notion of trajectory implies "a certain directionality to change" (Aminzade 1992, 459), the conjuncture is more open to the idea of contingency and therefore to different and contradictory results (see Goldman 2005). Thinking in terms of conjunctures enables us to complicate the narrative of social movements as responding to a predetermined structure of opportunities and constraints, located outside of the movements themselves (McAdam 1982; Meyer and Staggenborg 1996).

Interdependent Trajectories

The concept of interaction is becoming central to most definitions of social movements. The latter are viewed as collective challenges to existing power arrangements by activists with shared goals and collective identities in interaction with opponents and competitors (Meyer and Tarrow 1998). In this literature, the interactions are defined as "interplay of contending movements" (Meyer and Staggenborg 1995, 1633), "oppositional consciousness" (Morris, quoted in Feree and Roth 1998, 627), and action/reaction, all referring to the ways in which movements and countermovements influence each other while affecting the "political process" (Andrews 2002; Fetner 2008; Marshall and Orum 1986; McAdam 1982; McCarthy and Zald 1977; Meyer and Staggenborg 1996). The conceptual framework provided by social movement literature paved the way for the study of social movements comparatively and in various contexts with more focus on questions of "boundaries" (Ferree and Roth 1998), collective identities (Melucci 1995), and framing (Ferree and Merrill 2000; Gamson 1992; Klandermans 1992; Snow and Benford 1992). My study of the interactions among the feminist and the Islamist women's movement is inspired by this literature. As we will see, I do not define these interactions in terms of reaction and influence, but rather in terms of interdependencies and intersections.

By interdependencies, I refer to the entanglement of the feminist and the Islamist women's movements and the ways they have constituted each other's discourses, politics, and forms of organization. As a matter of fact, these movements' interactions did not begin with the controversy of March 2000, but two decades earlier with women's writings in the respective feminist and Islamist press. As chapter 2 will illustrate, women's writings had developed on two different paths during the 1980s, but started to merge around similar concerns about gender inequalities and equal opportunities for women in the Islamist movements.

Despite their different trajectories, these writings expressed similar aspirations among a growing population of young professional women from the urban and middle classes to define women as agents in projects of social change. It is the purpose of this study to show how the changes that have occurred in these movements' politics of women's rights only take full meaning if one considers the entanglement among their politics of protest. In order to illustrate this point, I will briefly discuss the impact of the feminist One Million Signature Campaign of March 1992 and the Islamist rally of 2000.

The One Million Signature Campaign was the first mass mobilization of feminist groups against the *mudawwana*. The goal was to collect one million signatures to push the state to reform this code and ratify CEDAW. As we will see, the petition campaign was a critical event in a conjuncture of constitutional reforms, structural changes, and a global mobilization toward the upcoming Beijing Conference of 1995. This campaign is still the entry point for analyses of the emergence of liberal feminism in the North African context, because of the transnational dynamics it instigated (see Daoud 1993; A. Freeman 2004). In fact, the campaign had a far-reaching impact even beyond the sphere of North African politics, and it continues to inspire feminist activism in the entire Islamic world.[6]

Contrary to most approaches to understanding this mobilization, I consider the One Million Signature Campaign as the moment of birth for *both* the feminist and the Islamist women's movements in Morocco. I use the petition campaign as a movement moment to identify its impact not only on Moroccan feminism, but also on Islamist women's agency as a force of change within political Islam. I argue that these changes take on full meanings only in the perspective of an articulation of a feminist discourse by Islamist women. As we will see, this campaign was instrumental in propelling Islamist women to reposition themselves within global feminism, and to dispute the legitimacy of feminist groups to speak on behalf of "Moroccan women."

In addition, as Islamist women were confronting the feminist arguments against the *mudawwana* with "Islamic alternatives," they engaged in public interpretations of the sharia, transforming the Islamist male-owned press into a podium for debates about the validity of the United Nations' regime of rights in comparison to these Islamic alternatives. This debate was not limited to questions of reforming family law, but encompassed questions of "cultural imperialism," neocolonialism, and antiglobalization claims. The "woman's-gaze" is the expression used by these activists to describe how women's particular positionality and standpoint changes the "malestream" (Zeleza 1997) interpretations of the sharia, was a powerful contribution by Islamist women to feminist methodology.

Two magazines played an instrumental role in this phase: *Al Forkāne,* an Islamist magazine launched in 1984, and *Thamānia Mars,* a feminist magazine created in 1983. Both became platforms for these emerging and interacting women's voices. As I was following the path of Islamist women's writings from the early 1980s in *Al Forkāne,* I could see how these activists had slowly begun to address critical issues, such as gender hierarchies in the Islamist movements, and to gradually incorporate a discourse of women's rights, notably after the feminist petition campaign. I term this process of change the feminization of the Islamist movements. This refers to the shifts that took place in Islamist women's discourse and activism in contact with the feminist movement, which brings me to my second point.

The perceived success of the feminist movement in affecting the state's gender policy after the petition campaign—the state's ratification of the CEDAW—propelled Islamist women to reflect on their "marginalization" in the Islamist movements and to position themselves as *women* with rights, rather than simply *members* of male-dominated organizations. Zoubida Oum Yassir, an activist in the organization al-Islāh wa-l-tajdīd (Movement for

Reform and Renewal) wrote in *Al Forkāne* to protest against the marginalization of women and its impact on political Islam. She contended: "It was the
marginalization of women by the Islamist movement, and the lack of Islamic
alternatives, that enabled feminist groups to take the lead of the women's
movement" (Oum Yassir 1992, 51).

Islamist women's demands for leadership positions translated into the
creation of the first "independent" women's rights organizations, working
within the framework of Islam first before incorporating the international UN
platform. This type of activism regained tremendous legitimacy in the post-
9/11 era, as the Moroccan state was eager to identify "moderate" voices from
within political Islam, notably in the aftermath of the Casablanca attack of
May 2003. In chapter 4 I discuss the importance of the rhetoric of fighting
terrorism on the respective agendas of the feminist and the Islamist women's
movements, as well as the losses and gains these movements have experienced
by mobilizing this discursive regime.

When I discussed the results of my study with leaders of feminist organizations as I was writing this introduction, they expressed doubts about my
understanding of Islamist women's agency. To them, Islamist women's activism
is not shaped by any genuine concern about women's rights, but only reflects
the way in which the Islamist movements instrumentalize their female leadership, notably in times of crisis. To them, Islamist women are mere followers of male politics. These arguments may reflect some of the struggles that
Islamist women have faced with the most radical forces within the Islamist
movements, preventing them from having a significant voice. However, they
do not account for the dynamics of change in these movements; nor do they
explain how Islamist women have managed to occupy influential positions
in the highest religious and political institutions of the state, namely the con-
gregations of the 'ulama—previously an exclusively male territory—and the
right to preach in state-controlled mosques, or to represent the Islamist party
in the Parliament.

Some of these gains were certainly made possible by the imperatives of
the "war on terror," to which I will return later, and the way Islamist women
used the Casablanca human-bombing attacks of May 2003 to make a strong
case about their inclusion as main players in the state's cultural and religious
reforms. Hence, subsuming Islamist women under the banner of "religious
fundamentalism" (Alami 2002; Zeghal 2005), or ignoring them altogether
(Brand 1998; Darif 1999; Tozy 1999), means overlooking the internal gender
dynamics in the Islamist movements on the one hand, and the importance
of feminism as a discourse in these changes on the other. This brings me to
my last point.

To explore the interdependent trajectories of these movements entails investigating how feminist activism has also been transformed in contact with the Islamist discourse of identity and grassroots politics. Bouchra Abdou, an activist in the Ligue démocratique des droits des femmes (LDDF; Democratic League for Women's Rights), called the changes that occurred in the feminist movement "crucial to its survival," notably after the Islamist March of 2000. She described the "revisions" that feminist groups needed to make to their "elitist and legalistic" approach of social change—as law reform—to "a politics of the street" in order to gain popular support for their project.

I analyze these changes in chapter 3 and also discuss the type of "cultural translations" (Bhabha 1994) that feminist groups engaged in to remove the *mudawwana* from the realm of the divine and the untouchable to the contingent realm of history and human interpretation. Islamist women's alternative discourse of rights and their grassroots politics have been instrumental in disrupting the regimes of truths informing liberal feminism and the "modalities of agency" (Mahmood 2005, 153) deployed by feminist groups in their struggle to reform the *mudawwana*. I term this impact the Islamization of the feminist movement. This refers to the changes that have occurred in feminist discourse, agendas, and practice in contact with Islamist women's activism, notably in the aftermath of the Islamist March of 2000. As this study will further explore, it is at the intersections of Islam, feminism, and global regulatory regimes that both movements have been formed and transformed.

Unsettling the Categories

The terms "feminism" and "Islamism" have genealogies rooted in colonial representations of Islam, postcolonial identifications with modernity, and the politics of identity in the Middle East and North Africa. Gender is at the center of these representations. The question of women's oppression in Islam was not only crucial to legitimizing the colonial enterprise (Ahmed 1992; El Guindi 1999; Said 1978) but also the nationalist resistance, couching modernization and developmental projects in women's emancipation, their participation in public life, and more importantly, their unveiling (al-Fassi 1979; Q. Amin 1992; El Haddad 1930).

The past decade also saw the proliferation of studies on the Middle East that questioned the orientalist representations of a monolithic, ahistorical Islam and a normative Western modernity (Abu-Lughod 1998; El Guindi 1999; Karam 1998; Moallem 2005; Treacher and Shukrallah 2001). This literature has instead shifted the lens of inquiry to the encounters of Islam and modernity at the colonial and postcolonial (dis)junctures. Since the field of sociology of religion is now considering modernity as the framework for explaining the resurgence of religion "as a public force" (Hefner 1998, 98), the entanglement of the Islamist movements and secular modernity came under a new light (Al-Azmeh 1996; Asad 2003; Emerson and Hartman 2006; Hefner 1998).

The other major contribution to the modernity debate comes from feminist scholarship on the Middle East, notably postcolonial and postmodern critics of the secularist, developmentalist, and liberal trends of Western feminism (Abu-Lughod 1998; Cooke 2000; Lazreg 1986, 2002; Mahmood 2005; Sabbagh 1996; Tucker 1993). This scholarship shifts the lens to gender in order to examine women's discursively based and politically grounded articulations of "modernness" (Deeb 2006), feminism(s) (Karam 1998), agency (Kandiyoti 1998; Mahmood 2005), and rights. By doing so, this scholarship has demonstrated that feminism is neither alien to the region nor foreign to Islam (Afshar 1999; Badran 1995; Mir-Hosseini 1999; Moghadam 2002; Tohidi 1991; Yamani 1996).

In order to account for articulations of gender, feminism, and Islam, this scholarship has designated intermediary locations for women, such as "Islamic feminism" (Moghadam 2002; Moghissi 1999), "Islamist feminism," and "Muslim feminism" alongside "secular feminism" (al-Ali 2000; Badran 1994; El Guindi 1996; Hale 1997; Karam 1998). These categories challenge entrenched representations of feminism and Islam(ism) in both Western media and scholarship as incommensurate, enabling us to see feminism as valid within Islam. More important to the purpose of my study, these new labels permit the exploration of the areas *in between* feminism as a discourse and practice targeting the multiple faces of patriarchal oppression, and of Islamism as a discursive site enabling the woman's gaze on the sharia (see Lamrabet 2002; Nassef 1999; Wadud 1999; Yamani 1996; N. Yassine 2003).

I would like to make two points: first, Islamic feminism, a very popular concept in recent literature about the women's movement in the Middle East, is often used as a descriptive category to define women working to improve women's rights within the Islamic framework. What this literature lacks are accounts that contextualize the emergence of Islamic feminism in various parts of the Middle East, as part of a process of exchange, not uniquely of opposition, between Islamist women's groups and feminist movements.

Many scholars living in the West got hold of the idea of Islamic feminism as a means to challenge the discourse about the incommensurability of Islam and feminism. In the aftermath of 9/11, this debate becomes even more relevant. However, this label is still the object of contention among feminist scholars and activists living in the Middle East (see Abou-Bakr 2001). Thus, while most of my feminist respondents endorse the term after redefining its meanings to better fit their spectrum of voices, Islamist activists reject the label altogether and refer to themselves as Islamist women, as a territorial identification. Their rejection of feminism stems from their understanding of feminist politics as secular and Western in origin, and therefore hostile to Islam.

The aim of this study is not to dispute the validity of these identifications and categorizations. Instead, its goal is to show how the boundaries of feminism and Islamism have been pushed and redefined as women negotiate the spheres and scopes of their rights. This enables us to see these boundaries as fluid and flexible, rather than fixed and stable. The focus on significant moments of mobilization by these two movements permits us to see this process of negotiations as it has been taking place at the borderlines (Anzaldua 1987) of feminism and Islamism.

Locations

As I stated earlier, the impetus for this book started with my own involvement in feminist movements during the 1990s. I had just started my PhD program in 1999 when the Islamists marched against a reform that I was personally involved in promoting. It was out of disenchantment that I decided to enlarge my ethnographic gaze to Islamist women, while positioning myself as an outsider trying to make sense of the scene. Looking at these two movements through the semiotic binaries of modern/antimodern and feminist/antifeminist was the very starting point in the journey of this book, and the first methodological and epistemological limitation my study had to overcome. As I began immersing myself in Islamist women's groups during different periods from 2000 to 2004, it became obvious to me that these binaries were too reductive, eluding complex connections, interactions, and exchanges among movements.

While I was trying to make sense of these connections, I ended up in a different location as a researcher and with a different political project as an activist. As a researcher, I had to shift the scope of my inquiry from a widely shared understanding of Islamist and feminist movements as antagonistic and separate to an analysis of their interpenetrations and changes. Departing from binary approaches, feminist versus Islamist—that is, antifeminist— also requires a methodological shift: to explore the arenas in between the politics of feminism and the politics of Islamism.

As some have already argued, feminist scholarship is definitely political (Alexander and Mohanty 1997; hooks 2003; McRobbie 2004; Mohanty 2003). My political project is enmeshed in this methodological shift. On a more personal note, questioning boundaries poses questions about my own positionality, that is, my choices as a woman whose political awareness has grown within the highly politicized Moroccan academy of the 1980s and a family background of nationalism. Both are complicated by my shift into the U.S. "corporate academy" (Mohanty 2003) in the late 1990s. Raised within the modernist ideals of nationalism, I came to view women as the mediators between the spheres of "tradition" and "modernity," and to see both of these spheres as constitutive of and constituted by Islam.

Thus, the story of this book is very much informed by my own intermediary location, my in-between "dis-locations" (see Moallem 2005), as well as my own transformation. Being part of what I used to call the Women's Movement, in the singular, I could not have been more disturbed during this research by the way my feminist community excluded Islamist women from meetings and activities and the realm of semiotic feminism. It was equally challenging for me to hear Islamist respondents depicting feminist activists as local instruments for imperialist penetrations in Morocco. Yet I could not agree more with their perceptions of neocolonial penetrations into the Middle East, and their imperative of building local alternatives, notably in light of an open-ended "war on terror" widely lived and perceived as a war on Muslims (see Akhter 2003). Thus, in this decisive "imperial moment" (Nederveen Pieterse 2002) of neoliberal wars in the region, in the name of fighting terrorism, the emergence of a new scholarship that would stress the intersections among women's different movements becomes crucial.

I was conscious that I was violating Durkheimian and Weberian rules of objectivity and value-free knowledge when I started inviting Islamist women to read the Moroccan feminist literature and get closer to feminist organizations. I also discussed with some feminist activists their exclusion of Islamist women from their meetings and events. Thus, from my initial position as an outsider in Islamist groups and an insider in feminist groups, I found myself trying to mediate between both leaderships and correct the way in which they perceived their opponents as the absolute Other. I came to admit that the paradigms of being an outsider, an insider, or an outsider-within limit the understanding of the complexity of relationships between the researcher and the "object" of research, and the way this relation is constitutive and transformative of both.

Faced with my respondents' doubts about my positionality in the U.S.-driven war on terror, I had to reflect on my own project, not only in light of power struggles among two local women's movements, but in the perspective of the place of Islam and feminism in a global struggle for self-determination and human rights. Thus, my study is equally animated by an activist concern about balkanization and divisions among women's groups which, as we will see, only benefit the disciplinary power of the monarchy, the forces of "neopatriarchy" (Sharabi 1988), and the naturalizing forces of the neoliberal/neo-orientalist and oil-driven "war on terror." It became very accurate then to explore the impact of these divisions on strengthening the disciplinary power of the state under the fight against terrorism. In the following chapters, I will show how women's divisions are mediated by these multiple forces.

Book Organization

In chapter 1, I identify the main players, including the 'ulama, the monarchy, the Islamists, political parties, and women's groups. I show the relevance of gender to their negotiations for access to a highly centralized political system. I define gender as a field in which tensions over political legitimacy rise and may unfold, and discuss the ways in which negotiations for access to political power had taken place in the gender field. These negotiations had relied on the manipulation of gender hierarchies and the inscription of these meanings in highly patriarchal codes, limiting the range of rights that women might enjoy in both the private and the public "spheres." I conclude this chapter with a discussion of women's location in the Islamist movements and focus on the case of the movement of al-Tawhīd wa-l-islāh and its related political party, al-'Adāla wa-l-tanmia (Justice and Development), and the movement of al-'Adl wa-l-ihsāne and its related Women's Section.

In chapter 2, I analyze the dynamics around the One Million Signature Campaign. I explore the impact of this campaign on the feminization of Islamist women. Far from being a localized event, the petition reflected broader structural changes and global regulatory forces. I depict three of these: the consequences of the economic restructuring decade (1983–94) on gender and the forms of mobilization by women; the pursuit of the negotiations around state liberalization; and the rise of Islamist radicalism as a new political force in neighboring Algeria. The feminist campaign was a critical factor in this conjuncture of domestic reforms, regional changes, and a global feminist mobilization toward the Beijing Conference of 1995. The contradictory nature of these changes shaped Moroccan feminism as a main instigator of the transnational feminist dynamic in North Africa.

The petition campaign had, in fact, a disruptive effect on the long process of negotiation that had been taking place among political players, and which had left women at the margin of debates about political change. This chapter shows how feminist groups had engendered this process through specific discourses and forms of mobilization. The second part of the chapter illustrates the feminization of Islamist women, in reference to three major changes: the endorsement of a discourse of women's rights and gender oppression by Islamist women; their repositioning in the women's movement; and their negotiations of leadership positions within the Islamist movements.

In chapter 3, I describe the dynamics of interactions around the Casablanca Islamist rally of 2000. I consider this rally as the second movement moment, because of the way it propelled feminist groups to rethink their activism in light of Islamist women's wide entry to the political field. In the year 2000, all signs pointed to the beginning of a feminist era in the Moroccan state. Many events seemed to indicate a full-fledged change in women's rights legislation in Morocco. These included shifts in political power, with access to the former socialist opposition to the government in 1997; the sudden death of King Hassan II in 1999 and the ascension to the throne of his son, King Mohamed VI, who in his first inaugural speech stated his commitment to women's rights; and the pursuit of economic liberalization, narrated in terms of democracy, citizenship, and free enterprise by the state-controlled media.

All these factors led to a consensus among leading political and economic forces to improve women's rights for both democratic and development purposes. The NPA was the most visible outcome of this consensus. However, the conjuncture of political liberalization also had contradictory effects. Principal among these, by all means, was the access of the first authorized Islamist party, al-'Adāla wa-l-tanmia, to Parliament in 1997, with fourteen seats. These were the same members who, a few years earlier, had opposed any debate on reforming the *mudawwana*.

The first part of this chapter describes the importance of the Islamist women's movement in this context. Women became a major force in the Islamist movements because of their grassroots politics and easy access to wide populations of women across social, cultural, and economic spectrums. I discuss this form of activism in the first part of the chapter, during my description of Islamist women's politics of space and their challenges to the private/public divide. The second part of the chapter describes the process of Islamization of the feminist movement. The 2000 Islamist rally formed a major turning point for this movement, because of the types of adjustments that feminist groups had to make to their discourse and politics of protest in order to keep the project of reform alive. I use *Islamization* in terms of an articulation of feminist and Islamist politics by feminist groups. This was mostly expressed through (1) a redefinition of the Islamic sharia to fit feminist demands; (2) an incorporation of the 'ulama in feminist activities as a means to legitimize feminist demands; (3) a return to political parties in order to create support within these male-dominated structures; and (4) a shift from exclusive targeting of the state to grassroots politics. This chapter illustrates my argument that these changes did not affect the identity of the feminist movement, which remained grounded in the United Nations' regime of rights, but were critical in validating this regime of truths through a feminist "progressive" reading of the Islamic sharia.

In chapter 4, I describe the contradictions related to the state's response to the Casablanca attack of May 2003. I use this attack as a movement moment to identify how both feminists and Islamists have shaped the conjuncture of the war on terror, all the while redefining their movement at the aftermath of the Casablanca attack. Everything since the Islamist Rally of 2000 had been pointing to the fact that feminist groups had lost their dream reform. However, the Casablanca attack undermined the legitimacy of political Islam in the official discourse and provided feminist groups with their missed opportunity to reposition themselves as the agents for the new era of fighting "terrorism" through "state feminism" (Hatem 1996). The Casablanca attack provided feminists with tremendous opportunities to assert their feminism in explicit and powerful ways, and to negotiate a privileged position as "representatives" of the forces of "modernity" and "democracy" in comparison to the "obscure" and "archaic" Islamist groups. Feminism became endowed with a normative value and was defined as a "fence" against Islamic radicalism.

Thus, the state's reform of the *mudawwana* came only a few months after the Casablanca attack, responding to the most radical feminist demands, putting the family under the equal authority of a man and a woman, prohibiting repudiation, abolishing from the law men's guardianship over women and the requirement of wifely obedience, among many other reforms. These positive changes notwithstanding, I show how the feminists' gains conflicted with major setbacks for human rights in the aftermath of the bombing attack, and how the monarchy used the reform of family law as a means to position itself within the U.S. discourse of democratization of the Middle East, without necessarily implementing profound changes to the structure of power still dominated by the king as a central player.

The second part of this chapter shifts the gaze to Islamist women's articulation of feminist politics in a highly hostile political environment. I show how these activists appropriated the discursive tropes of the war and redefined their meanings to occupy political positions. The discourse of "moderation," a key component in post-9/11 American discourse, was appropriated by these activists as a means to locate "motherhood" and "womanhood" at the center of the agenda of fighting terrorism.

I conclude this study by pointing to some arenas where the feminist and the Islamist women's movements are now overlapping. These overlaps are visible in the practice of veiling by women, independent of their political agenda and affiliations; in their representations of feminism; and in their approach to activism, in which "education" becomes a key component. My goal is to emphasize intersections while keeping notice of the way these two movements remain divided along ideological lines.

1

Gender and the Nation State: Family Law, Scholars, Activists, and Dissidents

On August 20, 1992, the Moroccan public was expecting to hear King Hassan's annual address to the nation. The women involved in signing the One Million Signature Campaign were particularly concerned with that year's address. They knew that the king would not keep silent after their mass mobilization, much less after the death penalty statement suggested in the Islamist press by one of the "independent" *'alim* (theologians). Both events, Moroccans knew, encroached on the authority of the king as Commander of the Faithful (Amir al-Mu'minin), with ultimate religious authority and the power to define the realm of the acceptable in political and religious matters (see Brand 1998; Waterbury 1970).

The scale of public controversy raised by the feminist mobilization disturbed the process of negotiations and consensus that King Hassan was attempting to reach with the opposition about reforming the constitution (see Brand 1998). In his speech, and for the first time since coming to power in 1963, King Hassan addressed the question of women's rights on national television, recognizing that the time had come to reverse the injustices cast upon women. At the same time, he reminded the nation that all questions related to the *mudawwana* belong to the realm of his personal authority, repositioning himself as the ultimate recourse of both Islamist "dissidents" and women's groups. I remember how frustrated I was to realize that perhaps women were being sent back to square one. That was, in fact, the case when King Hassan decided to return the question of the *mudawwana* not to women but to the 'ulama for reflection and suggestions. Why is the *mudawwana* so crucial to so many players? What does the question of reforming the *mudawwana* say about shifting political arrangements in Morocco? What does it say about the importance of gender in these arrangements?

These questions led me to rethink the meanings of gender, not only as "a system of unequal social relations between men and women and . . . ideologies to justify these relations" (Moghadam 2001, 129), but as *a field of struggle* and a *marker* of specific shifts in power arrangements. Bourdieu defines the field as a social arena within which struggles or maneuvers take place over specific resources or stakes and access to them. The political field is, therefore, "a structured system of social positions occupied by either individuals or institutions and a system of forces which exist between position, domination, subordination, or equivalence centered on the actors' logic, strategies, and practices" (Jenkins 1992, 84). Raka (1999) adds another dimension to the definition of political fields by viewing them as "dynamic outcomes of local and regional processes" that shape women's movements. I would like to shift the focus, however, from a definition of the political field per se, to the interaction of this field with gender. I expand Bourdieu's definition of the field—seen as economic, political, religious, and cultural—to gender, understood here as a "field" of struggles within which various elites' interests are confronted, negotiated, and unfolded.

In Morocco, struggles over political power have been played, disputed, and negotiated in the gender field. This also means that women's interactions are mediated by these struggles and grounded in the particular history of the nation-state formation. Following this line, I understand the *mudawwana* as an expression of power arrangements among various elites, including the monarchy, the 'ulama, the Islamists, and women's groups.

Since Morocco's independence in 1956, negotiations over political legitimacy have relied on the manipulation of gender meanings and the inscription of these meanings in codes and regulations about women's rights. It is no wonder that both the promulgation of the *mudawwana* in 1958 and its reform under the new name of the Code of the Family in 2003 followed two major events, respectively: the independence of Morocco and the Casablanca bombing attacks of 2003. In both cases, the state had to reaffirm its sovereignty by reforming the codes regulating women's rights. It is my purpose here to introduce the meanings attached to family law by multiple players, and to situate the debate about women's rights in its historical context.

Gender and the Nation State

The political system in Morocco is characterized by the centrality of the king and the importance of religious symbolism in legitimizing his authority. Morocco gained independence from French and Spanish colonizers in 1956.[1]

The Moroccan constitution, written in 1962, put the king at the pinnacle of political and religious power. The king is the first legislator, supreme political arbitrator, and Commander of the Faithful (see Laroui 1993; Maghraoui 2001; Waterbury 1970). The constitution recognizes political pluralism, with Islam as the state religion and Arabic as the national language, interdicting any assault on these symbols of national unity. The *makhzen* is the term used by Moroccans to define the type of political system that emerged over centuries of formation of the central power. The *makhzen* currently refers to the administrative structure, legal apparatuses, military personnel (see Brand 1998; Maghraoui 2001), and attendant patron–client relations.

The legitimacy of the king rests definitively on his ability to represent the religious sphere as the source of his authority. The *mudawwana* is central to this legitimization. It is the only state law that claims adherence to the sharia, and therefore falls directly under the authority of the Commander of the Faithful. This fact testifies to the kind of challenges facing feminist activism, which has targeted this law precisely and required its discussion within elected institutions, notably the Parliament.

To understand the importance of these challenges, let us remember that the *mudawwana* was also the place in which the monarchy inscribed the meanings of national identity and state sovereignty immediately after independence. First, the codification of family law by the newly independent state in 1957 affirmed the national unity of the Arabs and Amazigh (Berber) populations after the 1930 French "Berber Dahir," which had divided Morocco into two contrasting zones of legal authority: one for the Arabs under the sharia, and another for the Amazigh under '*urf* (custom). This attempt to divide Morocco on an ethnic basis helped, I argue, to inscribe the process of state formation within the contours of a unique source of identity, which is secured by the submission of all Moroccans to one god and one father-king.

Promulgating family law was the first statement of unity that the urban nationalist elites, in charge of codification, made immediately after the independence of Morocco. This law, known also as the Code of Personal Status, *mudawwana*, was grounded in a conservative interpretation of the *māliki fiqh*—the school of interpretation of the sharia followed in Morocco—giving men the upper hand in questions of marriage, divorce, and child custody while subjecting women to men's guardianship and permissions throughout their lives (see al-Ahnaf 1994; Moulay R'chid 1991).[2] As a means to understanding the complexity of this moment, Charrad (2001) links the highly patriarchal family law to the importance of tribal and ethnic alliances at work during the formation of the nation-state in Morocco. She argues that the

French did not affect preexisting kinship relations but used and reinforced them in their system of indirect rule (Charrad 2001; see also Mamdani 1996). This explains, according to Charrad, the prevalence of the patriarchal extended family model in the Moroccan legislation, as compared to what she calls the more progressive Tunisian code or the moderate Algerian code.

While this argument is well taken, I would also add that the entrenched values of the agrarian patriarchal society have surely played a role in the new configuration of power within the state, and therefore in the Moroccan legislation of family law. But a more important political goal was achieved through such codification. It instituted the sovereignty of the king over the territorial state, while inscribing national unity in the Islamic sharia at the expense of *'urf*, Amazigh customary law. Thus, by recognizing the sharia as the unique source of legislation in the private sphere, the monarchy, backed by nationalist leaders, managed to place the religious identity of the state at the heart of the Moroccan family, and to make any change to family law a threat to the unity of the small family before the big one, the nation.

As Joseph argues, family law "is the testimony to the centrality of women's bodies and behavior to scripts of nationhood and statehood and a testimony to the centrality of 'family' to social and political projects in the region" (2000, 20). This explains, Joseph argues, why this code became "both a benchmark of feminist struggle" and "a site of contestation in the making of state and nation" (20). In the Moroccan case, the modernist convictions of nationalist leaders were then sacrificed to neonationalist imperatives of unity under the authority of the highly patriarchal law and a holy father-king. These struggles offered the first ingredients for polarizing views of the reform of this code along the political spectrum, and shaped feminist and Islamist articulations of their competing definitions of national identity, state sovereignty, and women's rights (see A. Freeman 2004).

It is also worth noting that the state's reference to a dualist framework of modernity/authenticity, and its discourse on women as "agents of development" during the 1980s, created cracks in this system enabling both feminists and Islamists to challenge it. For instance, Mernissi (1987) points to the contradictions between a rigidly patriarchal law regulating the domestic sphere—family law—and a more sex-egalitarian legislation in the public sphere for Arab women—the constitution, public administration, regulations, and so forth. Mernissi's perception underscores women's agency, in the sense of women navigating between these contradictions to engage significantly in higher education and public institutions, notwithstanding their definition by family law as housewives (Mernissi 1987, 2001).

The Religious Scholars, 'Ulama

The 'ulama were major players in both the legitimization and delegitimization of women's demands for reforming the *mudawwana*. Their authority is acknowledged through state training schools, degrees, and wages, and falls directly under the supervision of the Ministry of Endowments and Islamic Affairs, which places them at the forefront of debates concerning the interpretation of the sharia. For all these reasons, they are perceived by both feminists and Islamists as part of the establishment.

The prevalence of the 'ulama throughout Moroccan history crystallized, in a predominantly agrarian society, the privileges of urban elites, formed in the tenth-century Qarawiyine University of Fez and through other prestigious institutions throughout the Islamic world. Thus, during the nationalist struggle, the 'ulama were the most equipped for leading the movement for independence, organized under the Istiqlal (Independence) Party, and were the unavoidable interlocutors of both the French authorities and the monarchy.

After the independence of Morocco, the king's control over religious symbolism materialized in the direct control of related religious institutions such as the 'ulama's councils. Under the authority of the Ministry of Islamic Affairs,[3] the 'ulama's representative bodies became a site of endorsement for official state policies and discourse. The vanishing authority of the 'ulama followed the damage to the previously prestigious status of religious studies, at the expense of bilingual and modern education. During the 1960s and 1970s, religious school graduates had very few job opportunities, and most ended up taking the modest position of *khatīb* (preacher) or *imām* (leader of the daily prayers) in state-controlled mosques. These agents formed the first base of support for the Islamist movement, and for its call for the implementation of the Islamic sharia.

My study, however, breaks with the common understanding of the 'ulama as a monolithic body, co-opted by the *makhzen* and hostile to women's rights. Already in the 1950s, a group of 'ulama had started questioning the authority of the king in religious matters and organized as "independent" preachers in private mosques and other informal settings (see Tozy 1999). This group planted the first marks of the fragmentation of the religious field into independent, mainstream, and Islamist religious scholarship.

The self-named independent 'ulama have evolved into organized Islamist groups, taking part in the production of Islamist discourse and literature. In this overt or covert alliance, the 'ulama did not miss the smallest opportunity to call for the implementation of the sharia as a code of ethical conduct in the state. The second, mainstream 'ulama enjoys recognition from the state, but lacks legitimacy among some Islamist activists. The latter coined the expression "'ulama of the *makhzen*,"[4] or "'ulama of the power," to dismiss this group's authority on questions of women's rights.

The independent 'ulama have been working more or less at the margins of the 'ulama's mainstream structures and used the Islamist press as a medium for disseminating their own interpretations of the sharia. It is through this press that calls for capital punishment were made for women petitioning against the *mudawwana* in 1992. This movement by independent 'ulama was nevertheless fundamental to the "modernization" of the religious phenomenon through its individualization and even its "secularization," as some have argued (Bishara 1995, 83; Hefner 1998).

Though the mainstream 'ulama did not necessarily adhere to Islamist politics, they did share with the Islamists a pressing concern about their political marginalization, the degradation of their representative bodies, and the silencing of their voices in the public sphere. They also shared a mounting anxiety over the secularization and modernization of state institutions, perceived as "West-oxication," to use Abu-Lughod's term (1998), meaning alienation and a loss of identity. Both groups perceived the *mudawwana* as the last resort of the Islamic sharia, to be secured from the intervention of positive law. Furthermore, both groups found in the rise of the feminist movement their missed opportunities to reposition themselves within a highly centralized political system and safely parlay their contestations and claims to the state. Gender became the main field for the 'ulama's exercise of control over social change, and their main access point to the state.

The Latent Pact, the State, and the Islamists

This study only includes the two Islamist movements that have developed an important women's leadership and a mass base of female membership. These movements are al-'Adl wa-l-ihsāne and al-Tawhīd wa-l-islāh. They offer two different versions of political Islam and encompass Morocco's largest component of Islamist women.

The rise of Islamist groups dates back to 1969, when al-Shabība al-islāmiyya (the Islamic Youth) was formed as a radical underground group, inspired by the teaching of the Egyptian Muslim Brothers.[5] Al-Shabība al-Islāmiyya is considered the mother organization of the Islamist movements in Morocco. According to Darif (1999) and Tozy (1999)—political scientists and experts on Moroccan Islamism—this group was tolerated, if not encouraged by the *makhzen* to counter the political left. Any open alliance, however, between the monarchy and the Islamists would require approval of the political legitimacy of the monarchy, by the latter's endorsement of the king's title of Commander of the Faithful, and recognition of the Islamic character of the state. Some of these groups willingly engaged in this process during the period of state liberalization in the 1990s. The organization al-Tawhīd wa-l-islāh paved the way for the normalization between this long-standing dissident group and the *makhzen*.

The Organization al-Tawhīd wa-l-islāh

The pathway from the radical al-Shabība al-islāmiyya to the current movement al-Tawhīd wa-l-islāh shows a long process of maturation, concession making, and alliance formation. The leadership of al-Tawhīd wa-l-islāh declared its rupture with al-Shabība al-islāmiyya in 1982 and formed al-Jamā'a al-islamia, which changed its name in 1992 to al-Islāh wa-l-tajdīd. Failure to get legal authorizations pushed this group to change its name once again, into the current al-Tawhīd wa-l-islāh, a fusion with another Islamist group, al-Mustaqbal al-islami (the Islamic Future), in 1996. Strategic changes, such as the endorsement of the legitimacy of the monarchy and recognition of the Islamic character of the state, allowed this movement to get a share of the political pie through a proper political party, al-'Adāla wa-l-tanmia. This party is the political extension of the movement al-Tawhīd wa-l-islāh in the Parliament since 1997 (see Willis 1999).

Al-Tawhīd wa-l-islāh has elected bodies, a general assembly, an executive committee, and local representatives. The movement is mainly involved in cultural activities, philanthropy, and social programs supervised by its web of representatives throughout the country. Most leadership positions, however, remain in the hands of male members, and the nine-person executive committee has only one female member, the teacher Naima Benyaich.

Al-'Adāla wa-l-tanmia—its affiliated party—is also viewed by the local media as one of the most democratic institutions of the country. In fact, since its creation in 1996, this party has held regular elections and has renewed its leadership four times. This democratic stance constitutes a major strength for a movement that operates in a political environment where most leaders of older political parties (left and right) have remained in office since Moroccan independence.

The Islamist Dissidents: Al-'Adl wa-l-ihsāne

The second Islamist organization of concern in this study is al-'Adl wa-l-ihsāne. The organization was born in 1978 and is led by a former high school teacher, Sheikh Abdessalam Yassine, now in his early eighties. Yassine marked the birth of his movement with a memorandum sent to King Hassan in 1974, at the peak of the monarchy's struggle with both the political left and the military.[6] The memorandum, entitled "Islam or Deluge," invited the king to implement profound political and economic reforms, ensure the conditions for social justice, and observe the Islamic sharia as a code of conduct. Furthermore, Yassine enjoined the king to renounce his title of Commander of the Faithful, recognize his implication with corrupt political institutions, and renounce his allegiance to the West. This memorandum earned Yassine three years of internment for "mental illness" and marked the beginning of a continuing struggle between his group and the *makhzen*. In 1989 Yassine was put under house arrest in an attempt to limit his influence and the scope of his movement. These constraints did not, however, prevent Abdessalam Yassine from building what today is the largest movement of opposition to the monarchy, according to most analysts (Darif 1999; Maddy-Weitzman 2003; Tozy 1999). Indeed, they also helped Nadia Yassine, the daughter of the sheikh, to position herself as the spokesperson for her father.

Abdessalam Yassine was a member of the Sufi Brotherhood (mystic congregation), *al-qādiriyya,* also known as the *butshishiyya.* This Sufi orientation of al-'Adl wa-l-ihsāne shapes most of the writings of Abdessalam Yassine, whose extensive intellectual production (twenty books to date) offers the cohesive ideological base for this movement. Abdesslam Yassine is considered the supreme guide, and allegiance to him is raised to a matter of a faith. Members of al-'Adl wa-l-ihsāne define their movement as a nonviolent organization, with a transparent agenda and an open political program, although it works outside of existing political institutions.[7] They stress the Sufi orientation of the group and endorse the authority of the sheikh as a spiritual guide (see Hammoudi 1997).[8]

These claims constitute the main differences between this movement and "mainstream" political Islam, represented by al-Tawhīd wa-l-islāh, which considers allegiance to al-'Adl wa-l-ihsāne a heresy at most, and a deviance from the pure teachings of the Qur'an and sunna at least. This is why the relationship between al-Tawhīd wa-l-islāh and al-'Adl wa-l-ihsāne has remained ambivalent and grounded in divisions over the Sufi orientation of the latter and the endorsement of "the political game" by the former.

Abdessalam Yassine operates as both a political leader and a spiritual guide in a fashion that does not authorize the separation between temporal and spiritual authority. The sheikh derives support from various social constituencies, ranging from the lower middle class, small businesses, students, working-class families, peasants, and housewives. The movement extends its scope to the Moroccan diaspora in Europe and North America, which seems to provide a substantial source of funding to the organization's different sections, active across the entire Moroccan territory.

Its membership is estimated to be in the tens of thousands (Darif 1999), organized in small networks of ten called *al-usra* (family), whose members regularly interact and work together while reporting both horizontally and vertically. This pyramidal type of organization grants adherence to the general guidelines of the elected *majlis al-irshād* (council of guidance) and ensures a bottom-up circulation of information and control over the various local councils and committees. Al-'Adl wa-l-ihsāne is also known by the discipline of its members, the efficacy of its structures, and its impressive mobilizing capacities. For example, in the 2004 rally against Morocco's hosting of the U.S.-sponsored regional conference Forum for the Future,[9] al-'Adl wa-l-ihsāne alone drew up to thirty thousand marchers, according to its members.

Al-'Adl wa-l-ihsāne has built consultative bodies, but the supreme guide, Abdessalam Yassine, possesses the most important decision-making powers. The general assembly is endowed with the right to elect a new leader(ship) under special circumstances. The general assembly also elects the different leaders of the numerous commissions and sections working across Morocco and abroad. The supreme decision-making structure is the *majlis al-irshād,* followed by the *al-majlis al-thanfidi* (executive committee) and the *al-jam'iyya al-'ama* (general assembly). Elections are used at all these levels, but they are called *shūra,* a Qur'anic concept requiring consultation of the base during the process of decision making and used in Islamist literature as an alternative to the term "democracy." Al-'Adl wa-l-ihsāne has developed many other institutional bodies, such as the *al-dāira al-siyyāsiyya* (political circle), which shapes the political agenda of the movement and its public image, and the women's section, which focuses on developing programs for women.

The differences between these two Islamist movements have deepened since the party al-'Adāla wa-l-tanmia accepted the opportunity to be part of the formal political institutions. However, they both share a similar concern over the reform of a *mudawwana* that is not shaped by the Islamic sharia, and they want to keep the debate about the reform under the control of the 'ulama and the conservatives within the state. They have also been very keen on securing their access to the state through keeping the controversy over the *mudawwana* alive and animated.

Nevertheless, the politics of these two organizations cannot be fully dismissed as conservative. It is now widely admitted that "Islamism" should be distinguished from religion and "popular religion," as well as from the "religious establishment" and "religious conservatism" (see Bishara 1995, 85–87). In North Africa and the Middle East, Islamist movements have built their legitimacy precisely by challenging practices defined as "tradition" and by questioning the power of the religious establishment or mainstream 'ulama, dubbed the 'ulama of *taqlīd* (imitation), and the traditional 'ulama. They stand in opposition to "independent" Islamist religious scholarship, developed alongside these structures or emerging from them. Furthermore, the legitimacy of the Islamist movements in many parts of the Middle East stems from their ability to articulate their activism on calls for social justice, equity, and solidarity. In Morocco, the marginalization of the Islamist movements from mainstream politics enables them to position themselves as a force of opposition and change, rather than as agents of the system. Moreover, their claim to represent "national interests" is supported by a politics of funding that exclusively relies on domestic donors and wealthy members—a venture in which women have played a key role.

Despite this grounding of Islamist activism in a narrative of "Islamic nationalism" (Zubaida 2004), the project of political Islam is transnational. It is shaped by a definition of an "imagined" community (Anderson 1991) of believers, or Islamic *umma*, and is animated by the feelings of kinship and solidarity among its members regardless of race, ethnicity, gender, or nationality. Nevertheless, many analysts link the legitimacy of these movements to the state's adoption of Islamist discourse, which I call *Islamist mainstreaming*. In Morocco, nothing illustrates this argument better than the policy of Arabization, which aimed to substitute Arabic for French as the language of education. This policy presented the Islamists with tremendous opportunities to extend their influence to the educational system.

Social movement literature uses the concept of the *political opportunity structure* to understand the rise and fall of social movements in relation to a changing political process (McAdam 1982; Meyer and Straggenborg 1996). This conception is based on a two-way analysis that explores how social movements are affected by a shifting structure of opportunities and constraints, and how in turn they affect this structure. The question remains: How do we understand the rise of antagonistic claims and movements as an outcome of the same structure of opportunity? Responding to this question requires, first, more emphasis on the contradictory nature of "opportunities" and recognition of the way in which antagonisms are constitutive of all social practices (Bocock 1986; Bowman 2002; Laclau and Mouffe 1985). Second, it entails the expansion of the definition of opportunities to the way they are perceived through culture, religion, and gender (Katzenstein 1995; Noonan 1997; Raka 1999). In what follows, I will briefly discuss the opportunities open to the Islamists by the state's cultural policy of Arabization in the 1980s. I will show how the cultural interventions of the state have been gendered, played on the battlefield of religious discourse, and entangled with structural changes.

Cultural Policy and Economic Restructuring

Studies on the Arabization of the educational system have linked this policy to the postcolonial struggles of nationalist elites, notably the Istiqlal Party (Party of Independence), to reaffirm the Arabic identity of the Moroccan state (see Baina 1981; Benchekroun 1992). Arabization meant the substitution of Arabic for French as the language of teaching in public education. The Arabization of education was a priority for the Istiqlal Party—which was in charge of education—in the years following the independence of Morocco. However, it was not until the beginning of the 1980s that the state espoused Arabization, implementing it at the secondary level of education, as a first step to universal Arabization of the whole educational system.

While this policy makes sense under a constitution that names Arabic as the national language of Moroccans, the goals of Arabization were nevertheless articulated in terms of a "return" to the "sacred" language of the Qur'an and of "cultural authenticity" (Keppel 1997), which implicated other measures to Islamize the educational curriculam. It is worth stating here that the policy of Arabization became intertwined with the implementation of the Structural Adjustment Program in 1981. Carrying a legacy of two decades of social and political unrest (Brand 1998; Clement 1992; Saadi and Berrada 1992), the Moroccan state entered into a decade of structural adjustment with financial reforms, privatization, and a shrinking of the public sector.[10] But moreover, the state embarked upon cultural reforms of the educational system through its Arabization and Islamization. The latter refers to a type of state intervention in the educational system during the 1980s as a means to reduce the influence of the dissident left.

Islamization took several forms: it first relates to the introduction of Islamic education at all levels of the schooling system, coupled with the elimination of philosophy departments—which also encompassed sociology and anthropology—from all newly opened universities. The second change was to marginalize the social sciences and Western philosophy from the high school curriculum and make prominent what was labeled as Islamic thought in philosophy courses in high school. The third measure was the creation of Islamic Studies departments at all universities, marginalizing philosophy and social sciences, considered the anchors of political dissidents.

According to Tozy, a major expert on the Islamist movements in Morocco, such a department started by recruiting professors from the Middle East—more precisely from Saudi Arabia—at the expense of professors trained in the local institutions and universities in Morocco (see Tozy 1999). If the former were perceived as politically neutral, the latter were viewed as overly influenced by the Muslim Brothers of Egypt, a highly political Islamist dissident group.

As I indicated earlier, these changes reflected the struggles of the two components of the nationalist movement: the conservative Istiqlal Party (IP), in charge of education; and the socialist Union Socialiste des Forces Populaires (USFP), very influential among students and teachers. By the same token, these changes benefited the monarchy by increasing the influence of the conservative and presumably apolitical Wahhabi discourse for a whole new generation of students. Such a move should also be understood in the context of the war of maneuver between the monarchy and the political left, itself grounded in logics of the cold war.[11]

Alongside the policy of Arabization, the monarchy's most immediate interest was fighting the left with the Islamists. It met with the Islamists' most strategic interests, seeking to create a new hegemony couched in the discourse of authenticity and identity instead of "revolution." In the 1980s this discourse was taken from the confines of isolated mosques, in which it was disseminated by Islamist preachers, and placed at the heart of the teaching curricula by the state. With the implementation of the Arabization policy, the Islamist discourse became state sponsored, enabling the Islamists—still operating in the shadow of formal institutions—to influence mainstream teaching.

The implications of the Arabization policy were not limited to the school system, however. Articulated in a narrative of Islamic identity, cultural relativism, and authenticity, this policy also responded to some of the imperatives of the Structural Adjustment Program, which opened further opportunities for the Islamists to step into the vacuum left by a shrinking state and provide social services. However, the social and economic crises amplified by economic restructuring also created other needs for moral support. The latter was supplied by the Islamist discourse of "equality of all before God," "individual responsibility," and the mandated "solidarity" among members of the *umma* during a time of crisis. This narrative formed the backbone of the Islamic educational course and the cornerstone of the Islamist discourse. Furthermore, stressing individual responsibilities before god and toward others, both core Islamic principles, along with the neoliberal capitalist requirements of citizen-entrepreneurship, the gaze shifted from the state's social responsibilities to those of the individual and the third sector, NGOs (see Kamat 2004; Poster and Salime 2002; Pratt 1998).

Arabization and Women's Rights

By skimming the headings of the textbooks published by the Ministry of Education in the 1980s, we can identify the wide range of subjects that are now defined through the sharia. For instance, the *hijāb* (veil) is the subject of one separate course, in which the practice of veiling is made a potent symbol of the boundary between the male and female spheres, and between the "true Muslim woman" and "others." In most textbooks, discussions of the (Muslim) "self" in opposition to the (non-Muslim) "other" lead to the conclusion that the "stagnation" of Muslim society is the result of its deviance from the sharia—rather than from global regulatory regimes—as symbolized by women's unveiling. In these courses, the sharia is presented as an unchallengeable source for rethinking social and gender relations. The authentication of the veil and of polygamy helped legitimize other calls for the "housewifezation" of women (Mies 1986), in the context of high unemployment rates facing men. All these changes were justified through the proliferation of a cheap Islamist press, glorifying motherhood and sold by unemployed, educated young men at the marketplace and the entrances of mosques, as well as inside of academic campuses. However, like any state intervention, the policy of Arabization had its unintended consequences.

In fact, emphasizing "equality of all before God," a core principle in Islam, raised the question of the inequalities observed between men and women before the law. The courses of Islamic education also became the place where female students started debating social practices in light of the Islamic ethics of fairness, justice, and equality. During my work supervising the training of high school teachers in Islamic education between 1987 and 1992, I witnessed the emotions linked to these debates among high school students. While the veil seemed to be largely endorsed and remained unquestioned, at least openly, by the female students, other issues were very controversial, including inheritance rights, polygamy, and repudiation, defined by some as clear assaults on women's rights.[12] The students carried these debates to the schoolyard, I was told. But in all cases, the Arabization policy also instigated a widespread debate about women's rights among high school students, while limiting this debate to the boundaries of the Islamic sharia, defined as superior to positive law. Moreover, the state's adoption of Islamist discourse undermined the dissident roots of political Islam, all the while shifting the focus of Islamist activists from the "unislamic state" to the "atheist left"—a polarization that shaped the interactions of feminists and Islamists for the following two decades. In the ensuing chapters, I will show how these debates are reactivated during specific movement moments and conjunctures.

Women in Islamist Organizations

The mid-1980s saw massive involvement of women in male Islamist organizations. The imperatives of gender division in space and labor, observed in the beginning by these organizations, had helped women gradually integrate into some leadership positions. Women were initially needed to provide services and literacy courses to other women. Considered free from sexual harassment and social differentiations, Islamist organizations represented the best option for a young generation of women looking for a safe public space for action. The two Islamist organizations of al-'Adl wa-l-ihsāne and al-Tawhīd wa-l-islāh include the most important women's component of the Islamist movements known to this date in Morocco. Women form up to 30 percent of these two movements' various structures. This women's leadership is important, politically salient, and publicly active working both within and parallel to these two mass organizations.

It is worth noting that the rise of this leadership owes a great deal to feminist activism. The latter propelled the Islamist movements to encourage alternatives to secular feminism from within. However, compared to the leaders of feminist organizations, the Islamist women's leadership is composed of a relatively younger generation of educated and middle-class professional women in their late thirties and mid-forties. These activists were in high school when they first encountered Islamist thought from their own readings of Islamist literature, notably that of the founding fathers: the Egyptian Muslim Brothers, Sayyid Kutb, and Hassan al-Banna. A woman, Zaynab al-Ghazali, detained by Gamal Abdel Nacer's regime in Egypt during the 1950s, is most venerated by Islamist respondents. The knowledge gained through these readings is shared with other women in the intimacy of their homes. In what follows, I introduce the spaces in which Islamist women started to develop their politics and collective identities in the 1980s.

Mediated Agency

In her study about the civil rights movement, Robnett stresses the importance of mediating factors in the formation of collective identities. She emphasizes the "conversion" process from one's personal identity to the political identity of a movement (Robnett 1997, 16) and defines women activists in the civil rights movement as "bridge leaders" who mobilized individualized and specific methods of recruitment to facilitate this conversion process. Feminist studies have also stressed the endogenous character of feminist organizations and their embeddedness in local communities (Robnett 1997; Sabdury 1998). In this part, I build on these arguments to discuss the mediating spaces through which Islamist women have collectively developed their pedagogies, leadership, knowledge of Islam, and communication strategies. I argue that opening multiple rooms for women's voices in various women's communities was a necessary step for the conversion of thousands of women who transited from these "private" and "intimate" spaces in the 1980s to the public arenas of the mosque and the Parliament at the turn of the century.

In her study of the mosque movement in Egypt, Saba Mahmood (2005) makes a distinction between Islamist political organizations that openly engage in the political process and the women's mosque movement, animated by a politics of piety. She also stresses the impact made by the piety movement and women's debates in the mosque on changing the gendered dynamics within families and between husbands and wives, transforming the socio-cultural landscape in the streets of Egypt. This is certainly a political impact. Though my study has a different focus, that of women who are part of polit-ically organized Islamist movements, piety remains a primary motivator of women's activism. The practice of *da'wa*—a call or invitation to others to follow the message of god—was in fact the gateway to political activity for these activists. It is the site where the religious and the political meet and intersect. Considered as a requirement of faith by my informants, this man-datory *da'wa* demarcates political Islam as a movement to change social insti-tutions and the social habitus, through Islam as a personal faith.

Da'wa was not confined to mosques. It indeed began with women con-verting their private arenas, homes, and family settings into spaces for politi-cal action. This enabled them to expand the social base of support to political Islam and to blur the boundaries between Islam as a faith and political Islam as a movement of change. Weekly meetings, collective readings, and interpre-tations of the Qur'an subverted the home and its related social events, trans-forming them into sites for debates about social change through a "rethought Islam" (Badran, quoted in Yamani 1996). During the 1990s it was hard to find a woman living in a city or a small town who did not witness this kind of uninvited intervention during a social event, a wedding celebration, or even a mere visit to a friend. Usually, these activists address their publics with sim-ple language, backing up their arguments with citations from the Qur'an and stories from *al-sīra,* the prophet's example.

Women's reconfiguration of private settings, and their transformation of them into sites for the dissemination of the Islamist discourse, provided a powerful stage for the articulation of growing social deprivation in contrast to the Islamic ethics of moderation, modesty (see Taarji 1992), and social solidarity. In a previous work, I also showed the pragmatism of "Islamizing celebrations" through the return of sex segregation to spaces as a means for job creation by hundreds of educated unemployed women (Salime 1997).[13] Within this politicized, feminized, and rationalized Islam, growing numbers of women have mobilized since the mid-1980s to propose "Islamic alternatives" within a culturalist understanding of social change, based on transforming mentalities and the social habitus. This discursively based politics has been the grounds for both Islamist "subject formation" (Mahmood 2005) and Islamist women's collective identities (Melucci 1995).

For these reasons, Islamist women consider their approach to activism more radical compared to that of the feminists. They claim to be targeting the cultural roots of patriarchy and the denigration of women, terms widely adopted by my informants. To an outsider this claim may not make much sense, given a context in which these same activists have been among the most vehement opponents of removing unequal conditions from the codification of family law, such as male guardianship over women. I will later present the type of rationalization that these activists have used to justify their practices by relating them to the economic security of women. One may endorse the fact that these rationalizations do the work of consolidation rather than subversion of patriarchal norms.

However, the "consolidation" (Mahmood 2005) of patriarchal norms, such as the gendered division of space, observed from the very beginning by these activists, had the double effect of first granting the inclusion of a subaltern women's population (e.g., the working class and housewives) into most structures. This has enlarged the popular base of support for these movements by attracting growing numbers to political Islam. Second, it was a very effective strategy in connecting these populations to upper-middle-class women, the main organizers and sponsors of the various activities offered to women. This involvement of educated women in organizing other women was central to the development of a feminine consciousness, which was not articulated in the rhetoric of gender equality but in a discourse stressing women's almost superior ability, compared to men, to lead the Muslim community in critical times. This participation is, however, contingent on women's observance of modesty as the embodiment of piety and a mode of inhabiting the public space (see Deeb 2006; Mahmood 2005). It is clear then that the discourse of gender equality, as feminist groups have articulated it since the early 1980s, was not the core issue in these activists' mobilization. As a part of larger male constituencies, Islamist women do share with their male counterparts the same concerns about increasing secularization and perceived colonization/Westernization of "life worlds" (Habermas 1985). In the aftermath of the first Gulf War (1991) and in a period of high unemployment rates (see Cohen 2005), the narrative of "Islamic alternatives" found echoes among a large public of high school and university graduates completely disillusioned with the discourse of human rights and international law. The irony is that at the same time, as feminist leaders were withdrawing from leftist political parties to form their independent groups, other women were integrating en masse into the male-dominated structures of political Islam.

Women of al-Tawhīd wa-l-islāh

Al-Tawhīd wa-l-islāh has developed a large base of support among educated professional women, who constitute about a third of its membership. An activist in the organization, whom I will call Hanan, revealed her reasons for joining:

> I have been veiled since the elementary school. It was not very common in the late '70s to see city girls wearing headscarves in schools. The administration found my behavior alarming. The school principal warned me, talked to my parents, and then started pulling my scarves off my head, keeping them with her. I found it offensive and continued covering my hair. One day she brought a collection of my scarves and burned them before my eyes in the schoolyard. I was radicalized by this experience. I kept asking myself, Why did she do that? Are we not Muslims? I understood that a headscarf is not a mere piece of cloth. I joined al-Shabība al-islāmiyya [mother organization of al-Tawhīd wa-l-islāh] and doubted of everything coming from the school. Now, as a founding member of al-Tawhīd wa-l-islāh, I am fighting for the right of others to veil.

This activist described her journey from the radical al-Shabība al-islāmiyya to the party al-'Adāla wa-l-tanmia. She was among the few women members who have been closely involved in the politics of the organization al-Islāh wa-l-tajdīd since it was established in 1992. She described how, alongside male structures, women have also managed to open alternative spaces in their own homes, in the neighborhood, and in the schooling system for women's meetings, voices, and interpretation of the Islamic sources. Within these spaces, she contends, women developed their communication skills and political awareness, their pedagogies and audiences. Despite the enormous impact of women on the politics of al-Tawhīd wa-l-islāh, only one woman is currently represented on its executive committee, Naima Benyaich. Nevertheless, during the 2002 legislative elections, six women were elected to represent the party al-'Adāla wa-l-tanmia in the Parliament, benefiting from a politics of quotas advocated by feminist and other women's sections in political parties to give women 10 percent of seats in the Parliament.

Women of al-'Adl wa-l-ihsāne

Nadia Yassine, the daughter of Sheikh Abdessalam Yassine, has the reputation of being one of the most vehement opponents of feminism in Morocco. She is the president of the Women's Section (*al-qitā 'e al-nissaī*) of al-'Adl wa-l-ihsāne and the spokesperson of the movement. She earned a bachelor's degree in political science in 1980 after her graduation from the French Cultural Mission in Morocco—a private French school—for her secondary education. Yassine views her movement as the major force behind the Islamist rally against the NPA. She gained an international reputation because of her eloquence in both Arabic and French and her virulent opposition to the NPA. For this reason, she is also perceived as the most vigorous "antifeminist" activist by most of my feminist respondents.

Before going to my first appointment with Nadia Yassine in the summer of 2003, I was anxious about how to explain the purpose of my study and how to justify my affiliation with a U.S. institution with convincing arguments. I was going to be meeting her only a few months after the mass demonstrations against the U.S. invasion of Iraq, in which al-'Adl wa-l-ihsāne was a key organizer. I was not sure how I would be received by such a vehement opponent of the feminist movement, especially since I had no intention of hiding my own affiliation with the movement. I thought this might be too much of a barrier to overcome for a productive encounter. I finally decided to put on my Moroccan djellaba, a dress adopted by all generations of Moroccan women independent of their politics or educational background, carefully kept for special occasions in my case. My hair was not covered, yet by wearing my djellaba I was conscious that I wanted to qualify for "authenticity."

Nevertheless, my defense mechanism fell apart when Nadia Yassine greeted me at her door with a large smile and warm welcoming words, and with her insistence that I should not take off my shoes before entering her guest reception room. I introduced myself, answered some of her questions about my research, and gained her friendship. During our conversation, Yassine shared with me her story about long years of struggle trying to educate not only the "sisters" but also indirectly the "brothers" in the culture of respect of womanhood. I was aware that Yassine was talking about femininity, described in her own words as a "balanced interest by women in their bodies, sexual life, and beauty besides the soul." Curious to know more, I asked Yassine to explain to me how she would claim to be fighting for women's rights while opposing the NPA. Her answer was more than unsettling. She replied, "To be honest with you, I marched in Casablanca with my heart turned to women marching in Rabat." She added, "For years, I kept repeating that women did not have problems with Islam. Now I am saying: *we do* have problems, *I mean* with the way Muslim men *stole* this religion from us."

At this point, I asked her if she would consider herself a feminist. Her answer pointed to some of the complexities I am trying to unfold in this study.

She said, "No, I am not a feminist. I am an Islamist, and Islam is feminist." Hence as an identity politics, feminism only becomes legitimate if redefined within a "feminist Islam" and a "gender-sensitive Qur'an," as Yassine likes to describe them. To Yassine, the *mudawwana* is not sacred. It is a human effort of interpretation that should be renewed. Thus, her mobilization against the NPA relates to the way it was *imposed* as "an up-down reform," which was neither inclusive of all women's voices nor accepting of the sharia as a source of inspiration. Commenting on the feminist march in 2000, Yassine said: "They wanted to blackmail the government by taking a few people to the streets. We showed them who can mobilize the masses."

The masses Nadia Yassine referred to are the thousands of women organized by the nationwide committees of al-'Adl wa-l-ihsāne who work according to a strict division of labor and a yearly calendar granting continual contact between the upper levels and the base. The busy schedule of these leaders, including that of Nadia Yassine, includes periodic visits to their membership all over the country, during which they are received by old and new supporters in their own homes and among their families. The purpose of the visit is to renew the allegiance of the base, learn its needs through direct contact, and eliminate "cultural" and "class" differentiations among the members, I was told.

The Women's Section of al-'Adl wa-l-ihsāne is active in every neighborhood of Morocco's big cities and towns. Not only do these leaders organize around women's issues, but they build their programs according to the particular needs of the neighborhood. For instance, in a campus neighborhood, the priority will be to respond to female students' needs in lodging, funds, books, and summer camps for high school students. In an industrial neighborhood, most of the training sessions, programs, and conferences relate to labor rights, unionization, and self-help organizing. However, it was not until 1998, with the birth of the Women's Section of al-'Adl wa-l-ihsāne, that its leadership could focus on women's needs with programs entirely created and supervised by women.

Feminist or Feminine?

Definitions of feminism have been part of most studies of women's movements. Most of these definitions acknowledge the differences among forms of mobilization by women that may or may not engage feminist politics. For instance, Alvarez (1990) noted the differences between a "proactive" and a "reactive" women's movement. Though both are forms of politicization of the women's movement, Alvarez only acknowledges the first to be a challenge to gender roles and therefore representative of feminist organizing. In the second case, women do not mean to affect gender roles but to protect their socially ascribed roles as women. This is what Alvarez calls "feminine organizing" (1990, 24). Klatch suggests a similar approach in her distinction between feminist consciousness and gender consciousness. The first "requires recognition of unequal and unfair treatment of women" (2001, 792) and "entails the formation of a collective identity as women" (792). Gender consciousness is a more encompassing category that includes "women who believe in gender equality but do not necessarily identify with the term *feminist*, as well as women who recognize a common identity and interest as women but who mobilize in support of the traditional conception of gender" (792). In contrast, Badran (1994, 203) used the phrase "gender activism" in the Egyptian context to denote women's common "feminist" modes of thinking and behavior in the public sphere without denying the reality of distinct feminist and Islamist "movements." She reserves the term "feminist" for "women who publicly declare their feminist identity and those who admit to being feminists in private but do not make public affirmation of this" (203).

It is the purpose of this study to contextualize this debate by relating it to the interactions among feminist and Islamist women's movements. I define feminism as an individual and collective awareness about women's oppression by various patriarchal regimes; a philosophy based on a vision of an egalitarian social order; and a practice to challenge gender inequalities at different levels of private and public institutions through individual and collective means. In fact, feminist groups' mobilization in the name of women's individual rights and gender equalities clearly set them within conventional definitions of liberal feminism. If their politics could be described within the realm of "feminist consciousness" (Klatch 2001), regardless of how much these groups endorse the term "feminism," understanding Islamist women's activism requires a more complicated argument.

To understand the type of gender consciousness articulated by Islamist women, we need to look into the ways these activists link women's oppression by a patriarchal system to men's oppression by authoritarian political regimes. Women's emancipation, argued Khadija Mufid, a leading activist in al-Tawhīd wa-l-islāh, is contingent on men's liberation. As long as men are ignorant of the true essence of Islam, as long as they are subjected to various political and economic regimes of oppression, there would be no real liberation of women.

While trying to understand Islamist women's activism in relation to "feminine" or "feminist" organizing, I found it difficult to establish a demarcation line. To Nadia Yassine, "femininity" rather than feminism should be the place for building a gender consciousness about women's oppression. This follows her perception that femininity is denigrated under certain forms of interpreting Islam, which perceive it as a threat. Restating women's right to recover their femininity—inner and outer beauty—should be the starting point for struggling against patriarchy, she contends. Accordingly, women from al-'Adl wa-l-ihsāne have been establishing programs to help their female membership recover their sense of self as a means of empowerment and a first step toward mobilizing them for the general cause of social change. Despite differences in their approach to women's rights, Islamists and feminists alike acknowledge *patriarchy* as the site of struggle for women's movements. While feminist groups only stress gender oppression and subordination of women, Islamist women espouse a more encompassing vision of social change based on the "liberation" of both men and women.

This perception of women's emancipation as an integral part of "people's liberation" resonates with the concept of *womanism* as developed in versions of black feminist thought and African feminism (Collins 2000; Walker 1983). Ogunyemi defines "black womanism" as a "philosophy" concerned both with sexual equality in the black community and with "the world power structure that subjugates" both blacks and women (quoted in Robnett 1997, 8). For Ogunyemi, black womanism pursues an ideal "for black unity where every black person has a modicum of power and so can be a brother and sister or a father or a mother to the other" (quoted in Robnett 1997, 6). This relational conception of womanhood as a connecting site for the black community as a whole defies the divisions assumed by white feminism between men and women, between private and public, and challenges the claims about rights as individual (see Gilliam 1991; Saldbury 1998; Zerai and Salime 2005).

In a similar vein, Islamist respondents believe that women's emancipation can only take place in a context where men themselves are liberated. Gender consciousness is grounded in the broader ambition of reforming society as a whole, as a means to change women's conditions, rather than the goal of emancipation of women as individuals. In this societal project, women occupy a central place since they are viewed as main players in the social structures that perpetuate the faces of oppression of women.

As the next chapter demonstrates, feminist organizing played an instrumental role in the rise of a "feminist consciousness" among Islamist women. This took the form of women's affirmation of their identities, needs, and aspirations within the Islamist movements, and confirmation of their central place in Muslim society. It is through their perceived "differences" as *women* that these activists started claiming leadership positions within the Islamist movement, putting an end to their marginalization. Khadija, a leading member of al-Tawhīd wa-l-islāh in the city of Fez, claims: "I do not accept that women should be assigned to women's committees. I do not accept working on women's issues just because I am a woman. I can make a contribution to all committees and I want to see both men and women involved in working on women's issues; I refuse the ghetto-ization of women's rights."

Nevertheless, the insider location of Islamist women, as members of male-dominated organizations, made their impact almost invisible to most studies on the Islamist movements (Darif 1999; Tozy 1999) and to the few studies on the women's movement in Morocco (Alami 2002; Daoud 1993; El Mossadeq 1995; Zeghal 2005). These studies disseminate a wide perception shared by feminist groups that Islamist women lack a political agenda of their own, and are therefore not worth scientific inquiry. This misconception may be due to the religious nature of these activists' discourse, to their attire—as veiled women—and to their positioning against the hegemony of liberal regimes of women's rights.

As I will describe in the following chapter, women's involvement in Islamist movements had a major effect on them, moderating the tone of the most radical voices and enlarging the social base of support. My informants like to describe their struggle as "a two-front battle": an internal one against the most conservative voices within their movements and an external one against the secular left. The struggle for recognition, on both fronts, took longer in comparison to feminist groups. While the 1980s marked the rise of autonomous feminist organizations, Islamist women had to wait one more decade to see the first women's "independent" groups emerging out of male structures. It was not until 1994 that the first Islamist women's organization was formed on a women's rights agenda. The Organization for the Renewal of Women's Awareness (ORWA) was created by the women's leadership in al-Tawhīd wa-l-islāh in the aftermath of the One Million Signature Campaign to provide Islamist women with an alternative structure for advocating women's rights.

The Feminist Movement

The Moroccan feminist movement is led by women who had been active in leftist political parties and student unions, as well as human rights groups, during the 1970s. In the 1980s, women started to wean their organizations from the political parties and unions that had spawned them. To these activists, the *mudawwana* stood completely at odds with the real changes that affected women's lives and with the ambitions of a growing population of urban, educated, middle-class women.[14]

When I started my meetings with feminist activists, I was surprised nevertheless to see major figures of feminism in Morocco rejecting the term "feminism," calling it Western and alienating because it allegedly refers to "sex wars," thereby dividing men and women. These representations of feminism as Western and reductive are definitely linked to personal readings of feminist activists, but also to direct contact with the discourse and practices of Western feminism in international settings. More important, these groups' rejections of feminism are also linked to the way its activism has been dismissed as elitist and illegitimate in the Islamist discourse. Indeed, feminist groups have adopted a different approach to social change, which starts with reforming state laws. Conscious that the state is crucial to any change in women's conditions, these groups have slowly reconciled themselves with the state, notably in the 1990s, and have started creating access points in all state institutions. Acknowledging the importance of the United Nations as a powerful platform for legitimizing their demands, these groups allied their movement to transnational feminism, and contributed to a global circulation of knowledge and representations of women's rights under the sharia. Any study of feminism in Morocco should begin with the leading role played by two organizations: the Association Démocratique des Femmes du Maroc (ADFM; Moroccan Women's Democratic Association) and the Union de l'Action Feminine (UAF). These two groups have formed the benchmark of feminist activism in Morocco since the mid-1980s. By defining the women's movement as a challenge to the legal source of the subjugation of women, these two organizations have shaped the whole range of women's activism and hundreds of women's groups, advocacy centers, and research programs active in Morocco to date.

Association Démocratique des Femmes du Maroc

The ADFM was formed in Rabat in 1985 and currently works more as an umbrella organization, federating numerous local NGOs all over Morocco. Most of ADFM's leaders were affiliated with the Communist party, Partie du Progrès et du Socialisme (PPS), before declaring their organization independent from any political party's agenda or persuasion. The leadership of the ADFM is composed of a group of academics, teachers, lawyers, and professional women with bilingual or exclusively French educational backgrounds. The ADFM is inevitably the entry point to any study on the women's movement in Morocco and remains, to this date, the cornerstone of secular feminism in the country.

The importance of the ADFM stems from its position as a federating organization for many NGOs working on gender issues. The ADFM played a leading role in building a transnational movement in North Africa under a unified agenda and discourse, organized around the Collectif 95 Maghreb

Egalité. This regional network was launched in 1991 with the participation of academics, lawyers, and feminist groups from Algeria, Tunisia, and Morocco. Rabia Naciri, a university professor and geographer, Amina Lamrini, a high school inspector, and Farida Bennani, a university professor of law, all from Morocco, have been key players in building these structures.

Through the Collectif 95, the ADFM launched sustained campaigns that targeted the Moroccan government with communiqués, "open letters" in the press, studies, and reports on the condition of women's rights in Morocco. This endeavor earned the ADFM consultative status with the United Nations' Committee on the Status of Women, to which the group submits yearly Parallel Reports on women's rights in Morocco. These reports aim to correct the government's official accounts to the United Nations.

Union de l'Action Féminine

The UAF was created in 1987 by women members in the leftist Organisation de l'Action Démocratique et Populaire (OADP). It is based in Rabat and has sections in the main cities and towns across the country. Similar to ADFM, the leadership of the UAF wanted their organization to remain independent from political parties and open to all women regardless of their political affiliations and sensibilities. The main figure of this group was Latifa Jbabdi, a former political detainee and a long-standing activist for human rights. The UAF group emerged out of the leadership experience of producing the monthly feminist magazine *Thamānia Mars* (March 8), the distribution of which was seemingly supported by the OADP. The UAF's ties with this party had lessened after several events, including a division within OADP, the enlargement and diversification of the UAF's base, and a split of the leadership between old and new leftist political formations. The UAF has been at the forefront of the feminist movement since it launched the One Million Signature Campaign to reform the *mudawwana* in 1992. This leading role was acknowledged by the United Nations' Committee on the Status of Women when it provided the UAF with its consultative status.

Rise of Feminist Groups, Conjuncture

The proliferation of women's nongovernmental organizations (NGOs) in the 1980s was shaped by the global changes affecting the Moroccan state. In this section, I will analyze the rise of these organizations in relation to three interrelated discourses: first, the discourse of women's rights, which was a major impetus during the second half of the United Nations' Decade for Women (1976–85); second, the Women in Development (WID) discourse, which formed the backdrop of the NPA; and third, the discourse of democratization and citizenship articulating the state's transition to neoliberalism. These discourses are interconnected in the way they articulate the shifts from a "developmentalist state" (McMichael 2004) to a free market economy. For this reason, I suggest first an analysis of the political and economic changes that shaped feminist groups' activism during late 1980s and early 1990s, before looking into the impact of the United Nations' process upon the same groups.

Like most of the indebted states of the Global South, Morocco entered the era of neoliberalism through the painful implementation of a structural adjustment program (1983–94). Mandated by the World Bank and the International Monetary Fund during the 1980s, the policies of structural adjustment were used as a means to establish the financial credibility of "developing" nations by the industrialized North. More precisely, as McMichael (2004) argues, structural adjustment facilitated the shift from nationally oriented growth to a globally oriented economy. This entailed policies of market deregulation and the state's withdrawal from the public sector in favor of private investment and voluntary organizations (Mercer 2002; Kamat 2004). The drastic effects of the structural adjustment program on women's education, employment, and health has been well documented—even by official state studies in Morocco (Akesbi 1991; Lacoste 1991; Moghadam 2000; Salime 1997). More important to the purpose of this study are the ways in which these policies heightened various forms of violence against women, which I will explore in the next chapter, making the issues of development and women's rights a priority in feminist groups' agendas.

The implementation of neoliberal reforms for a free market entailed political transformations as well, reshaping the Moroccan state's relationship to women's groups on the one hand, and to the Islamist opposition on the other. The transformation of both forces into players in the implementation of neoliberal reforms was central to the policies of co-optation and containment followed by the Moroccan monarchy during the 1990s.[15] Brand (1998) refers to this process as state liberalization and describes it as a transition from centralized political institutions to a decentralized and democratized political life.

This process followed three main paths: first, a constitutional reform authorizing the gradual participation of the opposition (leftist and nationalist) to the government; second, indirect negotiations with the Islamists of al-Islāh wa-l-tajdīd, giving birth to the first Islamist party of the country, al-'Adāla wa-l-tanmia, authorized in 1997; third, an opening of the state institutions and media on the discourse of citizenship and human rights (Waltz 1995). The state's co-optation of the discourse of rights was tangible through the creation of a Council of Human Rights in the 1990s, and later a Ministry of Human Rights,[16] the first in the history of independent Morocco.

Pratt contends that as "a cultural intervention," neoliberalism creates categories of belonging, structures of possibility, and forms of agency (1998, 435). In this context, civil society is perceived, Yudice argues, as "the medium through which the conventional compromise between the state and the diverse sectors of the nation was renegotiated" (1998, 353; see also Gibbon 1997). Feminist groups played a major role in these renegotiations. Implementing neoliberal reforms necessitated the alliance of some state departments, notably the ones working on development issues with women's rights organizations who started articulating their demands within the liberal WID discourse.[17] Backed by the various development and UN agencies active in Morocco, the WID discourse legitimized a modernist, liberal, and developmentalist framing of state social programs and many of the alliances between these programs and feminist organizations.[18]

As a hegemonic program, the WID created its own spheres of inclusion and exclusion, favoring women's groups that were ready to use the liberal narratives of development and individual rights in their lobbying and their approach to foreign funds.[19] As a discourse of power, the WID also shaped the creation of new institutions supervised by women and new state actors. The Office for the Integration of Women in Development (IFD) is one of these institutions. Created within the Ministry of Foreign Affairs in the 1990s, this office's mission was to channel funds for NGO projects, monitor the work of women's groups, and facilitate their access to global funds and conferences. The office itself was funded through different UN programs and other sponsors interested in gender and development (Brand 1998), and was directed by a young woman named Farida Jaidi, who is currently Morocco's ambassador to Brazil. The office was instrumental in this phase of "NGO-ization" (Alvarez 1997), through the opening of state institutions and international funds to women's groups (Belarbi 1997; Denoeux and Gateau 1995).

The production of knowledge and local expertise has accompanied the work and rise of feminist groups. In this case, it was the Ministry of Population and its affiliated Demographic Center for Studies and Research on Population (CERED) that contributed to engendering the state's development rhetoric by providing data and studies on population and, more particularly, on Moroccan women. Most of these studies were also funded through the various UN programs and have been released regularly on an annual basis since the mid-1980s. These publications formed an incredibly important source of information about gender and women's rights in Morocco during the phase of economic restructuring and beyond.

Goldman (2005) and others have shown that the transformation of subjectivities is a fundamental phase in the building of hegemony, which takes place through consent and participation (see Escobar 1994). The dynamics described earlier were crucial for the transformation during the 1990s of the feminist leadership from being women's rights advocates and feminist "dissidents" to local "experts" on gender and development, working alongside state officials and providing expertise for international funding programs—positions some of them occupied during the controversy over the NPA.

The United Nations' Process

As I discussed earlier, the UN process has played a central role in the globalization of women's rights discourse and activism. The scholarship on social movements viewed globalization as an enabling "opportunity structure" that has provided actors with external possibilities and resources for their mobilization (Keck and Sikkink 1998; Marks and McAdam 1999; Moghadam 2005). Other studies see the relationship between globalization and social movements as dialectical. In this case, globalization is not defined as an external opportunity structure (Guidry, Kennedy, and Zald 2000), but as a "spatial expression or domain, a condition and medium of collective action" (Nederveen Pieterse 2001, 25). In this sense, not only has the globalization of women's rights discourse shaped particular social movements, but in turn "these movements have become globalizing forces in their own rights" (25). I will now explore this dialectical relationship through the case of feminist groups in Morocco.

The international dynamics created by the United Nations' Decade for Women brought significant momentum to liberal feminist groups. The cluster of UN summits held in the 1990s, such as the Vienna Conference on Human Rights (1993), provided feminist groups with a public forum and stimulated debate, both domestic and international, over policy and reforms (see Bayes and Tohidi 2001; Moghadam 2005; Molyneux and Razavi 2002). One of the most effective tools that came out of the UN Decade was the Convention on the Elimination of All Forms of Discrimination against Women (CEDAW), also called the Copenhagen Convention, which laid out the duties of states to promote gender equality in all areas of life, from family to workplace and government. The CEDAW was central to the legitimization of both feminist claims that women's rights are universal and Islamist protests on behalf of the "cultural specificity of the Moroccan family."

The slogan of the UN Decade, "Equality, Peace, and Development," culminated in the 1985 Nairobi Resolutions. The NGOs' participation in the Nairobi Conference managed to shift the priorities from questions of rights as defined by women in the Industrial North to questions of rights defined around development issues by women in the Global South. The first NGO forum held in parallel to the official United Nations meeting in Nairobi (1985) helped activists to organize transnationally in order to promote the CEDAW. For instance, the International Women's Rights Action Watch (IWRAW) was started in 1985 as a result of discussions at the Nairobi meetings that closed the UN Decade for Women. Launched in Nairobi, Women Living under Muslim Laws (WLUML) is also part of this transnational activism by women (Moghadam 2005). Moroccan feminism took part in this process. For instance, the ADFM is a founding member of various transnational networks, including the WLUML.

In Nairobi, member-states (alongside NGOs) had to assess the achievements of the UN Decade and lay down the strategies to be implemented by the year 2000. Women were players in this process. As noted by Stamatopoulou (1995), until the turning point of the 1993 World Conference on Human Rights in Vienna, the human rights of women were not a priority at the UN. By the early 1990s, activists had laid a substantial groundwork and benefited from the astonishing rate at which communication was then taking place. Knowing that both the process and substance of international law is gendered, these activists had to ensure that women's voices and experiences were included in the definition of all human rights norms as a strategy for the advancement of women. The developmentalist agenda of global feminism made it difficult for the Moroccan government to keep ignoring its local women's groups. The latter articulated their demands in terms that resonated with the agenda of the UN Decade.

Two years after the Nairobi Conference, the Ministry of Social Affairs in Morocco, which oversees women's issues, organized workshops to develop national strategies to respond to the Nairobi resolutions with concrete policies. For the first time, women's groups and women's wings in political parties and unions were invited to join a national committee that was debating these strategies. In the same year, women's sections in oppositional parties held meetings to press the government to ratify the Copenhagen Convention without reservations. The NPA was the culmination of this process of globalization of the United Nations regime of women's rights.

Dynamics of Contention

In this chapter, I have outlined the different trajectories of the feminist and the Islamist women's movements. In conclusion, I would like to suggest a few places in which these trajectories have been overlapping. The articulation of feminist demands within the discursive regimes of rights and development has created powerful spheres of identification and empowerment for these groups. It has shaped feminist subjectivities as the "agents of change" in modern Morocco. However, these identifications also created sites of contention and subversion, built by Islamist women targeting both the discourse of development and that of universal women's rights. For instance, during the 2000 Casablanca rally against the NPA, Islamist women responded to the title of the NPA, National Plan for the Integration of Women into Development, with the slogan: "Here are women! But where is development?"

Though Islamist women's activism has grown at the margins of both the UN process and the state's appropriation of the discourse of equality and development, their activism has shaped the agenda of global feminism by undermining its universalist claims. The United Nations' legal instruments and norms are redefined as agents of "imperial sovereignty," to use Hardt and Negri's (2000) wording, of the Industrial North over the Global South. This articulation of the United Nations' framework brought issues of cultural relativism to the forefront of feminist discourse.

Framing this debate in oppositional terms of universalism versus cultural relativism is very misleading. Scholarship on the Islamic context of the debate discusses the concept of human rights as a "historically circumscribed and context-bound phenomenon" (Rao 1995, 117; see also An-Na'im 1992; Mamdani 2000). This means that any debate about universalism will have to articulate cultural relativism. To An-Na'im, the merits of a certain degree of cultural relativism stem from challenges to the ethnocentric claims of universalism (1992, 24) and demands for "the acknowledgment of equal validity of diverse patterns of life" (24). An-Na'im's perspective resonates with the way women in the Islamist movements define the legitimacy of their "Islamic alternatives" in comparison to "imported Western solutions to false feminist problems." The following chapter illustrates dimensions of this debate in the context of the first movement moment: The One Million Signature Campaign.

2

Feminization of the Islamist Movements: The One Million Signature Campaign

In 1992 the feminist group UAF launched the One Million Signature Campaign. As its name indicates, this campaign aimed to collect one million signatures against the *mudawwana*. The petition contested this code's consecration of gender inequalities and proposed an egalitarian codification based on equal rights and shared responsibilities of husbands and wives within the family. The UAF's project of reform was inspired by the liberal discourse of women's rights and by international treaties, notably the CEDAW. Since the early 1980s, the debate about the reform of the *mudawwana* had become more intense and widespread, but never were the controversies more vehement than during the UAF's petition.

As a movement moment, the UAF petition had a far-reaching impact on both feminist and Islamist women's groups. Not only did this campaign send a powerful signal about the rise of the feminist movement in Morocco, it also demonstrated the scope of its mobilizing capacities. It is the goal of this chapter to illustrate how this mobilization also paved the way for Islamist women's voices and discourse, and influenced their forms of organization. Perceived as an *assault* on the sharia, the petition campaign stimulated Islamist women's interpretations of the "sacred history" (Zubaida 1987) of Islam as it pertains to women's place in Islamic society. This mobilization by Islamist women raised questions: Who may speak on behalf of Moroccan women? Who may engage in *ijtihād*—a renewed interpretation of the sharia?

Upon closer inspection, broader questions were also at stake: How did the feminist mobilization contribute to engendering the state liberalization that had been in progress since the mid-1980s? What was the impact of the

UAF's petition on the reframing of religion and politics at this juncture? This turn in the discussion relates to the emergence of women as political agents holding varied—and sometimes competing—definitions and agendas surrounding key issues such as democracy, citizenship, development, women's rights, and Islam.

I address these questions by emphasizing the impact of the UAF campaign on the *feminization* of Islamist women's discourse and activism. I define feminization as, first, opening Islamist women to the discourse of "women's rights"; second, their positioning *within* the women's movement; and, third, their negotiations of leadership positions in the Islamist movements. I argue that the articulation of a politics of feminism by Islamist women did not occur in a vacuum. Besides the internal dynamics of change at work within the Islamist movements since the mid-1980s, the UAF's petition gave these dynamics a significant external momentum.

The point is when the UAF spoke on behalf of *all* women, the Islamist "sisters" had to reposition themselves as *women* advocates of an alternative discourse and agenda, rather than as simply *members* of Islamist male organizations. This meant a reconsideration of these activists' positions vis-à-vis the women's movement and a negotiation of their marginal location in the Islamist movements. Accordingly, Islamist women embarked on not only defending the sharia, but also rereading it as it pertains to their own marginalization in the Islamist movement. The "woman's gaze" (*al-'ayn al-nissäiyya*) is the expression used by these activists to describe their particular understanding of the sharia from a woman's standpoint. The "woman's gaze" replaces the term "gender," which these activists consider Western feminist terminology that divides society into two clashing components of men and women while also paving the way to gender crossing. The woman's gaze stresses the unique location of women as negotiators and mediators of social relations, highlighting how this location shapes their perception of social, political, and economic issues. Suad al-Amari, an active member in al-Tawhīd wa-l-islāh and current deputy on the City Council of Casablanca, contends that the woman's gaze was a "methodology" that instigated gender debates in the Islamist media and groups. I asked Suad to explain the difference between the woman's gaze and a gender lens, since both seem to have similar effects. To her, it is the "colonial" baggage that comes with the term "gender" that is most disturbing. At the same time, the woman's gaze does not reduce "femininity" to a question of personal choice, but makes it the lens through which one perceives the world.

These alternatives to the feminist discourse of gender equality have been expressed in an earlier stage of Islamist mobilization against the UAF's petition campaign of 1992. As I argued earlier, the UAF's petition deeply affected women's activism in the Islamist movements by shaping their discourse of women's rights and their modes of organizing. As the present chapter illustrates, changes in the discourse of these groups do not necessarily translate into changes to the core value of their movement, which remains grounded in the supremacy of the sharia over the international conventions of women's rights. If the latter have provided feminist groups with tremendous opportunities to use a hegemonic platform to support their claims, Islamist women drew legitimacy from a different, yet equally powerful, source—the configuration of state power in Morocco in which religion and politics are intertwined.

The One Million Signature Campaign

When the UAF launched the One Million Signature Campaign, it knew that it was playing on very risky ground. Women's issues were not on the king's agenda for reform, nor did the Moroccan constitution, under negotiation, determine the range of rights that women would enjoy. Political parties negotiating the conditions for the rise of real democratic institutions did not put women's demands on their calendar, and the Islamist groups were already powerful, massively organized, and watching closely. The feminist mobilization could therefore divert attention from "more important" issues facing the nation, notably the king's normalization with political opposition groups: the Islamist and, more urgently, the leftist and the nationalist ones (see Brand 1998).

The political process of democratization, however, left women's demands out of the agenda of reform. Thus, the feminist petition campaign was a powerful stage on which feminist groups brought gender *back* to mainstream political debate. The petition was backed by the major human rights organizations (active since the mid-1980s), women's rights organizations, and sections of labor unions and political parties. These groups recognized that the time had come to move from elaborating programs that focused on women in dispersed organizations to creating a movement that would place women's issues on the mainstream agenda. The UAF reform suggested readings of both the Moroccan constitution and the sharia as they pertain to women.

First, by articulating a more inclusive definition of democracy that takes into account women's contributions and voices, the petition campaign aimed to transform a gender-blind process of liberalization into a gender-sensitive one. As Joseph (2000) rightly argued, family law is the place where the three spheres of gender, the state, and citizenship meet and conflict. Across the Middle East, women's struggles to reform family law undeniably intersect with their definition of the meanings of citizenship. The state is critical, argues

Joseph, to "the gendering of citizenship" and the regulation of this citizenship through a set of laws. Infused with sacred meanings, gender divisions were jealously sanctified by sharia-based codes of family in the region.

Second, to redefine the sharia as a human endeavor of interpretation made by male scholars centuries ago and to activate the Islamic principle of *ijtihād* meant opening the religious field to feminist interventions. Third, to enjoin the state to ratify CEDAW with no reservations is to inscribe the women's movement in Morocco into a global dynamic that takes universal definitions of women's rights as the basis for all negotiations with the Moroccan state. The campaign also enjoined the state to take into account what they call "a reality criteria or principle," which refers to the changes that affected Moroccan society and the women's population while also considering the question of reforming the *mudawwana* (see al-Ahnaf 1994). In other words, the petition stated that the *mudawwana* opposed the advances that women had made and their contributions in all sectors of the economy, as compared with their marginal status in the *mudawwana*.

Though the petition was claiming to speak on behalf of all Moroccan women, it is clear that its demands were informed by the needs of a middle class of professional women whose free circulation was obstructed by male tutorship. It is, then, at this intersection of class and gender that one should understand the focus of the petition, aimed at achieving gender equality and eliminating male guardianship rights over women, as it is clear from the demands below.

The One Million Signature Campaign called for the following amendments: (1) suppression of the *wilāya* (marital guardianship) and acknowledgment of legal competency for women at the age of twenty-one; (2) instituting equality and complementarity between husband and wife in the family; (3) stipulating that husbands and wives have the same rights and obligations within marriage; (4) equal guardianship rights for men and women over children; (5) the right of women to keep the conjugal home in case of divorce; (6) abolition of polygamy; (7) abolition of repudiation and regulation of divorce through the courts; (8) equal rights for women to obtain a divorce from the courts; and (9) indisputable rights to education and work (al-Ahnaf 1994; Daoud 1993). The first version of the UAF petition also demanded equal inheritance rights, but this demand was withdrawn from the petition because of its direct challenge to Qur'anic directives. The petition also called for the ratification of CEDAW with no reservations, and for the revision of the *mālikī fiqh*, which is the school of interpretation of the sharia followed in Morocco, and for the activation of the Islamic principle of *ijtihād*.

To argue that the sharia is a human endeavor of interpretation made by male scholars centuries ago, and that the *mālikī fiqh* is only one possible interpretation among others, is to expose the movement to multiple fronts of opposition: first, the Islamist opposition to the universalist framework of gender equality; second, the authority of the king as Commander of the Faithful; and third, the conservative forces in society and within the government that equate the sharia to god's law. The three challenges exposed feminist groups to a wide range of conservatives within the state, political parties, society, and religious scholarship, as well as the 'ulama, all of whom used the sharia in conflation with god's words for political bargaining and mobilized the *mālikī fiqh* as the main defining element of national identity.

In order to locate this debate within contemporary scholarship on Islam, let us revisit al-Azmeh's (1996) very insightful study *Islam and Modernities,* which is one of the most comprehensive approaches to the sharia as a human interpretation. Al-Azmeh warns against confusing Islamic law with the requirements of Islamist ideology and stresses the "technical nature" of the sharia as shaped by different juridical schools of interpretation of the Qur'an and sunna. He defines the sharia as a "repertoire of precedents, cases and general principles, along with a body of well-developed hermeneutical and paralogical techniques" (al-Azmeh 1996, 12). Islamic law as a corpus, al-Azmeh argues, "is predominantly private: it treats obligation, contract, personal status (including succession), and other aspects of secular life" (12). He argues that the "the practice of Islamic law has been one of wide latitude in opinions over special points of law, *ikhtilāf*" (11).

Following the same line, Bishara (1995) states that the Qur'an defines the sharia as the "way" or the "path" rather than a set of strict regulations. According to Bishara, the sharia signifies currently "all Islamic *fiqh,* that is the commentaries and branches of theology that have developed around the Qur'an and sunna" (1995, 93). Thus, he concludes that the Islamic *fiqh* is "a human product, a cultural enterprise that arose as a function of changing historical circumstances" (93). For Bishara, even in the time of the prophet and the first caliphs, the sharia did not provide the principle of ruling but was rather produced by ruling (95).

Building a Movement: Feminist Culture

Feminist scholarship has stressed the centrality of culture, ideology, and discourse in women's organizations (Ferree and Martin 1995; Ryan 1992). While defining the term "culture" in the more encompassing sense of experience, knowledge, and emotion, Ferree (1992) contends that feminism has been particularly concerned with consciously and deliberately constructing perspectives grounded in women's own experiences. Alvarez, speaking in the context of Latin American authoritarianism, uses the term "feminist politics" to express the way feminists fashioned a distinct cultural politics based on radical practices and autonomy in reaction to both exclusionary and repressive regime institutions and the "democratic centralism" of the leftist opposition (Alvarez 1998, 298).

The importance of a feminist press as a means to disseminate a feminist culture, politics, and "ideology" (Ryan 1992) was acknowledged by the scholarship on the women's movement in the Middle East (Moghadam 2002; Paidar 2002; Skali 2006; Thamānia Mars Collective 1993). The feminist press played an essential role in the phase of mobilization characterized by a consciousness-raising type of activism. In Morocco, the feminist magazine *Thamānia Mars* (March 8) played an instrumental role in this phase of mobilization. Launched in 1983 by the same group of activists who later formed the UAF organization, *Thamānia Mars* is still perceived by many women's groups as marking a crucial moment in the invention of a feminist culture of equality and rights in Morocco. The magazine also helped federate women from the secular left around an ideal of gender equality.

The slogan of *Thamānia Mars,* "for a mass progressive and independent women's movement," aligns this group with other leftist organizations involved in class struggle. Khadija Amiti, a university professor of sociology and founding member of the UAF, describes *Thamānia Mars* as a "podium that allowed women from different educational and social backgrounds to voice their experiences, ambitions, and suffering under the existing *mudawwana*." This magazine was the primary source of information and consciousness-raising for students and professional middle-class women. *Thamānia Mars* targeted the *mudawwana* by directing public opinion toward the various violations of women's rights taking place under this codification. To reach this goal, the magazine devoted the column "Let Me Speak Up" to women's testimonies, stories, literary texts, and artistic expression. Through *Thamānia Mars,* the UAF was able to sway public opinion and to accumulate an impressive amount of firsthand material for its One Million Signature Campaign. *Thamānia Mars* is in fact credited as the only publication that prioritized the issue of gender equality and provided new perspectives on law, politics, society, and economics from a feminist standpoint.

The publication of *Thamānia Mars* coincided with the implementation of the structural adjustment program by the Moroccan government in 1983 (see Thamānia Mars Collective 1993). This period saw various violations of even the few rights that women did enjoy under the existing *mudawwana*. Most of these violations, argues political scientist Zakya Daoud (1993), were justified by the economic crisis, in which there was high unemployment. In her study on feminism in the Maghreb, Daoud provides examples of abuses made by legal agents in charge of enforcing the law. This ranged from withholding alimony to refusing to inscribe marriage contract conditions, such as a wife's right to work or to forbid her husband from taking a second wife, as permitted under the existing family law. As Daoud notes, these violations are legitimized by women's definition in the *mudawwana,* first and foremost as housewives and second-class citizens.

Throughout its first decade and more (1983–95), *Thamānia Mars* was the forum from which the readership composed of students, young professionals, and members of leftist political parties could publish poems, short stories, and journalistic reports on the state of women's rights in the country. The use of Arabic as the language of publication facilitated the reception of the magazine by students who sold and read it on their own campuses. The magazine was almost the only forum from which women's rights groups could articulate their responses to growing Islamist activism on university campuses.

These experiences had a significant impact on the feminist movement in Morocco as a whole. First, through *Thamānia Mars,* the UAF group launched the first public debate on the different forms of discrimination against women and showed their connection to the definition of women as subordinate to men in family law. Second, the magazine allowed women who were organizationally dispersed in various party structures, unions, and human rights organizations to be connected in what Katzentein calls a "discursive community through shared narratives and newly named experiences" (1995, 45). The magazine bridged women working within different leftist political groups and parties, uniting them around the same goal: that of reforming the *mudawwana.*

When asked to evaluate the impact of *Thamānia Mars,* Fatima Maghnaoui, the vice president for the UAF, responded that this magazine "was the place where women's identity politics was formed and the stage that allowed women to move from a politics of protest to a politics of participation in building alternatives." Khadija Amiti, sociologist and founding member of the UAF, stated that " *Thamānia Mars* helped the feminist movement to enter the political realm from the back door." In fact, the UAF petition campaign instigated the first interactions of women's groups with policy makers throughout the political spectrum.

The petition campaign was launched on March 5, 1992, during the conference Women, Democracy, and Civil Society. A report detailing the study's findings was sent to the different political parties, the president of the Parliament, and parliamentary groups, urging them to take into account women's demands in their discussions of constitutional reform (see Daoud 1993): "The consequential changes in women's conditions, besides the increasing ambition of women to implement equality and emancipation in the context of social and political democracy, urged the feminist movement to target first and foremost the reform of the *mudawwana*" (al-Ahnaf 1994, 10).

Feminist Strategies

In their mailing, the UAF articulated their demands through multiple frameworks: first, through the Moroccan constitution, which "enshrines full equality for all citizens," by showing how the *mudawwana* was indeed a violation of this constitution; second, through the United Nations conventions, by reminding the state of its obligations to respect international law and comply with the definition of women's rights, as determined by the Copenhagen Convention and the Nairobi Resolutions; and third, through the discrepancies between the concrete contributions of women at all levels and their inferiority before the law.

Regarding this third framework, the UAF argued that the *mudawwana* was "far behind the concrete evolution of Moroccan society and the changes impacting family structure," and called for "the adjustment of the *mudawwana* to these changes." Fourth, and finally, they pointed out that although the Islamic sharia "describes full rights for both men and women," some of the regulations enclosed in the *mudawwana* are not based on the sharia but rather on the Napoleonic Code inherited from the colonial French legal system (Moulay R'chid 1991). Hence, the mailing challenged the exclusivity of the *mālikī fiqh* and called for a reactivation of *ijtihād,* while asking the legislator to determine more precisely the range of rights that women enjoy under the amended Moroccan constitution. Further, the mailing also requested that all elected bodies include a quota of 20 percent women.

On March 7, 1992, the UAF held a press conference to announce the campaign and published the petition in *Thamānia Mars* the following day. The UAF used various strategies to sensitize the public, including media blitzes and the creation of neighborhood-based committees in different cities and towns. The group also organized countless meetings, conferences, and workshops outlining the campaign to the public. The National Coordinating Council, created on March 5 in the offices of the Organisation Marocaine des Droits de l'Homme (Moroccan Organization for Human Rights, OMDH), was in charge of coordinating this impressive mobilization. It comprised women from leftist political parties, labor unions, women's groups, and human rights organizations. This mobilization was highly effective and, according to Fatima Maghnaoui and Khadija Amiti, more than one million signatures were collected in less than three months' time.

The second key contribution of the UAF came through the "Court for Arab Women." This is a transnational mobilization launched in the aftermath of the Islamist protests against the One Million Signatures Campaign. It was a highly publicized annual meeting of lawyers, academics, activists for women's rights, and decision makers from all over the Arab world. The purpose of this court was to simulate trials and present cases on questions related to family law while building a transnational movement for advocating reforms of the various codes of the family in the region. The Court for Arab Women launched a transnational dynamic of communication, exchange of experiences, and solidarity between Arab feminists that originated in Morocco.

A decade later, the UAF's leaders still view transnational mobilization as the articulation of the human rights discourse emerging from the Vienna Conference on Human Rights (1993), which enabled a framing of women's rights as human rights. Through the annual Court for Arab Women, the UAF exposed the shortcomings of Arab legal regimes and their inability to respond to women's calls for justice, economic security, and legal protection. What made this experience so powerful was the involvement of lawyers and judges of both sexes in the simulation of cases that were also open to the public and the press. The Arab Women's Court also exposed the commonalities between women's struggles with the various family laws in the Arab world and led to another dynamic of reflection, research, publication, and compilation of data by women's centers and study groups across the region.

Open Secularism

The ADFM led the second transnational mobilization for reforming family law, by creating the Collectif 95 Maghreb Egalité. The Collectif 95 was the outcome of feminist groups' mobilization in Algeria, Tunisia, and Morocco at the conjuncture of the creation of the Union du Maghreb Arabe by the political leaders of Morocco, Algeria, Tunisia, Libya, and Mauritania in 1991. ADFM seized this opportunity to call for a meeting in Rabat of women's NGOs, academics, and lawyers from Tunisia, Algeria, and Morocco, who joined their effort to launch the Collectif 95. In the English version of the Collectif 95's mission statement, one can read:

> The *Collectif 95 Maghreb Egalité* is a network whose action is inscribed in the dynamic of the women's movement in three countries of the *Maghreb region*. . . . Its goal is to promote a regional approach and a co-ordination of efforts in preparation of the 4th World Conference on Women in Beijing

1995. The women who initiated this network believe that struggle for equality between women and men is a prerequisite for access to citizenship. The
commitment to de jure and de facto equality, of paramount importance
for democracy and sustainable development, is at the heart of the fundamental choice between progress or regression which our societies are facing.[1]

Since their earliest publications, the Collectif 95 articulated the feminist
slogan "the personal is political" by claiming that "women's inferiority" in
the public sphere is closely linked to their secondary position in the private
realm of the family. The Collectif states: "The woman's struggle for a real
equality and an effective citizenship must be founded on the respect of these
rights, not only in public life but in private life as well. The juridical inferiority of the woman, within the family, is indeed at the origin of discriminations against her in the public sphere" (Collectif 95 1995).

As women's rights advocates, this transnational feminist network engaged
in advocacy campaigns, lobbying their respective governments to ratify the
Copenhagen Convention without reservations and to promote codifications
that would respect full equality between men and women in the Maghreb.
Though sharing with the UAF group a focus on reforming family law, the
Collectif 95 did not initially incorporate the sharia into their framework of
advocacy, creating the first openly secular and transnational feminism in North
Africa. The founding documents of this network used the discourse of democratization and citizenship—disseminated by the state-controlled media—to
legitimize the UN regime of rights, notably CEDAW. These arguments were
articulated in some of the Collectif 95's publications: "The development of
women's NGOs and the defense of human rights both contribute, at the same
time, to the democratic movement and process of secularization of morals
and to the reinforcement of civil society . . . a decisive move toward the real-
ization of democracy and the objectives of durable human development. The
pledge for juridical and effective equality of rights is therefore at the heart of
the fundamental choice between progress and regression which our societies
face" (Collectif 95 1995, 8).

This discourse on equality is informed by international norms as this
statement testifies: "The universality of the values and principles on which are
founded the international deeds of promotion and protection of the human
person's rights constitute an essential reference" (Collectif 95 1995, 6).

The Collectif 95 specified its long-term strategies. The first was to com-
pile data on the state of women's rights in order to complete or challenge
government reports. The Collectif's report reflected on the extent of the three
North African governments' compliance with the Nairobi Resolutions and

other international conventions. Second, it suggested a "unified platform for a nondiscriminatory codification of women's rights in the Maghreb," based on equality of all before the law. The most important outcome of this transnational network was a proposal for a unified codification of women's rights: the One Hundred Measures and Provisions for a Maghrebian Egalitarian Codification of the Personal Statute and Family Law.

This is the first openly secular proposal for a reform of family law in the three North African countries. The document opposes the grounding of family law in the sharia and suggests a new codification that respects the universal framework of gender equality and rights (Collectif 95 1995). In addition to the One Hundred Measures proposal, Collectif 95 continued to publish reports on the state of women rights drawing to their forums and public campaigns academics, activists, researchers, and decision makers from North Africa and the Middle East. By acting exclusively within a secular framework, the Collectif 95 intended to first disarm the Islamist opposition and its discourse of cultural authenticity, and then subvert this discourse by validating the universalist framework through Islam, as the following quotation shows:

> The international rule concerning women's rights is based on three fundamental principles: freedom, equality and non-discrimination. These principles . . . are also the values referred to by millions of men and women for whom Islam is the just medium of tolerance, respect for human dignity, and love of knowledge. . . . In fact, it is from this system of values that an international consensus was elaborated. . . . This reference to universality does not at all appropriate any Western monopoly whatsoever to the person's rights, and the stress should be put on the diversity and multiplicity of the origins of thoughts that, through many millenniums and over all the continents, have converged in the emergence of an intercultural consensus, as a culture of human rights, founded on the respect of the human person and her dignity as well as the rejection of all forms of discrimination. (Collectif 95 1995, 8–11)

This discourse reflects the Collectif 95's response to the regional struggles and challenges posed by the rise of radical Islamism in Algeria and the fear of it spinning over to Tunisia and Morocco. In Algeria the 1990s beheld the rise of the radical Islamic Front du Salut (Islamic Salvation Front), which targeted women's secular organizations, among others. Tunisia followed a different path. The government ensured its hold on political institutions by curtailing human rights, including the right of women to freely circulate. In

Morocco, the Islamists were on the rise and were getting ready to occupy political positions. In this context, opening the debate on the modernization of Islam was a risky task, but one worth taking according to members of the Collectif 95. They expressed this goal—of modernizing Islam—in a very straightforward manner through meetings, conferences, and publications: "The challenges set in motion by modernity require actions not only in the economic, political, legislative, demographic and educative levels, but cultural [as well], [as a test] of the ability of Islam to question itself and draw its dynamics of evolution" (Collectif 95 1995, 8–11).

To understand the importance of situating the feminist movement in a *modernized* Islam, we need to keep in mind that Islamists have been articulating a discourse of "Islamizing modernity." This would bring the Islamic sharia back to the forefront, as a foundation of the norms that regulate modern life. It is within the borderlines of these two discourses of modernity and Islam that both movements organize their campaign around the reform of family law.

Global Funds: Feminist Divisions

The question of funds has been another source of contention, even among feminist groups. Both the UAF and the ADFM acknowledged that it is easier to connect with transnational (i.e., northern) donors when demands are framed in the rhetorics of development and gender equality. Their divisions stem, however, from the way they have handled the question of foreign funds in relation to the petition campaign. Many founding members of the UAF restated their choice to keep the struggle over reforming the *mudawwana* outside of all kinds of foreign influence or funds.[2] They saw the *mudawwana* as a highly sensitive issue and a question of "national interest" that they did not want to subject to the agendas of foreign donors. Behind this fear, there was also a deep awareness and concern about how Islamists could use the usual charge of Westernization to dismiss feminist demands.

The ADFM group did not pursue a similar path. Most publications, workshops, and meetings of the ADFM and the Collectif 95 were supported by European funds, notably from the German foundation Friedrich Ebert Stiftung (FES), an affiliate of the German Social Democratic Party. This foundation sponsored the formation of the Collectif 95 and its publications. This is why it is inaccurate to assess the impact of the feminist movement in Morocco without looking at the major role played by feminist activists in the production of knowledge regarding women and gender outside of academic structures (see Brand 1998).

Women's Research Groups

Any study of the feminist movement during the 1980s and the 1990s is incomplete if it does not include the role played by women's research groups. The lack of women's and gender studies programs in academic institutions enabled the emergence of new groups of scholar–activists willing to bridge academia with feminist politics. The sociologist and leading Moroccan feminist Fatima Mernissi played a major role in this phase through her publications and global networks. In her writings, Mernissi used a feminist methodology to counter the legal definition of women as dependent housewives. Her book *Doing Daily Battle* (1988) voices the concerns of working-class women living in poor urban neighborhoods, and illustrates their struggle as heads of households. The aim of the book, as she puts it in her introduction, is to illustrate the discrepancies between social and legal representations of women as housewives and their lived reality. Mernissi also mobilized her international network and used her notoriety as a prominent figure in Arab feminism to attract funds for supporting feminist research and activism. This effort to connect local players with international donors culminated in several academic conferences, workshops, and book series (see Brand 1998; Paris 1989).[3] These forums were instrumental to the recognition of women's voices within and outside of academia and to the production of feminist knowledge and scholarship that countered the existing regimes of "truths" about women.

Thus, the 1980s and 1990s brought forth a proliferation of publications on women written by a generation of scholars who had benefited from the state-sponsored bilingual education of the 1970s and early 1980s, and who were educated in the Marxist tradition dominating the social sciences in Moroccan academia. This collective production of books on gender and women started during the 1980s and was sponsored by the German foundation Konrad Adenauer Stiftung (KAS), an affiliate of the German Christian Democratic Party. The latter started collaborating with Moroccan academics in 1985 by allocating funds to the prestigious University Mohammed V in support of the group Approches, first directed by Fatima Mernissi and later by sociologist Aicha Belarbi. These funds allowed for the production of the first book series (ten volumes) on Moroccan women. This series and the others that followed helped to fill the women's studies gap within Moroccan academia and sharply boost interest in women's issues among the male scholars who contributed to them.

During the 1990s some of these series approached hot issues such as citizenship rights and Islam. The series "Women: Future Citizens of the Maghreb" and "Humanistic Islam" are the culmination of these efforts. The funds for related workshops and the publication of these books came from numerous transnational and international organizations including FES, KAS, the U.S.-based National Endowment for Democracy, and the United Nations University for Women, to name but a few. Later, other funds were secured through the Canadian Agency for Development, ACDI, Oxfam, and many others. These books were written in both Arabic and French, though French publications remained predominant. However, reaching a greater readership required competing with Islamist groups, who were prolific in sponsoring publications in Arabic. The Collectif 95 took on this challenge by providing Arabic translations of all its publications, notably those sponsored through FES.

Feminism and the State

Feminist groups' relationship to the state saw major shifts during the 1990s. The issue of co-optation was very present in women's activism, especially when the political left was still heading the opposition. But there were many ways in which these groups had to deal with the state regulations about associational life, foreign funds, and the required authorizations and mediations that these groups had to endorse in order to operate. The following statement by Fatouma Benabedenbi, the president of the ESPOD (Espace Point de Depart) association for promoting women's micro-businesses, illustrates the main shifts that occurred in the relationship between feminist groups as a whole and the state: "During the 1980s, we used to be very cautious about engaging the state. We were so sensitive to co-option that we wanted to keep the state out of our business. We wanted independence, but that meant working at the margin of the state and in parallel to the state institution. This was a mistake. In the 1990s we changed our approach. We realized that we need the state as much as the state needs us. This change in perspective helped us to penetrate most state institutions and create interest in gender issues with most of them."

The opportunities opened by the Beijing Conference, the negotiations between the state and its opposition, and the neoliberal orientations of the economy gave this drive a major impetus. Not only did feminist groups realize they needed the state, but the reverse was also true. As the state was enduring deep economic and political changes, new allies were needed to support the liberalization project. Equipped with funds and international conventions on women's rights, feminist groups became natural allies to the state, at least as far as the discourse of citizenship, rights and development was concerned.

The political liberalization of state institutions and the inclusion of the former opposition into the government had both certainly shaped the categories of belonging (see Paoli and Telles 1998, 99) and modes of subjectification adopted by liberal feminism in the 1990s. Nevertheless, the challenge for these groups stems from how to expand the notion of citizenship to the codification of family law and its definition of women as second-class citizens and dependents. The other challenge was to question a process of liberalization that was not truly inclusive of women's voices. How did feminist mobilization enable or obstruct this process? One way to consider this impact is by analyzing the meanings of the petition campaign for political liberalization of the state.

First, when feminist groups directed their claims to the Parliament, they were in fact putting their movement ahead of the process of democratization that was still under negotiation by other actors. Their goal was to shift the amendment of family law away from the realm of the king's and the 'ulama's authority, and into the legislative purview where it belonged. Getting Parliament involved in an issue considered up to that point as the private domain of the king provided the legislative branch with the legitimacy it was missing.

Second, by launching their public campaign, feminist groups meant to place the debate in the civil arena, where it would be appropriated by non-religious actors. Without a doubt, the debates launched by the One Million Signature Campaign were widespread. Controversies broke out in homes, schools, university campuses, cafes, and the press (see al-Ahnaf 1994; Daoud 1993). It was also the first time that a large audience could watch, on state-sponsored television, young women with a modern education challenging the 'ulama's interpretations of religion in broadcast debates (see al-Ahnaf 1994; Brand 1998).

Third, feminists' use of the upcoming Beijing Conference (1995) as a framework for the debate about reform compelled the state to have something in hand for the conference. The government's ratification of CEDAW and the first changes made to the *mudawwana,* both occurring in 1993, were concrete responses to the feminist mobilization. Obviously, the success of feminist groups in affecting state policy did not leave the Islamist leadership undisturbed. During the month of April 1992, there were major attacks in the Islamist press on the petitioners, including calls for capital punishment to be applied to women for apostasy, which also put in question the king's authority as the Commander of the Faithful.

Thus, only the king's address to the nation in August 1993 could put an end to the controversy launched by the petition campaign. In his address, the king did promise revisions to the *mudawwana,* but he decided to bring the issue back to his realm of personal authority. It is worth noting here that during the passionate debates caused by the petition, political parties remained silent. Some, including the Istiqlal and the USFP, the two major components of the opposition, had even enjoined their female members to withdraw from the National Coordinating Council, established by the UAF (see al-Ahnaf 1994; Brand 1998; Daoud 1993). According to some analysts, the UAF's campaign put at stake the unity of the *kutla* (oppositional bloc), which components might split over the support of the OADP (one member of the kutla) for women's demands (Brand 1998; Daoud 1993). The *kutla* was very cautious about whether their unconditional support for feminist demands would benefit the OADP (main party of affiliation of the UAF's members) in the upcoming elections.

Hence, in the face of vigorous mobilization of Islamist activists against the project of reform, feminist groups found themselves deprived of any significant support from political parties and divided about the leadership of their movement. These challenges would not prevent them, however, from shaping Islamist women's activism and their collective identities around the question of women's rights and family law reform. This is the process that I describe in terms of the feminization of Islamist women.

Feminization of Islamist Women

I have defined the One Million Signature Campaign as a movement moment that enables us to explore the contradictions and tensions but also the intersections among the feminist and the Islamist women's movements. In this part I will describe the effects of this mobilization in changing discourses, agendas, and types of organizations set in motion by Islamist women.[4] *Feminization* refers not only to changes in Islamist women's organizing but also encompasses the strategic changes adopted by the male leadership of these movements as they were attempting to respond to secular feminism with the rise of Islamic feminism. Thus, I do not limit the term "feminization" to the opening of Islamist women to the discourse of women's rights, but rather I extend the term to the transformations that began taking place within the male-dominated Islamist movements.

While stating this, I do consider Islamist women as main players in what most studies have called the Islamist countermobilization. The latter was an overwhelming force, directed by a male leadership and members of al-Tawhīd wa-l-islāh as well as the independent and mainstream 'ulama. All these agents used the Islamist press to publish various forms of condemnation of the petition and its petitioners. In what follows, I will expose the most significant reactions of the Islamists to the petition campaign before focusing on women's agency and their instrumental role in this mobilization.

Most studies of the Islamist mobilization have focused on the death penalty *fatwa* (religious statement) issued in the Islamist press as the point of entry for understanding the disruptive effect of the feminist movement and its potential for social change. The fatwa was issued by al-Tajkani, a leading activist in the movement al-Islāh wa-l-tajdīd (Reform and Renewal) (see al-Ahnaf 1994; Brand 1998; Daoud 1993). Al-Tajkani was one of the "independent" Islamist 'ulama, who was also a columnist for the Islamist newspaper *Al-Rāya*. His fatwa came one month after the feminist petition, in April 1992, as he was responding to readers' questions about the petition in his column. His fatwa paved the way for more accusations and defamations published by a proliferating Islamist press, such as *Al Forkāne* and *Al-Rāya,* in the months following the petition.

The second significant reaction came from an executive member of al-Islāh wa-l-tajdīd and director of *Al-Rāya*, Abdelilah Benkirane. On April 21 Benkirane expressed the official position of his movement in the opening pages of the magazine. He declared the petition unconstitutional because of its marginalization of Islam as the religion of the state and the foundation of its laws (Benkirane 1992, 17). He also dismissed feminist challenges to "divine precepts" through the use of "a quantitative source of pressure" (one million signatures). Nevertheless, he cynically agreed that "the *mudawwana* should be reformed, along with *all the state's laws,* but toward more compliance with the Islamic sharia" (17, emphasis added). He concluded his reaction with another call, this time enjoining everybody, including "the 'ulama, the state, and the Moroccan Muslim people," to rise up in order "to protect the Islamic faith and the Muslim family" from the feminist threat.

The 'Ulama Reaction

Compelled to respond to these various calls, the 'ulama joined the Islamist mobilization. They organized their representative councils across the country and published their collective statement in the form of an open letter to the prime minister and the president of the Parliament in *Al-Rāya*.[5] Attached to the statement, they presented a counterpetition signed by prominent figures. Both the statement and the counterpetition were published in the Islamist press in July 1992. In their three-page statement, the 'ulama addressed the "Moroccan people," to remind them that the campaign was indeed the continuation of a global assault on Islam and on Muslims, no different from what was happening in Palestine, Afghanistan, Iraq, and Bosnia. Feminist groups were accused of being "the instrument of the new crusades launched by the colonial order on the Muslims everywhere." In order to assess the seriousness of these accusations, it is important to keep in mind the general mood in Morocco after the attack on Iraq in 1991 and the widespread opposition to the Gulf War, which was expressed by one of the largest rallies in the history of independent Morocco. It is worth noting that all feminist leaders and organizations took part in the rally, but it seems that this piece of information went missing from the Islamist debate.

In their counterpetition, the 'ulama also stipulated that the sharia does not conflict with the international conventions or with the Moroccan constitution (articles 13-12-8), which enshrines equal rights for all citizens. They also stated that the sharia asserts the equality of men and women before god. While acknowledging these points of convergence, however, the 'ulama reaffirmed the supremacy of "god's law" over all human regulations. They dismissed the legitimacy of any practice of *ijtihād* by feminist groups, who lack the mandatory expertise in Islamic knowledge. To bring the king's authority back into the debate, the 'ulama argued that the "feminist petition puts at stake the state's sovereignty and challenges its authority over its citizens." In their petition, they reminded the state of the necessity to raise the local norms above international conventions, and prompted the state to "discipline" the citizens who do not respect these norms. The feminists were once again accused of apostasy and found guilty of "creating divisions among Muslims at the time that Muslim peoples are the most fragile and exposed to global-scale oppression." It is worth noting, however, that during their campaign to reinstate the primacy of the sharia, the 'ulama appropriated the same strategy used by the UAF by launching a petition—signed by representatives of the 'ulama's council all over the country—to the president of the Parliament and to the prime minister.

Engendering the Islamist Response

Most studies about the One Million Signature Campaign have focused on the Islamist male response. To them, feminist groups lost the case because of the forceful mobilization by the Islamist male leadership and 'ulama. I would like to propose here a counterargument that shows how much of this response was in fact instigated by young women activists within Islamist organizations. In contrast to previous studies, I want to locate Islamist women in a central position as agents who fueled the controversy in the Islamist press, in forums, and in society at large, because of their embeddedness in many state and nonstate institutions, such as schools, mosques, and women's communities. I illustrate this argument in the following parts.

I want to start by making these few points. First, Islamist women started their mobilization against the UAF's campaign as soon as the latter was presented at the press conference on March 9, 1992. Most systematic responses appeared in the press of the al-Islāh wa-l-tajdīd movement during that same month of March. Second, even the most vehement fatwa of al-Tajkani, which implied capital punishment for the petitioners, was in fact prompted by a group of Islamist women who enjoined the male leadership to react with a public statement. In a nutshell, the reactions outlined earlier were instigated by Islamist women and based on their immediate mobilization against the feminist campaign. I will now detail these points.

As I introduced earlier, the encounter of feminist and Islamist women did not start with the UAF campaign but rather with the publication of *Thamānia Mars*. This magazine was indeed the only feminist paper that was challenging a wide range of proliferating Islamist periodicals, such as *Al-Nūr, Al-Sahwa, Al-Rāya,* and *Al Forkāne.* The latter was created in July 1984 and became the privileged forum for young women who were either members or supporters of al-Islāh wa-l-tajdīd. Early contributions by women to the Islamist press were not, however, concerned with issues of gender equality. Instead, they stressed the new choices made by a growing population of educated women who adopted the veil as an Islamic form of attire during the 1980s, and who started writing in the male-owned Islamist press about their alternative views on society, "tradition," "culture," and "womanhood." In what follows, I will present some of these voices to show their feminist implications and how they gradually encompassed a discourse of women's rights and power, notably after the One Million Signature Campaign.

Early Writings

Islamist women's writings in the magazine *Al Forkāne* can be traced back to the early 1980s. The young activists who pioneered the movement of veiling were mostly concerned with defining womanhood, men's and women's separate territories, and the various "civilizational" meanings of the hijab, called also *al-libas al-shar'i* (Islamic dress). These activists constructed the veil as a potent symbol of identity and a marker of the boundaries between the authentic Muslim woman, veiled, and the nonveiled, also called *mutabarrija* (literally, on display) or *'ariya* (unveiled, with the literal meaning of nude) (see al-Sareh 1984, 35). But it is worth noting that since the early 1980s these writings have linked what al-Sareh called the "culture of seduction" to consumerism on the one hand, and to the commodification of the woman's body on the other (al-Sareh 1984). To her, the hijab provides a counternarrative to widespread beliefs about women's responsibility for preserving public morality. Another activist, Oum Naoufal, sees the veil as the means to regulate men and women's interactions in the public sphere. She claims that the veil does not limit women's circulation nor hinder their public contribution, but rather it allows them to "recover the full range of their roles in the public sphere, and to discover the true meanings of their humanity" (Khalil 1991, 10). Whether one considers the veil as a civilizational choice, a symbol of struggles over cultural identification (Charrad 1998, 65), or the embodiment of piety (Mahmood 2005), in this first phase of rising Islamist movements, the veil seemed to be first and foremost a *marker* of the boundaries between the "authentic" Muslim woman and the alienated other. Nevertheless, Islamist women's glorification of the hijab was not only at odds with a feminist understanding of women's emancipation, it also defied the trend to unveil by older generations of women, as well as the drive toward the European fashion that was dominant in public administrations.

Concomitant to this glorification of the veil was another discourse honoring Muslim women as role models and the Muslim family as an ideal type. Some of these arguments were discussed on the pages devoted to reader feedback in *Al Forkāne*. For instance, a reader named Adrit Suad wrote: "Motherhood is your natural mission. But it is also what gives you privileges over men. . . . You are the first person that your child sees and feels, your child is a blank page on which you may inscribe whatever you want. You are the first instructor and role model. You should be aware to ingrain the good; it is your noble mission and religious duty."[6] Another reader, al-Azami, writing in the same section devoted to reader comments, defined motherhood as a "mission," and highlighted the central position of women in the family: "Women are one of the two pillars of the family but the most important creature in a man's life. . . . In the Muslim family, the relationship between husband and wife is built on love, compassion, mutual understanding, trust, and loyalty. These are the seeds that should be cultivated by both men and women. It is not a matter of individual choice but rather an act of faith, because God links the *istikhlāf* [perpetuation of the divine order] to the preservation and strengthening of the family ties."[7] These themes were central in Islamist women's discourse in this early phase. Most of these writings have countered feminist groups' emphasis on gender inequalities with a rhetoric of equal rights and shared responsibilities. The feminist focus on gender hierarchies constituted with no doubt a direct challenge to the patriarchal foundations of the legal system and the family. Conversely, Islamist women's focus on equal responsibilities and rights before god does a different kind of work. Their starting point was to restate the divine origin of "equality in rights and duties" within the Muslim family, before even embarking on any claims about gender oppression. Their approach steered clear of a direct accusation or open challenge to the status quo. It nevertheless drew tremendous legitimacy from engaging the unquestionable sources of the Qur'an and the sunna as a means to buttress their claim about men's and women's *mutual* responsibilities toward each other and *equal* duties before god.

The other recurrent theme in these early writings is *tradition*. For these activists, tradition seems to be a signifier with shifting and contradictory meanings. It refers first to "corrupt" practices carried out by "women who were kept ignorant of the true essence of Islam," as many of my respondents restated. Curiously enough, "tradition" is also the term used to challenge allegedly alien Western values that are taken for granted by "ignorant" women. Tradition is reclaimed as long as it refers to the "authentic" Moroccan values, which shape gender relations in the "Moroccan Muslim family" and provide protection to women. There is then a sense of "good" traditions, referring to the "uncorrupt Moroccan self" and used to depict feminists as *mutagharibat* (Westernized). Another set of meanings articulate the notion of a purified tradition constructed closer to the sources of the Qur'an and sunna by self-educated women. Curiously enough, women are set as symbols of both the authentic and the inauthentic.

In all these cases, the purification of tradition is a practice mediated by a human effort of interpretation and by women's agency. As Mahmood shows, agency does not refer solely to the subversion of norms but also to the way in which norms may be "consolidated" and "inhabited" by women (2005, 15). The reconfiguration of certain meanings of tradition by Islamist women works to both mark and blur class and social boundaries within various women's communities. By activating a broad range of meanings for tradition, the modern and educated veiled woman marks her privileged position in the social hierarchy by her access to the power of knowledge, at the same time as she states her legitimacy in correcting the corrupt practices carried out by women who were kept ignorant of the "true" essence of Islam. My respondents consider tradition as the borderline at which modern subjects of Islamic knowledge meet and interact with the practices of their communities. "Modernness" is the term used by Deeb (2006) to define this modern subject, constructed in the arenas of encounters with modernity, piety, and an "authenticated" tradition.

It is worth noting, however, that conceptions of "good" versus "bad" traditions are postcolonial articulations of modernist discourses that shaped the nationalist struggle for independence (see Lazreg 1994; Narayan 1997; Said 1978). The colonial regime established in Morocco by General Lyautey, the Resident General of the French government, demarcated itself from the regime of "assimilation" that was falling apart in Algeria by insisting on the

Moroccan peoples' "right" to preserve and "keep" their traditions. Lyautey's policy of "respect of the local customs" and "traditions" put the ingredients for a dualist definition of national identity in terms of "authenticity/modernity" (Laroui 1993; Benchekroun 1992; Waterbury 1970), a notion reproduced in Islamist women's articulations of their identity politics.

In fact, the nationalist movement reacted to Lyautey by representing tradition as both an obstacle to the modernization of Morocco and the emancipation of women, as well as a site for fighting against colonial penetration by the French (see al-Fassi 1979). The articulation of the colonial discourse on preserving traditions and the nationalist modernist discourse of fighting "backward traditions" set the limits, I argue, of the contemporary debates of both Islamists and feminists, in which women became the shifting symbols of both.

Furthermore, a selective use of the meanings of tradition enabled Islamist women to position themselves as "agents" and to counter "role encapsulation," as Klatch describes in her study of right-wing women in the United States (Klatch 1986). As we will see, the Islamist women's leaders had been, since the early 1980s, among the most vehement advocates of women's presence in the public sphere as long as modesty was observed. It is my purpose here to show how the feminist mass petition campaign gave this drive significant momentum.

Alternative Discourse of Rights

Islamist women defined women's rights in a very singular way, by drawing on two Qur'anic terms: *istikhlāf* and *da'wa*. *Istikhlāf* is used in the Qur'an to signify the responsibility of humankind to fulfill the divine order. *Da'wa* refers to the duty of all Muslims to invite and call upon others to follow the message of god, namely Islam. Having defined *istikhlāf* and *da'wa* as "inclusive of women," Islamist women articulated these new definitions in their writings to claim their share of responsibility in practicing *da'wa*. To this end, they brought to the forefront a Qur'anic verse: "Believers are protectors of one another: they enjoin what is just, and forbid what is evil" (al-Maida, Surat 71). The Qur'anic term "believers" (the faithful) is defined by all my respondents as an "inclusive category, not a gendered one." This leadership maintains that not only women have the same responsibility to undertake *da'wa,* but they are also better positioned than men for this task. As mothers, women possess natural qualities that prepare them to be *more* effective in communicating the message of god.

This discourse has important gender and political implications. It legitimizes women's presence in the public sphere as a pledge of faith—a religious duty rather than a feminist concern. Islamist women's writings reversed liberal feminist claims that a woman's emancipation is contingent upon her rupture with a religious tradition. On the contrary, Islam stands as an emancipatory faith to Islamist women because it does not reduce women to one dimension of a commodified, objectified body. Al-Hilali, writing in *Al-Rāya,* expressed her opposition to the "one-dimensional woman": "Women's large contribution to social change was restricted by her definition as first and foremost a consumer. Reducing women to their appearance challenges the more complete Islamic definition of women as equally responsible, alongside men, for building a just society and a balanced world order. The Qur'anic message is inclusive; it addresses men and women as believers and *umma* [a community of faith] and puts no restriction whatsoever on women's large contribution to all spheres."[8]

Emphasizing the equal responsibilities of men and women enabled Islamist women to tackle the question of rights in a very singular way. What they propose is a duty-bound approach that consists of endorsing mutual obligations in order to turn them into mutual rights. Obligations are closely related to the allegedly mandatory contribution to *da'wa* of all Muslims, independent of gender, underscoring the centrality of *da'wa* to the coherence and welfare of the *umma*. Within this framework, the family is defined as an interdependent structure of "complementary roles" and "mutual responsibilities" (Khalil 1991, 10–11). This definition excludes any notion of power relations, since the *umma* is this "imagined" community (Anderson 1991) of sisters and brothers who are equal before god. "Womanhood" is central to this conception. As stated by Khadija Mufid, the leading activist in al-Tawhīd wa-l-islāh, women are not "only half of the society, they are also educators of the other half."

This location of women as educators is a strategic point of entry to instigate deeper changes in the private as well as the public sphere. In one of my numerous meetings with Khadija Mufid, she defined *da'wa* as "Islamic education" and made it central to the Islamic faith while restating women's pivotal role as *dā'iyyat* (agents of *da'wa*). This discursive effort to define *da'wa* as closer to women's nature and social location enables Islamist women to place their activism at the center of both the Islamic faith and the Islamic *umma*. Furthermore, by emphasizing women's roles as educators of the *umma,* this leadership was negotiating its access to the public sphere, but without using the conventional liberal feminist terminology of individual rights and gender equality.

The feminist motivations of such discourse were disclosed immediately, nonetheless, when I asked leadership figures to define the goals of *da'wa,* defined as "Islamic education." Women in both al-'Adl wa-l-ihsāne and al-Tawhīd wa-l-islāh agreed that the purpose of education should be to "uproot the seeds of the culture of denigration of women that is widespread in society and culture." This goal defined the common grounds for Islamist women's activism in both movements, and demarcated the difference between the cultural argument put forward by Islamist women and the legal argument (changing the law) articulated by the feminists. The Islamist leadership argued that a legal reform would not lead to a real cultural transformation, nor would it grant a considerable transformation of women's conditions of life.

In this view, women are not viewed as victims of this "culture of denigration of women" but rather the bearers. Because they are kept ignorant of their privileged place in Islamic doctrine, women have come to endorse their marginalization as a social destiny. Any challenge to this state of mind, however, would need to come from women themselves. Thus, the goal of the women's movement should be to "reconcile women with the culture of respect of womanhood, found in the Qur'an and the sunna," claimed Soumiya Benkhaldoun, a computer engineer and current Parliament deputy from the party al-'Adāla wa-l-tanmia. Reconciling women with the true essence of Islam, other activists add, is the means to fight against corrupt practices based on "superstition" and "emulation of the West."

These representations of women as victims of superstitions and backward traditions are still deeply influenced by the same patriarchal "culture of denigration of women" that these activists claim to be challenging. There are also class and generational struggles. Articulated as "false consciousness," these representations of women's corrupt practices represent, in fact, the projection of widespread images of "poor illiterate women," victims of ignorance, by an educated, urban, middle-class younger generation of "enlightened" women. This condemnation of women's practices is grounded in a framework of modernity that is more clearly articulated in Islamist women's views of "other" women. It carries the legacy of an old nationalist debate about the modernization of women that started under the French colonial regime and was adopted by the urban male bourgeoisie leading the nationalist movement. The latter was heavily influenced by the modernist Salafi school of thought, represented by Egyptian theologians and scholars such as Muhammad Abdu at the turn of the nineteenth century (see Mitchell 1988). In this framework, women are accused of being the main perpetrators of alien traditions that need to be corrected through a return to purified sources of Islam (al-Fassi 1953).

These representations found their way to generations of educated men and women through the textbooks of elementary and secondary education, which become vehicles of a discourse that victimizes women and denounces their "culture" of superstition and ignorance. This explains why one of the main actions taken by feminist groups, notably the ADFM, during the 1990s was revising these textbooks through a gender lens. Hence, despite their pronounced differences, feminists and Islamists have inscribed their activism similarly in the master frames of modernity, rationalism, progress, and emancipation.

I would like to suggest that the problem posed to Islamist women by feminist organizing in this period had more to do with the disruption of this process of constructing a culture of women's rights *within* the discursive platform of the Islamic sharia. The feminist campaign, its gender equality discourse, and its articulation of the international conventions all encroached on Islamist women's efforts to construct a culture of respect for womanhood from within Islam. As a matter of fact, the feminist petition campaign propelled Islamist women to organize their movement in response, rather than simply parallel, to feminist activism.

The Rise of an Islamist Women's Movement

Prior to the feminist petition campaign, Islamist women's identity politics was shaped by their adherence to male-dominated Islamist organizations. As members of these organizations, women had endeavored to advance the general cause of political Islam, namely the rise of "Islamic institutions" in an Islamic state. This insider location of Islamist women was challenged by the perceived political gains of feminist independent organizations and by their focus on women's "strategic interests" (Molyneux 1985). Islamist women had to respond not only to the successes of the feminist movement, but also to the threats it posed to the sacred grounds of family law. Therefore, they had to reposition themselves as "the authentic movement of Moroccan women." As one activist in al-Tawhīd wa-l-islāh stated: "There is only one women's movement in Morocco; it is Islamic."

Islamist women responded immediately to the feminist petition through articles, interviews, counterpetitions, and the mass mobilization of networks nested in the educational system and modern public administrations (see Daoud 1993). It is worth noting that Islamist women's activism underwent a major shift in focus during the feminist campaign. The latter paved the way for the former's debates about women's rights in Islam, and prompted their reflections on the discrepancies between rights and social practices. At the same time, while this leadership was trying to position itself within a movement for women's rights, it also made sure to demarcate the movement from the liberal feminist discourse of individual rights. In what follows, I will illustrate Islamist women's responses to the feminist petition campaign.

Islamist women started organizing their collective responses to the petition as early as March 1992. On March 9 of that year, the newspaper *Al-Rāya* published interviews with the leadership of leaders of various Islamist women's groups.[9] The interviews show the ways in which women started positioning themselves within the women's movement, all the while rejecting the liberal framework of gender oppression and individual rights. One of these activists, Fatema al-Sareh, expressed her doubts over the validity of the feminist approach to the "woman's question" (*qadiyyat al-mar'a*). She claimed: "Many terms have been used to define women: a problem, a question, a dilemma. . . . Yet this terminology only reflects a worldview based on sex wars. It shows the pervasive nature of Western categories propagated in the heart of our society by proponents of the political left who view social relations through the prism of class conflict, now reduced to sex wars. The woman's question has no relevance to Muslim women. Islam offers a fair and just vision of relationships among men and women."

The second question in these interviews opened the way, however, to more expressions of discomfort by these young activists regarding women's conditions in Moroccan society. Aisha al 'Asri, a young activist in al-Tawhīd wa-l-islāh, couched her response in an open criticism of the way women have been "used" and "marginalized" in Muslim society, while making sure, however, to address both Muslim conservatives and liberal feminists: "The Muslim woman has been exploited, alienated, and confined to a marginal position. Women's subordination profoundly affected Muslim society by obstructing women's capabilities as active agents of social change. Nevertheless, the real liberation, *tahrīr,* of women should not be understood in the individualistic and very limited terms of women's rights, nor is it solely contingent upon the liberation of men from the legacy of despotism and political oppression. The real emancipation is collective. The goal should be a civilizational liberation."

In another interview another activist, Khadija Mufid, demarcated herself from both the discourses that use women's rights to "alienate women" and those that mobilize religion to curtail their rights. Mufid argued in the same interviews: "A Muslim woman has to struggle against two restricting models. One impinges on her rights to education, participation, and expression, through defining her as humanly inferior to men. The other gives her these rights while placing her in alien situations and molding her into forms with no content, and lifestyles with no essence. . . . Muslim women bear responsibility for their own oppression; they have left the teachings of Islam and adopted the superficial aspects of emancipation that show nothing else but their colonized mind."

In addition to interviews and press articles, Islamist women held round-tables, conferences, and meetings to organize their collective response to the demands made by the UAF campaign. For instance, during the roundtable called "Moroccan Women: Realities and Aspirations" held by the group al-Thaqāfa al-bāniyya (the Constructive Culture) on March 7, 1992,[10] participants dismissed the UAF's campaign as the "outcome of a distorted understanding of Islam." In her opening statement to the roundtable, al-Hilali challenged "these Westernized advocates of emancipation" by restating women's inalienable rights in Islam. She pointed to a broad range of rights, ranging from "education to free expression, free choice, political rights, and the right to work, to own property, and to manage freely her property."

In addition, al-Hilali discussed the feminists' claims against polygamy, the *wilāya* (marital guardianship), and the *qiwāma* (men as the providers), and rephrased the three as "responsibilities for men rather than privileges, and therefore as rights for women." More particularly, polygamy was defined stipulating "a right" of the second woman to be considered as "a full partner, rather than a lover living in the shadow of the first and with no rights at all." Though polygamy was defined as the right of the second woman to live in a legal marriage situation, it was restricted by al-Hilali to exceptional circumstances. Polygamy, she said, is merely tolerated by Islam and is surely subjected to strict conditions: "Polygamy was not tolerated by the sharia to become the rule, but rather to regulate men's and women's relationships in specific and exceptional cases. Polygamy is also submitted by the sharia to conditions of absolute fairness, equal treatment of the spouses, and preservation of full rights of the spouses and their children. Yet, to abolish polygamy is to violate the right of men and women who may see it as an alternative to divorce."

Curiously enough, despite Islamist women's rhetoric against Western categories, most of these meetings and conferences were organized "in commemoration of the International Women's Day." In fact, the month of March 1992 became the site of disputes over the appropriation of this feminist icon by both feminist and Islamist women's groups. In the case of Islamist women, the appropriation of the Women's Day enabled the leadership to position itself within an international dynamic, which was not inclusive of their voices. In addition, the use of March 8 allowed Islamist women to co-opt and subvert the podium created by the feminist magazine *Thamānia Mars* and use it to build their alternative discourse of women's rights.

To define their new identities as an integral component of the women's movement, members of al-Islāh wa-l-tajdīd took a further step by creating the first women's rights organization with an Islamist agenda: the Organization for the Renewal of Women's Awareness (ORWA). One of the founding members of this organization, Bassima al-Haqaoui, a current Parliament deputy, explained that her organization was created to address "the injustices witnessed and experienced by women in the society." I was also surprised to learn, despite al-Haqaoui's denial of any influence over the petition campaign, that discussions about creating ORWA had started in 1994, only a few months after the first reform of the *mudawwana* in 1993. Al-Haqaoui acknowledged, however, that the forthcoming Beijing Conference was an additional motivation for women who wanted to be included in the international dynamics of women's rights.

The Organization for the Renewal of Women's Awareness (ORWA)

The founding members of ORWA, such as Khadija Mufid and Jamila Masdar, have been active in the movement of al-Islāh wa-l-tajdīd since the early 1980s. As Mufid argued, the leadership of this organization was concerned about "the different forms of violations of women's rights, including their right to veil, but were not satisfied with the existing approaches." ORWA aims at presenting women with Islamic alternatives. Bassima al-Haqaoui, its president, defines the organization as "the place in which women can fight for their rights, without losing their identities."

During the controversy over the NPA, the ORWA members produced translations of their mission statement in French and English, as a means to communicate the goal of their organization to an international audience. In the English version, the ORWA defines its mission around five concepts: humanity, complementarity, equality not similarity, accomplishment of the mission, and independence. Let us see the meanings articulated by these concepts as explained in the mission statement: "Independence means that [the] Woman is responsible for her choices, her own decisions, her principles, not depending on any one else[,] . . . bears full responsibility of her acts . . . and enjoys entire independence in the management of her funds [property]" (ORWA 1995, 20).

"Accomplishment of the mission" is articulated in a nationalist rhetoric: "[The] woman needs to have a goal in her life and . . . live up to her aspirations. The challenge our nation is confronted with concerns both men and women, and requires that the woman must transform by a psychological revolution her piety from simple historical belonging to a real and actual belonging, considering that she is the source of a civilizational potential that must be extracted and invested in a placement that corresponds to the appropriate role" (ORWA 1995, 20).

The term "equality" implies here a notion of equity, not to be understood as "similarity" or the erasure of men's and women's "natural" differences. "Equality" implies a woman's right to recover her full "human potential" without losing her womanhood or femininity. The divine source of "equality" grants women their full humanity and equal responsibility before god. These claims are important as a legitmation for the women's claims for equal treatment within the male-dominated Islamist movements (ORWA 1995, 19). To the ORWA, "humanity" is another term for dignity as the mission statement confirms:

> The organization (ORWA) starts from the rehabilitation of the *humanity* and dignity of women with all the meaning of respect and consideration included in this expression . . . [and from] the affirmation that the relationship of the Woman with the Man is one based on human equitable principles. The discourse of the holy Qur'an focuses on men and women to explain the role, duties, and obligations of each . . . in order to facilitate the creation of an equitable society where humanity will be happy. The Qur'an addresses the Humans in these terms: "Fear God your creator, who created you from one and the same soul," and the prophet, may the peace of the lord be upon him, said: "the women are but the matches of men." (ORWA 1995, 19)

In the euphoria of the upcoming Beijing Conference and feminist debates about gender equality, the ORWA adopted the women's rights discourse, most probably as a means to participate in global debates and set the grounds for its members' participation at the Beijing Conference, as it is clear from the paragraph below:

> We, as a group of women, focus our care on the issues of our like [women] in society, being ourselves close to their problems, ascertaining and witnessing the crushing of their rights, to improve their social standing and the protection of their being by the affirmation and defense of their rights. . . . It has become necessary to claim the safeguarding of the right God has granted to woman [but which society] has belittled. We therefore agree with all the claims internationally requested, which are not in contradiction with our religious, cultural, and social reference [background]. (ORWA 1995 25)

The next quotation shows a shift from a glorification of an ideal type of "Muslim family" in which gender inequalities are almost nonexistent, to a feminist methodology that relies on concrete case studies and "scientific" inquiry:

Our organization (ORWA) aims at renewing the awareness of Woman in the fields neglected by past generations including laws, regulations, and scientific methods of thinking and analysis . . . by means of a fresh reading of the texts and the facts, [and] according to our Islamic reference . . . [the] identity of our society and . . . the dignity of its members. We believe that the scope of awareness [about] women's rights and obligations . . . is likely to provoke a revolution on [the] pitiful [pathetic] situation of the woman. (ORWA 1995, 28)

It is worth noting that the ORWA benefited from the support of its base, notably the funds devoted by some of its members to the various campaigns, publications, and activities. Most probably, the ORWA also drew on the financial support of al-Islāh wa-l-tajdīd and its successor al-Tawhīd w-al-islāh. Its capacity to mobilize large numbers of women was overt during the different phases of struggle between Islamist groups and the feminist movement regarding the reform of family law. Smaller women's groups and younger activists saw in this organization a place to work on shared goals and to coordinate responses to both liberal feminism and Islamist conservatives.

Without doubt, the ORWA has facilitated the constitution of an Islamist women's leadership that in recent years became part of the formal political process. Most founding members of ORWA have held seats in elected assemblies and in the Parliament, including Bassima al-Haqaoui, Jamila Masdar, Fatiha El-Baqali, Fatema Benlehssen, and Soumiya Benkhaldoun, all Parliament Deputies, and Suad al-Amari and others as elected representatives in various city councils.

To conclude, it is clear that ORWA has paved the way for the articulation of a feminist discourse and agenda by Islamist women. The leadership that formed ORWA acknowledges that the search for recognition of their movement, and their desire to be part of international debates on women's rights, pushed them to mold their activism into forms immediately visible to the state and to international institutions. During one of my interviews with her, Khadija Mufid, a founding member of ORWA, confirmed my thoughts by stating that her group was animated by the need to create a structure that allows Islamist women to be part of the international dynamics initiated by the upcoming Beijing Conference in 1995. Khadija Mufid confirmed that they indeed took concrete steps in this direction when they wrote to the United Nations announcing the birth and the goals of their new organization and their desire to be included in the United Nations' process. She claimed that their requests remained unanswered at that time. Obviously now, Mufid became part of that process after she founded al-Hidn, an organization for supporting low-income families and children. Her organization has even gained a consultative status within the United Nations.

Despite their feeling of marginalization from the international process on women's rights, the ORWA members drew a lot of legitimacy from both their affiliation to the al-Tawhīd wa-l-islāh movment and from the network of women's groups for whom the ORWA became the umbrella organization. A founding member of ORWA was clear about the importance of creating this independent structure for Islamist women. She claimed that without this kind of organization, Islamist women would never have reached leadership positions in the Islamist movement.

Positioning in the Islamist Movement

As I illustrated earlier, Islamist women used the press not only to challenge the petition campaign, but also to question the male leadership of al-Islāh wa-l-tajdīd and its silence about the campaign. What these women lacked was the authority to issue a fatwa, because it was a male prerogative. It was important, then, for women to use an appropriate strategy to attract public opinion to the threats posed by the feminist mobilization. By requesting this public statement, Islamist women were putting themselves *ahead* of their male leadership in terms of defending the Islamic sharia. For instance, in April 2002 the newspaper *Al-Rāya* published, under the anonymous byline "a group of Muslim women," a request for a religious opinion about the feminist petition campaign. The group began by defining the campaign as an "assault on God's law" and an "attempt to challenge inalienable Qur'anic precepts." The group then addressed their question to al-Tajkani, the theologian who was responding to readers' questions in his column in the newspaper. They phrased the question as follows: "We have been aware of a circulating petition that requires Moroccan women to support the amendment of certain codes of the *mudawwana,* in particular the ones based on the Islamic sharia such as polygamy, *wilāya,* and inheritance law. We need to hear the position of the Islamic sharia about women's participation with and signature of this type of petition" (Group of Muslim Women 1992, 11).

In response to this request, al-Tajkani first confronted the UAF's demands with specific verses in the Qur'an and the prophet's *hadīth* in order to show that these demands posed an open challenge to inalienable divine precepts. Second, al-Tajkani made sure to resituate the feminist campaign in the international context of the Gulf War and the ongoing struggles in Afghanistan, Palestine, Chechnya, and so on, before coming to the conclusion that the feminist campaign was "the local expression of this Western plot against the integrity of the Muslim family." His final verdict was that "any form of participation in the UAF's petition, whether through signing or disseminating, is condemned by the sharia, and should accordingly be punished." To be more strategic, al-Tajkani launched a call to Muslim women, published in *Al-Rāya* (April 20, 1992): "It is time for Muslim women to rise up and start their women's organizations to advocate respect of the Islamic sharia, prevent the Muslim family from splitting into two antagonistic fronts, and preserve the identity of the Moroccan family, this unit based on complementary roles and Qur'anic principles of stability, affection [*mawadda*], and compassion [*rahma*]."

Though very significant, this call was not unprecedented. As early as 1984, Islamist men's writings began responding to the feminist press of *Thamānia Mars* by advocating the building of alternatives from within the Islamist movement. Abu al-Saad wrote in *Al Forkāne:*

> The growth of secular women's organizations and their effective use of the weapons of information and communication would not have been possible if the field were already occupied by the Muslim Woman. Western alternatives have prevailed in the void left by Muslim women. . . . It is imperative that the Islamic movement encourage the growth of a woman's constituency that would redefine the discourse of women's rights, and establish the true emancipatory model for Muslim women, which consists of their freedom from emulation [read: of the West]. It is also important that Muslim women invest in the technologies of mass communication and print information by creating a women's magazine that focuses on the rights provided to women in Islam. The rise of an Islamic women's leadership will make the younger generation of Muslim women self-confident, provide them with role models, and promote women's leading role in the society. (1984, 39)

A combination of factors explains this interest in the rise of a female leadership within Islamist organizations. The most important one relates to the division of spaces and tasks observed by these organizations at this initial phase, and the attempt to attract more women to Islamist politics. But generally speaking, this discourse reflects the internal dynamics of change operating in leading Islamist groups in the 1980s, which was also an outcome of women's increased penetration into these organizations. My interviewees described this process as "self-criticism" or "revision" (*murajaʿāt*), which entails assessment by the Islamist intelligentsia of the pros and cons of their movements, and a reflection on the way these movements have included or excluded the woman's component.

In the al-Islāh wa-l-tajdīd movement, this evaluation was led by young male activists with a modern education and expertise in the humanities, sciences, and social sciences. One example is Saad Edin al-Othmani, a PhD in psychology, founding member of al-Islāh wa-l-tajdīd, and former secretary general of the party al-'Adāla wa-l-tanmia. Beginning in 1984, he wrote a series of articles in the magazine *Al Forkāne* under the title "Women and the Psychology of Despotism." In this series, al-Othmani uses selections from the Qur'an and the sunna to reject women's exclusion from the public sphere and denounce the violations of their god-given rights. These efforts were joined by the writings of leading Islamist women such as Khadija Mufid, Oum Naoufal, and Oum Yassir. Oum Naoufal, for instance, wrote in *Al Forkāne:* "Treating women with the mentality of a jailer is exactly what allowed others to rise up against this injustice by promoting degenerated Western norms and values. This jail mentality has continued to crush women's humanity and to violate her religious, civil, and educative rights. We need to recover women's position known during the brightest days of Islam" (1991, 51).

During the 1990s, some of these activists were involved in another considerable effort of religious interpretation, in order to establish arguments against segregated spaces and work within the Islamist movement. This work is documented by videos and meeting minutes carefully catalogued in the library of the movement in Rabat. Referred to as *al-amal al-mushtarak,* or "participatory task," this effort laid ground for the largest participation of women in all the institutions and elected bodies of al-Islāh wa-l-tajdīd. Some women, such as Khadija Mufid, Jamila Masdar, and the current Parliament deputy, Fatema Benlehssen, played pioneering roles in this process.

Women's advocacy on behalf of their increased participation in all the institutions of the movement could not have found a better opportunity than the UAF campaign. The petition against the *mudawwana* made this call pressing even to the most conservative components of al-Islāh wa-l-tajdīd: the senior theologians and activists. Thus, as I mentioned earlier, al-Tajkani's call to women to establish their own organizations is extremely significant because it came from a senior Islamist scholar. His call for "Muslim women to rise up" was a powerful statement by the first generation of Islamists, recognizing the threat presented by feminist activism on the one hand and acknowledging women as political agents on the other.

It is worth noting here that Islamist women did not take this call for granted, but rather turned it into an opportunity to push forward their own agendas. Questioning women's subordination within Islamist groups, they also challenged the fact that women's rights were marginalized from the political agendas of the movements. Islamist women are convinced that Islam has developed advanced conceptions of social organization and gender relations that should be the focus of their movements. They also believe that most well-equipped settings in which to teach and advocate for women's rights are Islamist movements. These movements' failure to do so explains, according to these activists, why other groups, namely the feminists, are taking the lead.

This feeling, still shared by most of my respondents, widened the scale of Islamist women's criticism of the male leadership in Islamist organizations during the controversy over the feminist petition. For instance, Oum Yassir opened her article in *Al Forkāne* by acknowledging that she had "finally decided to speak out and make public what has been whispered in private or even silenced by Muslim women." Because of the importance of this reaction, I will summarize the main points that Zoubida Oum Yassir made in her five-page statement:

> Today the Islamists are divided along two trends. The first, minor but hopefully growing, believes that women and men have equal responsibilities for *da'wa* and maintains that without women's full contribution it is impossible to provoke any considerable social change. This trend is championed by the few thinkers who believe that women must recover the same podium they occupied during the time of the prophet, and take back the totality of their roles in the Muslim society. The second and most prominent, by all means, represents the majority of Muslims who have stolen women's rights and deprived women from leading the Muslim community. Why then, after this deliberate exclusion, is this majority upset to find out about a mass campaign that aims to demolish the last resort of the Islamic sharia? We have no right to be offended when our opponents accuse us of backwardness. How would we convince them if we cannot convince ourselves with the superiority of the civilizational alternative we are bringing? How would we show them the way Islam has raised the equality of men and women to the highest levels, while the Muslim woman is still excluded and marginalized? (1992, 51–52)

After this questioning, Oum Yassir explained why the feminists took the lead: "The women who are leading the campaign against the sharia benefited from the free stage left vacant by the Islamists. These women found no challengers whereas the most legitimate voices are kept silenced, dismissed from the podium, assigned marginalized tasks, and confined to narrow spaces" (1992, 51). Oum Yassir pursued her advocacy by comparing women's leadership in feminist groups to women's membership in Islamist organizations. She admits that "the leaders of the petition campaign are a well-trained and highly educated group of women," and therefore, she advocates "the rise of a women's leadership in the Islamist movement capable of challenging them." In this same article, Oum Yassir also summarized her own reaction to al-Tajkani's call in which he had encouraged "Muslim women" to form their own organizations. She stressed once again the male leadership's accountability in holding women back. Her response to al-Tajkani was as follows:

> We certainly need new organizations led by Muslim women, but more vital to us must be the change in the attitude of Islamist men toward women. The Islamists should learn how to help the women's membership overcome their negative feelings of helplessness and how to abandon the false conviction that their veiling is the ultimate goal. Asking women to form their organizations should not be used by the Islamists as a pretext to withdraw from stimulating their women's components throughout Morocco, and supporting them in their endeavor to reach *all* women. We have no time to waste. In a country where secularization is making swift gains, immediate action should be taken to protect our families from this trend. It is high time we reconciled our movement with the true teachings of Islam, and with the belief that women and men have equal responsibilities for *da'wa,* because without women's full contribution, it will be difficult to implement a large scale of change, and almost impossible to enact the crucially needed change in the Islamist movements.[11] (1992, 51–55)

The State Steps In

The purpose of this chapter is to describe the interactions of feminist and Islamist women's movements in the context of the feminist mass petition campaign. I have illustrated how this movement moment propelled Islamist women to slowly engage a discourse of women's rights, position themselves within the "international" women's movement, and make concrete demands about equal opportunities for Islamist leadership. I also discussed the impact of Islamist women's agency on bringing the issue of women's rights to the forefront of Islamist activism. I related these changes to the conjuncture of state liberalization, which kept women from both the feminist and Islamist sides at the margin of the political negotiations that were taking place among political elites. In the upcoming section, I will highlight the significance of feminist and Islamist women's activism for redefining the sphere of religious and political authority at this conjuncture.

Previous studies have already shown how the Islamist fatwa of apostasy called into question the authority of the king (al-Ahnaf 1994; Brand 1998; Daoud 1993). None of these studies considered this implication as an outcome of the articulation by Islamist women of political Islam and feminist agendas. In fact, both the feminist petition and the Islamist response calling for the death penalty threatened the highest authority of the king as Commander of the Faithful. The king's reaction came after six months of heightened controversies and public debates about the feminist campaign.

In his annual speech to the nation on August 20, 1992, King Hassan directly addressed women's groups, enjoining them to immediately end their petition and be sure not to use it for political ends. To recover his authority as Commander of the Faithful, King Hassan invited the petitioners to send their plea in writing directly to his cabinet. This step took a more concrete turn when the king invited forty-four delegates from several women's organizations (none of which were Islamist) to a reception in his palace the following month. Among these delegates, only one representative was from the UAF while the majority belonged to the Union of Moroccan Women. This is a women's organization created by the palace in 1969, headed by Princess Fatima Zohra. It used to be the sole representative body of Moroccan women in international forums. Other women came from various state departments, the king's cabinet, and political parties, none of whom had played a significant role in the One Million Signature Campaign (al-Ahnaf 1994; Daoud 1993).

In his broadcast speech to these delegates, the king admitted the validity of the women's demands and their calls for revision of the *mudawwana,* yet he reminded his audience that this kind of decision belonged in his personal sphere of authority. Moreover, the king restated the ultimate legitimacy of the 'ulama to pursue *ijtihād* on behalf of women. A council composed of mainstream 'ulama and judges was appointed by the king, and the women's campaign against the *mudawwana* was put to an end (al-Ahnaf 1994). Furthermore, women's groups were entirely removed from the discussions of this council, which ultimately made what most activists consider insignificant changes to the *mudawwana.*

First Amendments to the *Mudawwana*

The year 1993 marked the state's response to women's demands with three significant breakthroughs: the election of two women to the Parliament, both from the Istiqlal Party and the socialist organization USFP; the ratification of CEDAW; and several amendments to the *mudawwana.* The changes to the *mudawwana* related to four domains. First, the new code limited the power of the *wālī* by requiring a woman's signature in the contract of marriage as proof of consent, suppressing the *wālī* for mature orphaned women. Second, the guardianship of children upon the death of their father would go to the mother, and not to a judge, as was formerly the case. Third, divorce would continue to be the exclusive right of the husband, but the modified *mudawwana* required the presence of both parties to register the divorce. It also required the permission of a judge to repudiate the marriage and levied a *mut'a,* a compensatory amount due to a repudiated woman, in cases of prejudice. Fourth, while polygamy was also maintained, it required permission from a judge, and the first wife would have to be informed. The political scientist and activist Zineb Maadi argues that these changes did not come close to the demands of women's groups and remained attached to the traditional definition of the patriarchal family, which does not reflect any of the changes that have significantly affected Moroccan society (Maadi 1997, 210).

What are the meanings of the king's intervention? Analysts of the UAF's campaign saw the king's invitation to women as a co-option of their mobilization that benefited the monarchy and the agents of official Islam (the mainstream 'ulama) by reinforcing their supreme power over the definition of women's rights. Moreover, the UAF's campaign allowed the king to reiterate his exclusive rights regarding the application of the sharia, along with his role as supreme political arbitrator. Thus, the king's interference was seen as a constraint to women's mobilization and their ability to influence the political arena (al-Ahnaf 1994; Brand 1998; Daoud 1993; Denoeux and Gateau 1995; El Mossadeq 1995). It shut down a successful campaign that had polarized political elites during a time when the monarchy was searching for new sources of legitimacy and consensus.

To most analysts, the king managed to distance the debate on the *mudawwana* from the political institutions (Parliament and government) and reclaim it as matter of his *personal* attention. Disbanding the campaign and effectively interdicting gender issues from constitutional debates clearly indicated, to these analysts, that the operative definition of democracy in Morocco did not include the constituency of women.

Women's Agency

Feminist studies do not limit the impact of the women's movements to their immediate outcomes. Rather, these studies define women's organizations as "a form of movement in the present and a resource for feminist mobilization in the future" (Ferree and Martin 1995, 11). To Staggenborg, a social movement consists not only of "political movement organizations, but of individuals, alternative institutions, and ideas, which are often perpetuated beyond the lives of the organizations" (1995, 354). Following this line, I do not reduce the impact of the feminist campaign to the insignificant changes made to the *mudawwana* on the king's behalf, but rather I direct my focus to the long-lasting effects of feminist activism. There is no doubt that the king was ordering women to end a disruptive campaign. Yet his invitation to them, addressing their plea without mediation, was also a symbolic abolition of the *wālī* (male guardian) and recognition of women's new identity politics as agents and persons with rights. Moreover, although the changes brought to the *mudawwana* were meaningless according to most feminist activists, they nevertheless initiated a shift in the definition of this code as a human effort subjected to further negotiations, rather than an immutable divine law. As minor as they may appear, these changes still showed that women's status is not entirely a matter of faith and destiny, but more important, a matter of social control and power.

Beyond its immediate impact, the UAF's campaign also shaped the identity politics of numerous women's groups created in the dynamics of this first movement moment. For example, three major women's rights organizations were created between 1992 and 1994: Ligue Démocratique des Droits des Femmes (Democratic League for Women's Rights, LDDF), Association Marocaine Pour les Droits des Femmes (Moroccan Association for Women's Rights, AMDF), and Jussūr (Bridges). Regardless of the different foci of these groups—labor rights for the LDDF, sexual harassment and domestic violence for the AMDF, literacy for Jussūr—they have all built their activism around the goal of reforming the *mudawwana* and launched their groups amid the euphoria of the petition campaign.

During my discussions with leading members of these organizations, there was a common feeling that the inequalities encoded by the *mudawwana* justify all the other discriminations against women in the public sphere. Although these groups vary in terms of their secular or "Islamic" feminism, and despite their different approaches to the state and foreign funds, they are all united under the goal of reforming the *mudawwana*.

It was also the purpose of this study to show how the UAF's petition was instrumental in the feminization of Islamist groups, and how it has shaped Islamist women's politics within and outside of male-dominated movements. The state's ratification of CEDAW and the changes brought to the *mudawwana* all stressed the political impact of women's organizations and the importance for Islamist women to build structures that would deal with the real problems women were facing, rather than with an idealized archetype called the "Muslim family." The upcoming Beijing Conference was not out of sight, either. Though Islamist activists were excluded from this international process, they wanted to build adequate structures that would allow them to be part of it later.

All these factors compelled Islamist women to position themselves as *women* rather than simply members of Islamist organizations. The creation of the ORWA and its appropriation of the framework of rights to advocate for changes in Islamist movements all point in this direction. Thus, while the feminists emerged as agents of the democratization and secularization of the state, through their endeavor to reach legislative institutions with the debate on *mudawwana* reform, Islamist women have emerged as the insider agents of change in Islamist movements.

As far as the state is concerned, the interactions between the emerging Islamist and feminist movements contributed to a renegotiation of power relations between the state, Islamist activists, and women's groups. The articulation of the discourse of women's rights and the politics of Islamic identity by Islamist women shaped the process of feminization of Islamist women and their new positioning as a force of mobilization in the Islamist movement. As a movement moment, the petition campaign helped women to locate gender at the heart of the liberalization project, as well as the effort to engender Islamic sharia.

3

Reversing the Feminist Gains:
The Islamist Mass Rally of 2000

The Islamist rally of March 2000 truly marked Islamist women's entry into the formal political field. I consider this rally a movement moment because it captures simultaneously the tensions related to political alternance and the new framework in which the feminist movement had to operate. In this chapter, I will show how this movement has been transformed in contact with the Islamist discourse of "identity" and grassroots politics. I coined the term "Islamization" to explore the various modes in which feminist groups have validated feminism in the aftermath of the Casablanca rally. The rally marked a distinct turning point in the interactions between these two movements, reversing the gains made by feminist groups in the new conjuncture of political alternance.

The government of "alternance" emerged after the elections of 1997, the most transparent in the country's history, brought the political opposition (nationalist and socialist) into office, with a majority of ministerial appointments going to the socialist party, the USFP, including that of prime minister. The event was unprecedented and indicated the new expectations of feminists, some of whom were members of socialist and communist parties, if not old friends and colleagues of the new ministers. With these appointments, the legitimacy of the feminist movement was no longer at stake. Feminist groups gradually managed to work out their demands through governmental institutions and to take an active role in writing the NPA, in a move to grant Moroccan women their first secular legislation of family law.[1]

The Islamist rally of 2000 disrupted this process, propelling feminist groups to reposition their movement in relation to the contradictions of state liberalization, on the one hand, and the imperatives of Islamist nationalist claims, on the other. The latter were articulated in terms of "national interests," "Islamic identity," and "nation-state sovereignty." Feminist groups were once again depicted as a "Francophone elite," instrumentalized by imperialistic forces and alienated from "real" Moroccans. Their alleged ignorance of religion was the key argument to undermine the NPA, denouncing it through the popular forums of the mosques. As for feminist groups, their task became enormous. Not only did they realize that rhetorics of gender equality did not resonate beyond limited circles of supporters—both in- and outside of the government—but they were also confronted with the scope of opposition to the NPA across the political and social spectrum.

When the government validated the Islamist protests by withdrawing the NPA, feminist groups understood that their old connections with the political left were not sufficient, especially considering that leftists were divided over the NPA. They knew they had to take the matter into their own hands, and that keeping the project alive would mean lobbying *all* political players in- and outside of the government, as well as the religious players, notably the 'ulama. There was also a new battlefield called the "street." The term is used by the Islamist press to describe "the Moroccan people" who rejected the NPA in a mass protest, the "street" further fueled feminist anxieties and shaped the debate over their new framing of the NPA—this time in terms of social "benefits" rather than legal arguments. They needed to make sense to the "street" by explaining how the amendment of family law would benefit the "consolidation" of the "family unit," rather than how it would enhance women's individual and citizenship rights.

I use the term "Islamization" to depict these changes. Islamization refers to the articulation of feminist agendas and Islamist politics by the feminist movement. This articulation entailed the incorporation of a religious discourse as a means to validate the reform; the implication of the 'ulama in feminist activities and publications; wider lobbying of political parties regardless of their right or left sensibilities; and the construction of a "politics of the street" through direct contact with "subaltern" populations. I am not making the claim that these changes meant to dismiss the universalist framework of women's rights; instead, they were the very means of its validation in the eyes of a sharply suspicious domestic audience.

Gender as a Marker of Political Alternance

The 1997 legislative elections initiated the era of political alternance.[2] This refers to a mode of governance in which an elected government would alternate between various political formations—left, right, and center (Daoud and

Ouchelh 1997; Leveau 1998, 2000). Political alternance took effect when King Hassan appointed Abderahman al-Youssoufi, the secretary general of the USFP and a former political opponent, as the prime minister, endowing him with the power to form the government. This experience injected a new dynamic into "depressed" political institutions, by instigating hope under a new government. Not only did the 1997 elections bring the former opposition to the government, but they also granted fourteen Parliament seats to the Islamists. With these seats, the movement al-Tawhīd wa-l-islāh came to be represented through a proper political party, al-ʿAdāla wa-l-tanmia.[3] The struggles of these two forces over the NPA unleashed old tensions among those in the political left—dubbed secular by the Islamists—while the Islamists were called "reactionaries" by the socialist press.

As a matter of fact, the NPA was the most significant outcome of teamwork between these groups and a sitting government. As "experts" on gender issues, feminist groups were invited to join the committee established by Said Mohamed Saadi, the Secretary of State for the Family, to formulate a national plan for action in 1998. Saadi is a university professor of economics and a member of the PPS. He had been a friend, colleague, and comrade of leading feminist activists before being appointed as a Secretary of State in the government of alternance. It was therefore easy for both feminists and state officials to work together under his supervision, preparing Morocco's response to the Beijing Conference recommendation that countries establish national platforms for action to enhance women's rights (see Freeman 2004).

Saadi defines the NPA as a "gender-sensitive" (Saadi 2004, 36) and all-encompassing approach to women's social, economic, political, and legal empowerment in Morocco. To stress the importance of a gender lens, Saadi contends that "gender is not only a tool for the analysis of the impact of policies and laws on women's lives, but also an effective instrument for the building of strategies to address these deficiencies" (36). Accordingly, the goal of the NPA was then to proffer an all-inclusive approach to the institutional and structural obstacles blocking the effective integration of women in development.

A select group of NGO leaders, women's wings of political parties, human rights organizations, labor and professional unions, academics, and various state departments took part in workshops and debates about the NPA. These groups were alarmed that Morocco had been ranked 128th by the most recent Human Development Report of the United Nations Development Program, and they sought to address these deficiencies through a concrete strategy. This effort was coordinated by two ADFM members, hired as experts on gender issues. The names of Amina Lemrini and Rabia Naciri, both founding members of the ADFM with old ties to the PPS, had been mentioned by other leaders of feminist organizations for being the two primary crafters of the NPA.

The first version of the NPA did not mention the Islamic sharia as a source of inspiration, meanwhile acknowledging the UN platform. Moreover, the NPA articulated a liberal rhetoric of gender equality and individual rights and was first written and circulated in the French language. The purview of the NPA covers the following four areas: (1) education and promotion of an egalitarian culture in the schooling system; (2) reproductive health; (3) integration of women in development—that is, fighting poverty through facilitating women's access to training and employment; and (4) women's access to political positions. To ensure the incorporation of a gender-sensitive approach to state institutions, the NPA also proposed the following: a plan to introduce "gender and development" units within all ministries from 2000 to 2004, dealing with the issue of integrating women into development; a Permanent Commission for the Follow-Up and Promotion of Women's Images within the Media; and the creation of the Moroccan-based North African Center for Research and Study on Female Enterprise, as well as a training center (in partnership with the European Union) and a national Commission for Family and Childhood. It is clear from this platform that questions of gender-citizenship, rights, and entrepreneurship became intertwined.

The NPA materialized feminist liberal ambitions for an all-encompassing approach to women's conditions while actualizing the old leftist discourse of human rights. It was no surprise that this project involved consultation and financial backing from major international institutions such as the United Nations, the European Union, and the World Bank. Notably missing, however, were the Islamist groups, who joined the 'ulama to oppose a plan that was hailed as "national," but to them had been "crafted behind closed doors." More forces and individual players joined the bloc, including members of the government leftist and nationalist majority. This historical bloc declared the NPA unconstitutional because of its "marginalization of Islam," the defining element of national identity in the Moroccan constitution. Indeed, as part of its "integrative" approach to women's empowerment, the NPA sought legal reforms that would encroach on the well-established interpretations and practice of Islamic jurisprudence. These changes would include abolishing repudiation, restricting polygamy by making it contingent upon the first wife's consent, granting women unconditional custody rights, abolishing the *wilāya,* and endowing unmarried mothers with the right to give their children a surname, on top of other measures related to increasing women's access to education, training programs, and decision making, and enhancing their image in the media and textbooks. The Islamist mobilization made it difficult for the government to implement this project and imposed a selective implementation of some of its parts—those that do not overlap with existing interpretations of the Islamic sharia. More important, the Islamist opposition to the NPA once again forced tensions and struggles over political alternance into the gender field.

A Feminist State?

The tensions that arose with the NPA illustrate the centrality of gender in this phase of state transition. For example, whereas King Hassan co-opted the discourse of women's rights to mark the liberalization of his regime, the political left now in power was using the NPA to declare its rupture with the conservative policies of former governments and show its determination to "modernize" and "democratize" social institutions through a more participatory style of governance. How better could they illustrate this than by including feminist groups in not only the discussions about but the very writing of the NPA?

In the minds and hearts of the members of feminist groups, the end of the 1990s was a period of both great hope and anxiety. The dream of a better future was fueled by a combination of major events: the end of the structural adjustment era; the first free elections, which brought the socialist opposition to power in 1997; the accession to the throne of King Mohammed VI, whose inaugural speech stated a strong commitment to women's rights; the National Plan of Action for the Integration of Women in Development in 1999. But feminist anxieties remained linked to the contractions of political liberalization, notably the neoliberal pursuit of the privatization of state-owned sectors, the definition of citizenship rights around questions of "free" enterprise and micro-credit, the sudden death of King Hassan in July 1999, with all the uncertainties that opened up regarding the transition from a powerful monarch to a young king who was widely perceived as inexperienced, and, last but not least, the Islamists that entered Parliament after the elections of 1997.

Their anxieties notwithstanding, alternance was perceived by the feminist movement as the right climate in which to make major breakthroughs at the level of state institutions. They managed to shape the conjuncture of economic liberalization by linking women's particular needs in training, access to funds, and job opportunities to the legal obstacles preventing their full participation in the economy. For instance, they proposed the amendment of labor, criminal, and electoral laws, and pushed reforms to the codes of nationality, obligations, and contracts, among others. Some of these groups worked to enact a law criminalizing sexual harassment and domestic violence, and advocated codes granting single mothers and their children basic rights.

The ADFM was more involved in policy orientation, while the UAF was more active in the creation of women's centers for training and "development" projects for women. The NGO Solidarité Féminine, founded in 1985 by social worker Aicha Echenna, was the precursor to the debate about single mothers' rights. Echenna provided single mothers with shelter, training, market opportunities, and day care, despite the death threats she received. Echenna challenged the moral register of adultery by showing that a substantial number of cases resulted in unwanted pregnancies under the circumstances of the sexual exploitation of working-class women employed as maids in the city. Echenna has been lobbying the state to enact a law recognizing single mothers' rights, and for the rights for their children to be registered and given a name.

The AMDF, LDDF, Jussūr, Amal, Ennakhīl (based in Marrakech), and many other groups have incorporated a gender lens into the questions of illiteracy, poverty, and domestic violence in their approaches and centers. Some of the relevant laws have changed because of the impressive work done by feminist groups over the course of two decades. Backed by militants within political parties, these groups made a major breakthrough in political institutions when 10 percent of all seats were granted to women in the legislative elections of 2002, a long-standing feminist demand. These gains were enabled by certain political players who were embedded in state institutions during the phase of political alternance. For instance, it was unprecedented for any Moroccan government to hear both the prime minister and the king devote important parts of their inaugural speeches to the question of women's rights.

King Mohammed VI, succeeding his father in July 1999, marked a rupture with his father's conservative gender policies by devoting part of his inaugural speech to the question of women's issues, defining women as individuals with rights. Unlike his father, King Mohammed VI did not view women as wives and daughters, but as political players. Within a year of his access to power, in March 2000, King Mohammed VI appointed a female royal counselor, Zoulikha Nasri.[4] In August 2000 he appointed a woman, Amina Benkhadra, to head the National Office of Oil Research and Exploration; in October of that year, he appointed the first woman to head the National Office of Tourism, which oversees a major sector of Morocco's economy, and confirmed the first-ever female ministerial appointment, in addition to several appointments of women to the ranks of ambassador and consul general. The appointment of Aicha Belarbi, a prominent sociologist and long-standing member of the socialist USFP, as ambassador to the European Union testified to the desire of the new king to market Morocco with a feminist face. In May 2002 the Moroccan Parliament approved a proposal backed by the king that set aside thirty-five seats for women in the national elections of September 2002, giving them 10 percent of the Moroccan government. The new king also approved the creation of a first-ever Ministry for Women in Morocco. These appointments left feminist groups with the feeling that the best was yet to come. The adoption of the NPA by the government would have been the first real gratification of the feminists' efforts to see the emergence of a truly feminist state, one that adopts gender equality as a top priority.

However, the dismissal of the NPA left feminist groups questioning the meaning of political alternance and the future of their alliance with the political left, and was an indication of the contradictory results of this conjuncture of political alternance. For the monarchy, the need for bringing together socialists and Islamists to the Parliament meant building a "national consensus" around the importance of the monarchy to political stability; neoliberalism as a way out of the economic crisis; and political alternance with a thoughtful incorporation of the "moderate" Islamists into the political field (see Daoud and Ouchelh 1997; Leveau 1998, 2000). The decision to appoint Abderrahmane el-Youssoufi, the former socialist dissident, to head up the government was inscribed in this logic, in which the former socialist opposition became the catalyst for social change (see Leveau 1998, 2000).

With the political left now in charge of manufacturing consent, it suffered from the inherent contradictions related to its shift from being a power of opposition to a force of participation. The uncertainties related to this (un)comfortable (dis)location were exacerbated by the tensions associated with the gradual incorporation of Islamists into the political field. These tensions surfaced in the form of inflamed passions during the two rallies of March 2000.

A Divided State

The state is not a homogenous or monolithic body (see Charles 2000). Certain sections of the state have always been more receptive to feminist demands than others in Morocco. But the divisions among these players were never as pronounced as they were during the controversy over the NPA. Even from within the government, a robust opposition was organized by the Minister of Endowments and Islamic Affairs, Abdelkebir al-Alawi Mdaghri. The latter became the catalyst of the forces opposing the NPA. Mdaghri, a theologian himself, was appointed by King Hassan in the mid-1980s and remained in office until he was dismissed by King Mohammed VI in 2000. Meanwhile, though not a self-declared Islamist, Mdaghri managed to gain the recognition of Islamists thanks to his openly antifeminist positions.[5] His friendly monitoring of Islamist groups, tolerance of their use of the mosques to campaign against the NPA, and endeavors to keep decisions about the *mudawwana* in the hands of the mainstream 'ulama all allowed him to reposition himself as a powerful figure in the government of alternance.

Mdaghri began by challenging the "equality" approach of the NPA with his own alternative, one that he called the "contractual approach." The latter, as he explains it, is grounded in the "*mutual* commitments of husband and wife to respect the spirit [*rūh*] and purposes of Islam [*maqāsid al-sharia*]" (Mdaghri 1999). Mdaghri made this position public at the Jāmi'at al-sahwa al-islāmiyya (University of the Islamic Revival) conference in 2000, a yearly forum that draws Islamists, mainstream 'ulama, and theologians of Islam from all over the world.[6] From this powerful and widely publicized forum, Mdaghri organized his opposition to the NPA and formed a council of 'ulama to deliberate the matter.

Obviously, the council found the NPA guilty of violating the Islamic sharia, and even declared it unconstitutional in the pages of Islamist newspapers *Al-Tajdīd* and *Al 'Asr*. This also paved the way for various associations of clerics and specialists in Islamic jurisprudence to make official statements opposing the NPA. As for the Islamists, they used both their press and the mosques to create an even wider opposition to this project within public opinion. Therefore, rather than confronting a monolithic state, feminist groups were struggling in the contexts of a divided government, mosques dominated by conservative discourse, and the state's recent admission of Islamists as equal political players.

Factional conflicts over family law reform are not unique to Morocco. In her work on family law in Tunisia, Charrad argues that Tunisian "gender policy" was shaped by "conflicts among state actors pursuing divergent interests, or between state actors and political competitors" (1997, 288). Building on this point, I view gender as central to these actors' negotiations of power arrangements within both the state and "civil society." The reform of family law bears implications beyond the scope of domestic politics; it also shows how global economic and political arrangements have been played in the gender field.

Without pushing this argument to the point of dismissing any genuine concern about women's rights by the state, I argue that the feminist state was a response to both internal calls for democratic changes and external pressure for the creation of more appealing conditions for foreign investment,[7] which explains the framing of the NPA in development discourse. My definition

of gender as a field of struggle relates thus to the ways state elites have inter-
acted in the gender field to negotiate these global arrangements. In addition,
when religion is a constitutive element of the state, these negotiations surely
involve religious institutions and agents. The Islamist rally was the culmination of these tensions and passions.

The Islamist Rally

The historic bloc that formed around the agenda of the Ministry of Endowments and Islamic Affairs was composed of heterogeneous political forces.
They included the major 'ulama's local and national assemblies and councils, the various associations of students and graduates of Islamic programs
and schools, and professionals in the field of Islamic jurisprudence. Taking
place in metropolitan Casablanca, the rally was championed by the Islamists
of al-Tawhīd wa-l-islāh and their affiliated party, al-'Adāla wa-l-tanmia. As
soon as the NPA proposal was announced, al-Tawhīd wa-l-islāh launched the
National Federation for the Protection of the Family as a federating structure comprising men and women who opposed the NPA. They were joined
by the Islamists of al-'Adl wa-l-ihsāne, making this event the first open collaboration by these two large movements in a campaign against the government.
But participation in the rally was not limited to Islamist groups. Surprisingly,
several royalist party leaders took part in the event,[8] as well as members of
the socialist USFP and the Istiqlal Party—the two best-represented political
parties in the government at the time.

This heterogeneous body defies the conventional division of the political field into a progressive left and a conservative right. However, the mobilization of such a broad range of political players also occasioned the revival
of old nationalist sentiments for some, and old anti-imperialist feelings for
others. In addition, the participation of members from both the political left
and the nationalist Istiqlal Party validated the Islamist claim that feminists
are indeed an alien species in Morocco's political configuration. During the
Islamist march, many slogans pointed the public to this conclusion as well.
Referring to the parallel march organized by the feminists in Rabat, the Islamist
slogans stated: "Our march emerged from the people's will; their march derives from the West's will"; "their march is international, ours is national";
"they are marching with the elites, we are marching with the people"; "they
are funded by the World Bank, we are self-funded"; "they represent their sponsors, we represent our people." Although participants in the march expressed
their contentions in a narrative of national identity, it is worth noting that
most of these players would not have had much in common if they were not

interested in repositioning themselves within the new conjuncture of political alternance.

Where Are the Women?

In the previous sections, I have stressed the heterogeneous nature of the forces opposing the NPA and their contingent alliance. Where did Islamist women stand vis-à-vis the NPA? In both al-'Adl wa-l-ihsāne and al-Tawhīd wa-l-islāh, women *proudly* announced that it took them only one week to mobilize their constituencies for the march. Disputes over the numbers of participants in both rallies and the obviously larger numbers of veiled women mobilized for the Islamist march demonstrated how Islamist women shift the scope of the feminist debate from "who can change the state" to "who can display hegemony in the street." It is worth noting that Islamist women's leading roles in the organization of the rally, and their writings, interviews, and photos published by the press, were all crucial elements in being identified by a public that, as a result, brought them to the Parliament two years later. Louna Chebel's interactive weekly show *Only for Women* on al-Jazeera devoted several of its Monday broadcasts to these voices, making their anti-imperialist claims and Islamic identity narratives available to a highly sensitive transnational Arab public.[9]

Regarding their leadership role in the march, however, Islamist women leave a more nuanced account. The views I will present here reveal other divisions among women and subtle gender struggles within their respective Islamist movements. Their divisions notwithstanding, it seems as though women played an instrumental role in the call for the march. When I brought up this question during my meeting with the women's leadership of al-'Adl wa-l-ihsāne and al-Tawhīd wa-l-islāh, they described the gendered nature of the tensions that took place during the decision-making process leading up to the march. We must first keep in mind that al-'Adl wa-l-ihsāne and al-Tawhīd wa-l-islāh are very different in their approach to politics and the state. These differences set them apart in the actual political process, despite their similar reception of the NPA and matched reading of it as an instrument for further "Westernization" of women. These tensions significantly shaped women's mobilization in both movements.

The Islamists: United Front?

Islamist women came to the Casablanca march with differing agendas and constraints. It took me more than one meeting to bring these tensions to the surface, and even then, women addressed the issue of the gender divisions in their respective movements with extreme delicacy, which I will try to describe in this account. Unlike feminist activists whose grievances about male politics, notably the government of alternance, made media headlines, Islamist women like to emphasize commonalities and solidarities. When speaking about the Islamist march, it was easier for me to get the bottom-line story.

Nadia Yassine, leading the front of al-'Adl wa-l-ihsāne, had been open about her desire to join the feminist march. She expressed this desire on many occasions, but admitted that she "was not sure about how she would be received by the feminists." Other leading activists in al-'Adl wa-l-ihsāne, such as Ghislaine al-Bahrawi and Mouna Khlifi, define their movement as "an integral part of a global mobilization to end poverty and violence against women." They also expressed reservations about the participation of their movement in the Casablanca march. These reservations related to the continuous ban on al-'Adl wa-l-ihsāne and the inclusion of al-Tawhīd wa-l-islāh in the political game. An activist from al-'Adl wa-l-ihsāne, who preferred not to reveal her name, outlined more reasons behind women's reluctance to march in Casablanca:

> We were not very enthusiastic about our participation in the Casablanca march. We were concerned about the co-optation of our force of mobilization by the Islamists of al-Tawhīd wa-l-islāh. We were convinced that they needed our mass-base in order to position themselves as a political opposition. We did not want to gift them with this opportunity, especially if we should remain excluded. The male leadership did not listen. They thought of it as an act of solidarity in support to our brothers and sisters. We accepted to join but we set our own conditions, we wanted women to be in charge of organizing the event. Something good came out of it, though. Despite our reticence, the Casablanca march was a turning point in our relationship with the male leadership. After they had drawn the lessons from the march, they started listening to us.

It seems as though women joined the Casablanca march under a pretext of internal gender struggles within al-'Adl wa-l-ihsāne. Nadia Yassine articulated this struggle as "women's respect for the majority vote" that took place before the march. It is worth noting that the most important decisions in al-'Adl wa-l-ihsāne are made by the consultative council, *majlis al-shūrā*, in which women are consulted but, as I have learned, only informally.[10]

Similar tensions were expressed by the leadership of al-Tawhīd wa-l-islāh. Bassima al-Haqaoui is one of the organizers, as well as a university professor of education. She is serving a second term as a Parliament deputy and she is an active member in al-Tawḥīd wa-l-islāh. As a vocal source of opposition to the NPA, al-Haqaoui was frequently portrayed as extremely hostile to feminism by the profeminist press. I met al-Haqaoui in June 2003 in the Casablanca-based office of the women's rights organization ORWA, which she was directing. Our meeting did not last for the full one to two hours that I usually devote to these interviews, given her new responsibilities in the Parliament and her busy schedule supervising the work of activists in ORWA. But I had additional opportunities to meet al-Haqaoui during other activities scheduled by ORWA, and I was very familiar with her writings in the press. During the interview, she tackled my most controversial questions with impressive, cogent answers. To my question about the gender dynamics during the preparation phase before the march, she responded:

> Men were at first very reticent. They were not ready for an open confrontation with the government of alternance. We waited for them to react to the NPA, then we decided to put them before their responsibilities. We told them, "if you do not rise up against the NPA, you may never be able to make your voice heard by this government." This is a government that is waging a war on so called "obscurants" and "anti-democratic forces," meaning us. This is a government that came through a democratic process of election, but does not practice democracy. Democracy is about inclusion; we were excluded. We are not against women's rights, but against letting others define them on our behalf.

Championed by Nadia Yassine, the participation of al-ʿAdl wa-l-ihsāne in the Islamist march drew even bigger attention from major European media, such as the BBC and Radio France Internationale. Speaking to these European audiences, Yassine articulated her concerns with the NPA in the same anti-imperialist rhetoric of domination, identity, and nationalist discourse of resistance. On Radio France Internationale she stated the following: "Our march is for cultural self-determination. I know that we use self-determination to talk about political issues, but I want to extend the use of this term to cultural issues. We march to state our opposition to all forms of foreign intrusion in our business. We do have problems, but we can sort them out as a family and with reference to our own Islamic values and culture."[11]

Yassine also felt that "the Islamists were marginalized from a project that concerns them, as citizens of Morocco, *as well*," as she sarcastically claimed. Therefore, if women from other Islamist groups marched to oppose the NPA, women from al-ʿAdl wa-l-ihsāne marched to *end* their own marginalization. To Nadia Yassine, the Islamist march was about "positioning" more than "opposing."

In al-Tawhīd wa-l-islāh, women organized their response under the leadership of ORWA. This organization played the role of a federating structure for a wide range of smaller and even marginal Islamist women's NGOs, operating nationwide. ORWA benefited from four sources of support: Islamist women's groups, both formal and informal; the symbolic, social, and economic capital of al-Tawhīd wa-l-islāh; its large network of women active members of the Islamist party al-'Adāla wa-l-tanmia; and the Islamist male-funded press and Web sites. To demonstrate its ability to work as an umbrella organization, the ORWA issued a memorandum contesting the NPA that was endorsed by twenty-two Islamist women's organizations working in both rural and urban areas. The statement rejected the NPA on the same grounds of identity and sovereignty, while also pointing to the way women position themselves differently in debates about women's rights. The call for *ijtihād,* renewed interpretation of the sharia, was an apt indication. One can read in this statement:

> While we share a deep concern about women's condition in Morocco, we believe that solutions should ultimately be worked out within the framework of the Islamic sharia. We call for the activation of *ijtihād* as the only way to overcome rigid views and narrow interpretations of Islam. We want to reverse the centrality of international regulations and norms, because they are the tools of a global oppression and domination. We view the NPA as one of these top-down policies, designed to submit the will of the people to the agenda of international agencies and donors. We denounce the alienation of the sharia and the exclusion of a large national constituency from the elaboration of the NPA. We stress the Islamic identity of the Moroccan state and the Moroccan people, and reject all foreign intervention that does not respect our religious and cultural authenticity. We respond to the calls by the free people around the world and ask for a trial of those responsible for selling out their nation to foreign interests. It is not a national plan, but rather part of a global plot for domination of the Third World by the West. We want to tell the public that the NPA is anti-constitutional because Morocco is an Islamic state, and therefore the highest authority in the state is that of Islamic law. We require a true national debate that is inclusive of all the active forces, in order to create a true democratic consensus.

Khadija Mufid, another founding member of ORWA and president of the charitable organization al-Hidn, highlights the different reasons behind her decision to march:

> Our goal was neither to open old wounds with the secular left nor to polarize the country. We are aware that the country does not need further

divisions. But for many years, we have been denigrated by the feminists because we choose to wear a headscarf. They call us archaic, traditional, backward, and antimodern, while in fact we are a continuation of them, of the movement they initiated back in the 1970s. The feminists started this struggle, fought for their beliefs, for an ideal of equality, democracy, and development. We are pursuing the same goals but along different lines. We are not against women's rights, but our struggle is broader. We want the sovereignty of our country, we fight for the dignity of our people, and we want inclusive governance that respects the diversity of voices. We are not blind followers of Western choices. The West did not solve its own problems; how can it help us fix ours? In Casablanca, people spoke back. Everybody needs to listen. The Islamists have been listening to the pulse of the people. That's why we could easily mobilize the street. We are the ones who can mobilize the people, and this march was crucial to us. If we did not organize this march, who do you think was going to listen to us, ever?

All these activists used the male-controlled newspapers to subvert the agenda of the NPA as a regime of truths imposed by the World Bank. The diatribe against the World Bank and the United Nations articulated by the Islamists was an effective way to undermine feminist discourse about Morocco's commitment to the international community. This discourse was appealing to the wider public exposed to the Palestinian intifadah and the consequences of the UN's embargo on Iraq via Arabic television networks, who were constantly questioning the meaning of international law and the legitimacy of United Nations resolutions as far as the Middle East was concerned. The NPA granted these activists the opportunity to draw scrutiny to the "hidden" agenda of the United Nations' conferences, and to link the Moroccan reform to alleged underlying policies of population control.

For instance, the United Nations' 1994 conference on population in Cairo and the 1995 Beijing Conference became privileged sites for illustrating that the United Nations' regime of rights is grounded in broader agendas that submit Arabs and Muslims to the will of the West. Policies of birth control and legalization of abortion, also understood as "biopolitics" to use Foucauldian terminology, are "weapons against the gaining grounds of Islam worldwide," according to one of my respondents. These policies are "an assault on populations of the Global South by Northern governments," contended another activist. The World Bank's policies of "impoverishment" are also viewed as an integral part of this agenda, aiming to undermine the only remaining power of the Global South: its human potential. Al-Fatemi wrote an article for the Islamist newspaper *Al-Tajdīd* (March 1, 2000) under the sarcastic title, "I have been integrated into development for fourteen centuries," which referred to the advent of Islam and its liberation of women: "I refuse as a Moroccan woman to let the World Bank manage the most intimate aspects of my life. I am a woman, not a bank account, and refuse to give the International Monetary Fund the right to interfere in my family life."

While this narrative represents the main framework through which the Islamists as a whole articulated their opposition to the NPA, a minor but interesting position was expressed by the Islamists of al-Badīl al-hadāri (the Civilizational Alternative).[12] The president of this group, Lamine Reggala— a university professor and one of the few men I interviewed in this study— explained why his organization abstained from participating in either rally. To him, the NPA was significant only in what it was silencing:

> The controversy over the NPA was orchestrated by the government to divert attention away from the reform of education. This is one of the most devastating of the World Bank's policies that undermine public education, in a country where illiteracy hits more than 60 percent of the population. At the very moment when the Islamists and the feminists were creating a huge controversy over the NPA, the government passed its devastating reform to satisfy the recommendations of the World Bank. We did not take part in any of these marches because in both cases we would have been marching with brothers and sisters against other brothers and sisters. We would have been happy to march as a united block against the World Bank policies, notably the reform of education that passed unnoticed in the euphoria of the NPA.

I have laid out these differing positions in order to break with most accounts that homogenized the Islamists' positions and players, representing them as a unified camp of opposition to women's rights. Islamists are not simply sharing the same political field or "opportunity structure," but rather they are struggling to shape a conjuncture from their various perspectives and political locations. The position expressed by al-Badīl al-hadāri also throws doubt on the depth of the grievances expressed by Islamists about the World Bank's involvement in the NPA. In fact, the World Bank policies are opposed by the majority of the feminist movement, as well as by ordinary people who took part in street riots against them during the 1980s and 1990s.

If the Islamists did not decide to mobilize directly against the World Bank's economic policies, it is because they, too, are beneficiaries of economic liberalization through both its privatization programs and social crisis. I argued earlier that gender is the field where these tensions and antagonisms have been played by political actors in Morocco, facing only minor risks vis-à-vis the monarchy's disciplinary power. In the case of women, these politics have been played in alternative spaces, which I will discuss in the following sections.

Feminist Responses

The Islamist march pushed feminist groups to question their strategies and discourse. The recurrent terms in their description of the march were the "trauma" and "shock," as a founding member of the ADFM and Espace Associatif[13] expressed during our meeting in Casablanca:

> The Islamists use Islam as a means to channel political grievances. They have prospered in the context of widespread illiteracy and inequalities of all kinds. They responded through charity, alternative education, and social networks of support. They provide hope and help people to recover their *dignity* as *humans* [emphasis added]. However, the Islamists' instrumentalization of religion has been very challenging to us because we speak a different language. We use the discourse of human rights and international conventions. Unfortunately, the Islamist march showed the resonance of identity claims for large portions of the Moroccan population, and for all those who have been disillusioned by the United Nations' handling of Middle Eastern crises. The Islamists mobilize people's subjectivity, speak to their subconscious, and instrumentalize their beliefs. They do not treat them as autonomous individuals but as members of the *umma* to which everybody is accountable. It was then easy for them to mobilize such huge numbers for their march.

It is worth noting that my meetings with feminist activists took place only one month after the Casablanca attack of May 2003, which created lots of anxiety and uncertainty among Moroccans in general and feminist groups in particular. The level of frustrations that was expressed during my meeting with feminist groups was overwhelming. Most showed doubts about the efficacy of feminist organizing in this juncture of rising Islamist political power and what some called the state's flirtations with the Islamists. They thought that, once again, women's demands would be sacrificed. The language of individual choice came also under question, especially in light of the "instrumentalization" of women by the Islamist movements. Najia Zirari, a board member of the ADFM Casablanca, articulated this awareness as follows:

> Our activism is shaped by modernist understandings of democracy and individual rights. We think it is unethical to dictate how our beneficiaries should vote or whom they should support. We do not instrumentalize nor do we indoctrinate women. For example, before our march we explained to

the women beneficiaries of our centers the reasons why we needed to march. We explained to them the importance of our mobilization for women's rights. We did not ask them to march with us, we did not want to put any pressure or be suggestive. We told them that there would be two marches and that they were free to chose. We left it up to them. It was their choice. Well, guess what, they marched with the Islamists. We were *traumatized* [emphasis added]. Should we change our approach? What discourse should we use? I feel so frustrated. Are there any alternatives to the religious discourse? How do we mobilize women without instrumentalizing them?

These questions formed the common ground to most feminist groups in the aftermath of the Islamist rally. Bouchra Abdou, an activist in the Ligue Démocratique des Femmes Marocaines (LDDF), drew similar lessons. She was also "shocked" when she found out that the women beneficiaries of the LDDF Center for Legal Assistance chose to rally with the Islamists. With a tremendous amount of emotion, she shared:

I feel like we are in the bottom of a well, we keep screaming but no one hears us. To me the hardest part about the Islamist rally was to learn that our beneficiaries walked with them. This compelled us to rethink our strategies and discourse if we were to reach all women. We engaged in a self-reflective phase, but we did not even have time to think. We needed to act quickly. We needed to occupy the street, be in the neighborhood, and reach those at the margin. The idea of organizing caravans emerged from this questioning. We started our first trips to rural Morocco and our first actions in the cities' poor suburbs. In these places, women do not connect with a discourse about international conventions, modernity, or democracy. They look at you wondering: are you representing the *makhzen* [the state]? We have to speak a language that appeals to people. Talking about the international conventions only reinforces the Islamist representation of us as a bunch of Westernized women representing foreign interests. Unfortunately, feminists have completely ignored the importance of incorporating religion into their discourse. We used to believe that religion was a personal matter, now we believe that Islam is open to different interpretations. We do like the Islamists: we pick and choose. We choose the progressive interpretations of the sharia, and we use them in our advocacy. The Islamist march was very disturbing; nevertheless, it presented us with the opportunity to change our approach. It was a question of survival, the survival of the feminist movement.

The changes in the discourse of feminist groups were already visible in the first statements published by the National Network of Support of the NPA

(Network) created in July 1999, immediately after rejection of the NPA by the national council of 'ulama. The Network responded to the 'ulama's rejection through a communiqué published by the daily newspaper *Bayāne al-Yaoum,* the mouthpiece of the PPS. Its rhetoric shifted drastically in favor of a religious argumentation, using the Islamic sharia as a means for legitimizing the NPA. As we will see, the communiqué claimed that *ijtihād*—renewed interpretation—is a core principle of the Islamic sharia, and that the reform of the *mudawwana* has always been informed by this principle: "The promulgation of family law in 1958, as well as its first reform in 1993, was shaped by the Islamic principle of *ijtihād.* The *mudawwana* is based on interpretations of the foundational texts of the Qur'an and the sunna. The NPA is equally informed by the same principle of a renewed reading of the sharia" (Network 1999). After restating that the NPA was informed by an "enlightened" reading of the sharia, the Network addressed the 'ulama with a statement that repositioned feminist groups within this effort of *ijtihād:* "The 'ulama's council does not have a monopoly over the interpretation of the sharia. . . . We would like to remind those who hold an obsolete vision of the *fiqh* [Islamic jurisprudence] that justice, equity, and progress are at the heart of Islam and that it is high time we reopen the gates of *ijtihād* " (Network 1999).

The Network that published this communiqué was an umbrella organization formed by feminist groups in the frenzy of the NPA, and immediately attracted more than a hundred NGOs representing various regions of Morocco.[14] Under the Network, the feminist movement became a clearly identified force with a national base of support. As stated by its president, the university professor and human rights activist Khadija Marouazi, "Informing the people and creating a larger base of support for the NPA was not an easy task, but it became inevitable after the Islamist march."[15] Through the Network, feminist groups "raced out across Morocco," confirmed Leila Rhiwi, the president of ADFM/Rabat. "We needed to talk to the people," she added. "We wanted to have direct contact." Meetings and conferences about the NPA took place in universities, schools, homes, public health centers, public administrations, and local markets. During these meetings, the priorities of feminist groups were to correct people's representations about the NPA and to bring the feminist movement closer to its potential social base.

Working through a nationwide network enabled the feminists to create channels of communication with local communities and NGOs, and to create a bridge between these groups and the local governing bodies, opening them to feminist organizations' resources and transnational networks. Direct contact with local populations also allowed feminist groups to speak in their own voices, instead of being defined by Islamist preachers and activists in local mosques, markets, and schools. A young activist at the LDDF explained the benefits of this new approach:

> Working with women from rural and poor suburbs taught us how to adapt our message to the context. The Islamists use a simple and direct message. They ask people not to listen to us. They enjoin men to warn their wives against us, as a religious duty. During our trips to the countryside, we were surprised to see that people knew about the reform. However, their knowledge was based on messages disseminated by the preachers in their local mosques. To them, we were a group of atheists, adulterers, prostitutes, and even Zionists, whose goal is to attack Islam and make Morocco a secular state. Still, there was nothing new about that. It was written all over the Islamist press, and everybody could read it. But when you knock at a woman's door and she tells you this right in your face, then the trauma is substantial. During our trips, we discovered that we first had to work on people's representations; we had to listen to them, listen to their demands and needs and go from there. The Islamists' power came from their co-optation of the old methods of the political left; in fact, they are the best students of the left. We have to go back to these methods. We have to reinvigorate our old methods, we have to work with the people, with the masses, and we have to create new spaces for the interaction with the people, with the youth, their educators, and women. We have to work together, unify our efforts. This is how the Islamists won the street. This is our approach to activism now.

The King's Response

Faced with resilient positions on both sides, King Mohammed VI decided to take the matter into his own hands. His response came through the creation of the Royal Advisory Council, a committee of experts endowed with the power to make recommendations about the reform. This time, in his public address to the council he commanded that the new project of reform had to be consensual but also had to provide a "profound reform." To the Islamists, seeing the debate removed from public opinion, the media, and a left-leaning or feminist friendly press, was very satisfactory. Furthermore, knowing that most members of the council were familiar and even friendly names provided the Islamists with another good reason to claim out loud a victory. In contrast, for feminist groups, having to deal with yet another royal council instead of "the people's representatives" in Parliament evoked bad memories, more fears, and deeper frustrations, but also some hope, for reasons I will enumerate.

The Royal Advisory Council for Arbitrage was created in February 2003, after a long year of heated controversies over the NPA. It had a mandate to tackle the issue of reform, but discreetly and behind closed doors, away from the media, Parliament, and the government, with the king as the sole arbitrator. Obviously, since the Islamists had managed to express their concerns in terms of an Islamic nationalism, the council had to be composed of predominantly religious players carefully selected by the minister of Islamic Affairs, the most virulent opponent of the NPA. The royal council was composed of thirteen representatives of nationwide 'ulama councils and a few members of the judiciary. Nevertheless, one sign of hope for feminist groups came with the appointment of three women to the council. This was in fact the first time in the history of this struggle that women were represented on the council, and they all came from outside of the field of religious expertise per se. The three women selected were Nezha Guessous, a professor of medicine at the University Hassan II and a member of the socialist party USFP; Zhor al-Horr, a judge and president of the Court of Ain Chock in Casablanca; and Rahma Bourkia, a sociologist and president of the University Hassan II in Mohammedia, and a long-standing militant in the PPS party. This type of configuration says something about the nature of the challenges that the council, and more precisely its religious and secular women's components, were about to face. All were ready to take on the challenge; it was a question of survival, I was told by a woman member of the council.

Appointed by the king, the members sitting on the council had to reach an agreement after consulting the various protagonists, inviting them to make their cases in hearings. Along with feminist groups, these sessions would include Islamist women's organizations, acknowledging them as equal partners in the women's movement. They also heard representatives from ministerial departments, women's sections of political parties, labor unions, and human rights organizations.

In sum, eighty women's organizations, with active membership nationwide, were invited to advocate their projects before the council. The presence of three women among the council's members did not attenuate the feminists' fear of an existing bias or a real gap between "progressive" members and the predominantly conservative and Islamist-friendly constituency. The hearings became sites of an additional struggle, because feminist activists anticipated a competition with Islamist women in their own area of expertise: religious discourse and argumentation. I will later discuss feminist groups' divisions over the royal council, but more immediately, I would like to show how the questions that feminist activists had to tackle in the aftermath of the Islamist rally were exacerbated by the creation of the royal council.

The Royal Advisory Council was a site of additional struggles for feminist groups, who attempted to put aside their divisions and respond *collectively* to the challenge. In order to advocate their program of reform, these activists had to first equip themselves with the tools of religious argumentation and reconnect with foundational Islamic texts, so that they might identify alternatives to the mainstream interpretations of the Qur'an and sunna. Second, the 'ulama's exclusive training in the Arabic language and their foregrounded knowledge of the sharia presented the feminists with yet more challenges, a conflict of communication styles, thus propelling the most bilingual groups, such as ADFM, to prepare their documentation and advocacy in the Arabic language.

Not only was this shift crucial to overcoming charges of "francophony" and Westernization, but it was also essential for efficient communication with the council. Leading activists from various feminist groups described how they looked among their members for those women who possessed a greater mastery of the Arabic language and prepared them to appear before the council. To enhance their negotiation power, feminist groups decided to speak to the council as one body, united in a new network.

Springtime of Equality

"Springtime of Equality" was created in March 2001 by the same group of NGOs that established the Network. It became the base on which feminist groups organized their collective response to the creation of the Royal Advisory Council. The Springtime of Equality first comprised twenty-five NGOs working totally or partially on gender issues, before expanding to fifty groups under the coordination of Leila Rhiwi, the president of the ADFM/Rabat. As stipulated in its statement, the Springtime of Equality aimed to "approach the Royal Advisory Council with a unified vision, and to closely follow the deliberation of the Council in the hope of influencing the emergence of a profound reform of the *mudawwana*."[16]

I was invited to the press conference in which feminist groups presented their first memorandum in the Farah Hotel in Casablanca in July 2003. The Farah Hotel was one of the targets of the series of bombings that had hit Casablanca a few months earlier. Hence, the choice of this place by feminist groups to present their project was a sign of solidarity with the people who lost their lives during the attacks, but also a powerful message to the decision makers about the "dangers of fundamentalism," as one organizer explained. During this press conference, attended by Minister Saadi and several other male supporters of the feminist movement, Leila Rhiwi addressed the public in Arabic after distributing a memorandum printed in both Arabic and French. Under the title "Equal to Equal," the memorandum stated that "Islamic law is a code based on respect of the person's dignity . . . and the values of justice and equality." Equal to Equal acknowledged the Islamic sharia as one of the sources of its inspiration, as follows:

> We consider that the inferiority of women conflicts with both the essence [*rūh*] and purposes of Islam [*maqāsid al-sharia*]. . . . Women's demands for justice, dignity, and equality are grounded in the ethics of Islam and thus take their full meanings within the framework of the Islamic sharia. The interpretation of the sharia by Muslim scholars has always aimed at preserving the moral foundations of Islam while keeping sight of changing circumstances. . . . Dialogue is a main directive in Qur'anic teachings. The Qur'an invites debates and deliberation and debate as a means to reach consensus on issues of collective concern; we inscribe our approach within this logic. (Springtime of Equality 2002, 13)[17]

In addition to this endeavor to approach the Royal Advisory Council as a united front, feminist groups also mobilized their separate structures. They used their various organizations to put more pressure on the council through communiqués, letters, press conferences, meetings, workshops, publications, and, more important, by compiling legal decisions disseminated through the press and mailed to the council. These activities bore witness to the shifts in the feminist narrative toward religious argumentation. For instance, the LDDF produced a study on the "Sharia and Women's Rights" and enclosed a selection of religious opinions and interpretations made by authorities of Islamic jurisprudence.[18] "Sharia and Women's Rights" is a document that comprised stories from the early days of Islam, focusing on the *sīra* of the prophet (behavior) and the lives of his four caliphs (successors).[19]

For example, to support their demand for the abolition of polygamy, the LDDF used the case of Ali, cousin and son-in-law of Mohammad, who was not authorized by the prophet to take a second spouse. The study claimed that the prophet wanted his decision to become public when he raised the issue during the collective Friday prayer. To the LDDF, this gesture set the Islamic precedent against polygamy, despite the tolerance of the Qur'an. Other cases were provided to prove that even the most unambiguous Qur'anic precepts were suspended by the *sahāba* (companions of the prophet) and *fuqaha* (experts in Islamic jurisprudence) to respond to specific circumstance. For instance, during times of drought and famine, the *hudud* (Islamic sanctions) for robbery were suspended by the caliph Omar Ben al-Khatab. The LDDF's study drew the general conclusion that the Islamic *fiqh* is based on human interpretation, *ijtihād,* and shaped by specific historical factors.

This study was one of numerous documents and books produced by feminist groups between the years 1999 and 2003. This effort shifted the terms of the debate from the claim that feminists were totally ignorant of Islam to the evidence that the 'ulama had failed in their mission to undertake *ijtihād* on behalf of Muslims. The next paragraph shows how the LDDF's study draws heavily on this rhetoric:

> Since its creation in 1993, the LDDF has endeavored to meet the essence of Islam [*maqāsid al-sharia*]. . . . The Islamic sharia regulates the two levels of *'ibādāt* [religious observances] and *mu'āmalāt* [social transactions]. While the first are unchallengeable, the second are open to interpretation. Women's demands relate not to the first, but to the second level. . . . Rationally speaking, no discussion of social transactions is possible unless it is contextualized and linked to specific time periods. For this reason, the Islamic *fiqh* is nothing else but an outcome of *ijtihād*. Hence, Islam's early *fuqaha* contributed to this effort of interpretation and helped to resolve issues and questions that arose in their time. Unfortunately, the gates of *ijtihād* have been closed since the fifth century of Hegir (between tenth and eleventh century) when repetition took over interpretation. This long period of stagnation led to the reproduction of fossilized and outdated interpretations, wrongly attributed to Islam. . . . In this book, we show the discrepancies between these interpretations and the lives, the views, and the acts of the prophet and his *sahāba*. We stress the *ijtihād* of the *fuqaha* who challenged some mainstream understandings of the sharia. We show how outstanding members of the Islamic community dealt with the issues of their time in the most creative ways, while preserving and meeting the essence and purposes of Islam [*maqāsid al-sharia*]. (LDDF 2001)

Nonetheless, this co-optation of religious rhetoric by these groups was not meant to replace the articulation of women's rights within the universalist United Nations framework. Instead, the sharia was used by the LDDF as a means to legitimize the UN regime of rights as valid within Islam. It is worth noting that feminist groups did not start from a vacuum, but rather from the breach already opened by other Moroccan feminists who, from the authority of academic research, had engaged the Islamic *fiqh* in their studies, publications, and dissertations. Farida Bennani, a professor of law, and Zineb Maadi, a social scientist, are known as two of the few Moroccan Arab feminists who are also experts in the Islamic sharia. Both have instigated a dynamic of feminist interpretations and both have located the *fiqh* at the intersection of history, gender, and power. As scholar–activists, these two women have been part of various feminist networks but have also managed to gain recognition from Islamist women who have invited them to speak to their own audiences. During my numerous visits to the Islamist organization ORWA, both professors' publications were exhibited in the hallway along with "proper" Islamist publications and videotapes. The prominence of these two feminist scholars stems from their positive engagement with the sharia, acknowledging that "a feminist reading of Islam is not only possible but also legitimate," as stated by Bennani in an informal meeting during the international workshop organized by the ADFM in June 2003 in Casablanca. These scholars have played a critical role in helping feminist groups make their claims more appealing to wider audiences and to connect with religious argumentations.

The 'Ulama's Feminist Voices

The legitimacy of feminist groups received a great boost when senior 'ulama, including Ahmed al-Khamlishi, one of the appointed members of the Royal Advisory Council, joined the feminist movement, backing feminist demands from within the council. More theologians and professors of Islamic law openly took a stand in support of feminist demands, including the notorious historian and theologian and president of the prestigious Islamic university dar al-Hadīth al-Hassania, Abdelhadi Tazi; the professor of Islamic law Driss Hamadi; and Abdelhadi Boutaleb, a former diplomat and 'alim. Their insider location, within the 'ulama's constituencies, gave these theologians significant leverage, adding to their symbolic capital as members of the nationalist liberation movement in colonial Morocco. Hence, when they raised their voices in favor of feminist demands, these voices could be ignored by the Islamist press but never challenged by the Islamists' own 'ulama.

Due to their support of feminist claims, these scholars were awarded the title of 'ulama al-i ijtihād, the "'ulama of interpretation," also known as the "enlightened 'ulama" by feminist groups. The latter granted a podium to these 'ulama through their access points in the leftist and independent press. Most of these interpretations stressed maqāsid al-sharia (purposes of Islam) such as justice, equity, and equality, rather than scripturalist interpretations of Islamic doctrine. These 'ulama's involvement with feminist groups in conferences, meetings, and studies spawned a new production of edited volumes and individual studies in which the 'ulama advanced their opinions about women's rights in Islam.[20] This teamwork between feminist groups and the "'ulama of interpretation" was instrumental in deconstructing Islamist truths about the opposition of religious scholars as a whole to the NPA and their assumed hostility toward feminism. Identifying these divergent voices was, in fact, one of the most significant aspects of this movement moment.

Nevertheless, the articulation of the discourse of equality and maqāsid *al-sharia* was not new. It was a revival of an old debate that was instigated by nationalist women and the 'ulama who had led the nationalist movement during the 1940s and 1950s. Curiously enough, during the controversy over the NPA, this old debate was reclaimed by feminists and Islamist women alike to legitimize their activism within an "authentic" Moroccan tradition of debate. During the nationalist struggle for independence, the discourse of liberation was not articulated in a theological framework but rather in modernist aspirations that were even very critical of the women's condition and marginalization. For instance, in his book *Al-naqd al-Dāti* (*Self-Criticism*), first published in 1953, Allal al-Fassi, the prominent Salafi scholar,[21] *'alim,* and nationalist leader, wrote: "Our society has maintained women in a condition which has *limited* their *potential and capabilities* [emphasis added]. These limitations are seen, by both men and women, as natural and grounded in physiological differences while indeed they are the mere outcome of the social conditions where society has maintained women" (al-Fassi 1979).

In this book, al-Fassi proscribed polygamy and repudiation, stressed the oppressive aspects of the veil, encouraged women's education, and challenged women's exclusion from the public sphere. In the euphoria of independence, another theologian, named al-Touzani, representing a minor yet important orientation of theologians from al-Qarawiyyīn University, addressed the newly sovereign king in an open letter through the press, urging him to reverse what he called "the archaic laws, including the ones based on the Māliki fiqh" (quoted in al-Ahnaf 1994, 4). These voices were concomitant to nationalist women's pressing demands for revision of the sharia and their enjoining of the 'ulama to open the gates of *ijtihād.*

Backed by the modernist trend of the nationalist movement, women questioned in an unprecedented fashion "the inferiority of women" in the Islamist sharia. They went so far as to challenge unequal inheritance rights, which remains to this day a taboo in demands for revision of family law throughout the Islamic world. They even questioned women's exclusion from leadership positions in the religious field. In their first congress of 1946, Akhawat al-safa (Sisters of Transparency), the women's branch of the nationalist party al-Shūra wa-l-istiqlal, addressed some of the prejudices faced by women before the court and requested the prohibition of polygamy, the regulation of divorce through the court, and the interdiction of early-age marriage (see Daoud 1993, 248).

More radical demands appeared in the nationalist press during the 1950s. One year after Moroccan independence, the newspaper *Democracy,* mouthpiece of al-Shūra wa-l-istiqlal, published a statement under the authorship of "a group of Moroccan Women," in which the group questioned the *māliki fiqh* and the 'ulama's affirmation of equality of men and women before god, compared to the inequalities encoded by the *māliki fiqh*. The article enjoined the 'ulama to explain why a woman's testimony was equal to only half of a man's, and why her share of inheritance was only half that of her male counterpart. The statement also renounced, not for the first time in this newspaper, the practice of polygamy, men's exclusive right to repudiation (unilateral divorce), the institution of marital guardianship (*wilāya*), and women's absence from religious leadership (see al-Ahnaf 1994, 3). These claims, though important, limited the terms of the debate to the Islamic sharia, and hence stretching the limits of this discourse to the universal framework of women's rights was the new challenge facing the feminist movement.

Back to the "Arab Family"

Overcoming the charge of Westernization and francophony entailed working through the transnational feminist structures created by women in Arab countries. The ADFM undertook this task by organizing their conference "The Evaluation of the Women's Movement in the Arab World" in July 2000. The conference, scheduled many months earlier, took place only a few months after the Islamist march in Casablanca. The latter pushed participants from ten Arab countries to evaluate their experiences in light of mounting Islamist activism in the region. Delegations representing women's groups in Morocco, Sudan, Palestine, Kuwait, Egypt, Jordan, Tunisia, and Algeria joined in two days of workshops on the challenges to and various strategies used by the women's movement in the context of political Islam. The ADFM conference was meant to bridge these movements and draw lessons from their diverse experiences and contexts. I joined the conference as an observer alongside representatives from United Nations programs in Morocco, including UNIFEM (United Nations Development Fund for Women) and the UNDP, in addition to other international human rights organizations such as Human Rights Watch and various European sponsors.

Yet, this attempt to ground the feminist movement in its Arab context was not entirely new. The UAF had been involved in a similar dynamic through the organization of the Arab Women's Court, which I will address later. It was rather the timing of this conference that was more significant, reflecting Moroccan feminists' new strategies to counter the charge of Westernization. This first entailed opening their structures to women working within the dual framework of the sharia and the international conventions on women's rights, such as in Sudan and Kuwait.[22] Second, it required the exclusive use of the Arabic language during the workshops, the plenary sessions, and the press communiqués. The conference further opened the secular

ADFM to alternative types of feminisms, as expressed by veiled activists representing Sudan and Kuwait. The sight of veiled activists being included in an ADFM conference was very surprising to me and pushed me to investigate even more those shifts. Knowing the firm position of the founding members of the ADFM against the veil, defined as a symbol of women's oppression, I could not help but ask a close friend on the ADFM board: How could the conference include veiled women from other Arab nations but not veiled women from Morocco? This friend exposed some of the tensions related to this choice by the ADFM members:

> We have been very strict about the veil, as you know. We did not want veiled women among our membership. To us, the veil symbolizes the oppression of women, but now it is becoming so widespread that we are reconsidering our position. The Islamists are doing the same thing. They are opening their membership to nonveiled women. They are competing with us over our audience. They are trying to attract the modern professional woman to their structure. We had to reflect on that and respond. I must also acknowledge that I had to negotiate with the other members the inclusion of these veiled activists in the conference. I heard them speak in another conference in the Middle East, and I was very surprised to see them articulate feminist demands despite the fact that they were veiled. I was both impressed and confused by the discrepancies between these activists' unambiguous feminist discourse and their veiling. I decided to invite them to this conference despite some resistance from other members.

Another ADFM member expressed her ambivalence about this inclusion. To her the veil raises serious questions about human rights and individual choice. "Islamist women have the right to veil," she claimed. "It is a *human* right and I would defend it," she added. However, her ambivalence stems from her doubts that Islamist women would rally to defend her right *not* to veil. In addition to the veil, another site of struggle was opened up during the final sessions by the most secular delegations that rejected any reference to the sharia in the framing of the conference declaration that was to be delivered to the press. While they claimed that referring to the sharia would put at risk the secular foundations of the feminist movement, those willing to compromise argued that it was the use of the term "secular" that "undermines the popular support" of the feminist movement and its image. Hence, between hard-line secularists and those willing to compromise, a third position emerged, leading to a consensus about framing the conference's minutes in terms of "our authentic culture, which does not conflict with women's rights."

These debates lasted for a whole day, illustrating the challenges facing feminist groups attempting to network across in the region.

Divisions

Studies on women's movements have tended to downplay questions of power struggles among women, attributing these struggles solely to men's organizations (see Martin and Collinson 2000). In the case of Morocco, the Islamist opposition to the NPA certainly helped feminist groups to overcome the fragmentation of their movement, forcing them to pool their expertise and resources together into broader coordinating structures, such as the National Network of Support to the NPA and Springtime of Equality. Nevertheless, they were not immune to struggles over ideological and political divisions. These contentions related to their differing stances toward the Royal Advisory Council, as well as disputes over the leadership of the feminist movement. Political allegiances to the socialist USFP compelled the groups supportive of the government's majority to shy away from openly opposing their government's handling of the NPA and from expressing concerns about the royal arbitration. I illustrate these divisions in the following sections.

Divisions over the Royal Council

As a mediating site, the Royal Advisory Council shifted the struggle from direct confrontations between Islamists and feminists to the feminists' ability to make a good impression on the council's male and most conservative members. In addition, feminist groups' rejection or endorsement of the authority of the council caused a major divide within Springtime of Equality, between those who have endorsed this mediation and those opposing it. The latter created a new network: the National Coordinating Committee for Women's NGOs.

While the Springtime of Equality remained unified under the leadership of the ADFM, the LDDF, and the AMDF, the National Coordinating Committee for Women's NGOs was led by the UAF, Jussūr, and other groups with links to government socialist majority. The rupture became unavoidable when the Springtime of Equality decided to organize a sit-in before the Parliament to oppose the creation of the royal council. Fifty women's groups from the core of Springtime of Equality took part in the sit-in,[23] despite a boycott from the newly formed National Coordinating Committee. The latter included the women's wings in the Istiqlal and USFP parties, those parties with the widest presence in the government.

Despite their unconditional support of the NPA, members of the National Coordinating Committee cultivated certain grievances about the way the initial framing of the NPA allegedly failed to respect their own recommendation—expressed during the workshops—concerning the importance of including the sharia into the final draft. They saw the king's arbitrage as the only way out of the crisis and thus opposed the Springtime of Equality's decision to organize a sit-in contesting royal intervention.

Another source of tension between these two networks relates to their position vis-à-vis religion. While the Springtime of Equality was dominated by the most secular trends of Moroccan feminism, the National Coordinating Committee for Women's NGOs united feminist groups that were open to the integration of the sharia in their advocacy. It was led by individual leaders who define themselves first and foremost as Muslim women. The constituent groups still wanted to base their advocacy on the United Nations' regime of rights; they were conscious that the "instrumentalization of religion" by Islamists had been a major obstacle toward effective communication with larger audiences, and its marginalization by the feminists had disastrous effects on their movement. It is worth noting, however, that while acknowledging their conflicting views, the leaders of these two networks spoke about their split with obvious signs of emotion. To them, the creation of a new network symbolized unhealthy relationships among women's groups, sending the wrong message to the "enemy."

In fact, more was also at stake. Women's groups were divided over not only the legitimacy of the royal council but also the leadership of the feminist movement. Each of these two networks blamed the other for disputing its well-established national and international standing, and accused the other of allegiance to a political party's agenda. But during my conversations with the members of the National Coordinating Committee, it became clear that they were more protective of the parties forming the government, and therefore saw any opposition to the king's intervention as putting these parties in a bad light. To illustrate these arguments, I will compare the perceptions of Rachida Benmasoud, one of the six women representing the USFP in Parliament and a member of the National Coordinating Committee, with those of Khadija Rougani, a lawyer and member of Springtime of Equality who represents the AMDF.

Rachida Benmasoud is a university professor, also known for being a feminist writer and a socialist militant. She explained her reasons for supporting the National Coordinating Committee for Women's NGOs by revisiting the meaning of the Casablanca march to the government of alternance. In what follows, Benmasoud also blames the way in which the NPA was established and presented to the public:

The Islamist march aimed to disrupt the new experience of political alternance led by the socialists. Now that the socialists are in the government,
the Islamists wanted to position themselves as the new force of opposition.
But since they lack any viable project of change, they jumped on the NPA
to blackmail the government and curtail the democratic process. We did
not want to gift them with the opportunity to sabotage this process. We
had to remain supportive of the government. The NPA failed to attract
enough support because of the way it had been handled and sold to the
public. We are still a hundred percent behind the NPA, but we think that
the government should not confront the Islamists; it is the king's prerogative to respond, hence, we support the king's arbitrage.

Members of Springtime of Equality had a different take on the king's
arbitrage and openly rejected it. To them, democratization should translate
into more power to representative institutions. Hence, the question of women's
rights should be the prerogative of any other bodies but the Parliament.
Khadija Rougani, a member of the FAMA Center for female victims of domestic violence and a lawyer, held the socialist majority directly responsible for
backing off. In more general terms, she held the political left responsible for
the polarization of the feminist movement and the dismissal of the NPA:

It is true that the "woman question" is at the center of the battlefield between the leftists and the Islamists. But the state also has an interest in stim-
ulating a certain opposition to feminism, because it fears the true democratic
potential of this movement. The state speaks to us through the Islamists.
It tells us through them that we should not trespass certain boundaries. It
shows us the frontlines through its agents: the Islamists. It uses the controversy over women's rights to restate its overall power. Obviously now, everybody calls for the king's arbitrage, the Islamists as well as the political left.
To us, members of the Springtime of Equality, the feminist movement did
not fail. It is rather the failure of the political left. The failure of the Socialist
prime minister who did not have enough courage to seize the great opportunity offered by the feminist movement to show his rupture with undem-
ocratic practices. We wanted the project discussed in the Parliament. This
is what democracy means.

While political allegiances seemed to have shaped feminist divisions, it
was also clear to me that more grievances were at stake. Though the NPA
implicated most feminist organizations, they did not all have equal power in
the decision-making about this project. In fact, the job of "expertise" was
given, I was told by members of the National Coordinating Committee, to

two leading figures in the ADFM, who were paid as experts on gender issues, while the rest of the participants were invited as volunteers to the workshops and debates. Nevertheless, most of the groups that formed the Springtime of Equality either had no declared political affiliation, as in the case of the AMDF, or were allied with leftist parties who were not part of the government, such as al-Talia, an alleged influence on the LDDF's agenda.

The ADFM was the only group whose members had well-known ties with the communist PPS and whose expertise was sought for the project by the communist minister, Saadi. Having said that, it is no trivial detail that most of ADFM's founding members left the PPS to show their disagreement with its failure to support its feminist minister, Saadi, who had become the target of personal offences and sustained attacks in the Islamist press. Not only did Saadi lose his ministerial appointment, but he also lost his seat in the Parliament after the elections of 2002. This news made the headlines of the Islamist press, which took it as a clear sign of political bankruptcy and the failure of Saadi's NPA to gain the support of the Moroccan people.

The external divisions among the Springtime of Equality and the National Coordinating Committee did not preclude internal discord among members of these networks. Within Springtime of Equality, some groups had their own concerns with the PPS. They did not like the "apologetic" approach of the party toward the Islamists after their march. Apparently, the charismatic figures of the PPS, including its secretary general Ismail al-Alaoui, approached the Islamists of al-'Adāla wa-l-tanmia in a move to appease the tensions between both parties, which had been caused by the NPA.

Despite the ambivalent relationships of feminist groups with leftist political parties, they drew lessons from the way Islamist women found support from their respective male organizations and parties. Feminist groups' autonomy was costly, reflected a founding member of the FAMA Center and the AMDF: "We were left alone on the battlefield." She explained why Islamist women have taken the lead as follows: "Islamist women rely heavily on men's support; they benefit from their party's financial resources, use the men's infrastructure, and mobilize the symbolic capital created by their alliances with the 'ulama. After the Islamist march, we started rethinking our approach to autonomy. We decided to engage again with political parties in order to build support from within the political institutions. We need to regain a negotiating power within political parties."

Despite their divisions, both the Springtime of Equality and the National Coordinating Committee for Women's NGOs had been convinced that political parties offer possibilities to maneuver. Both realized the importance of advocating their project of reform through political parties.

Back to Political Parties

Unlike Islamist women, who kept their groups nested within larger political structures and who have worked side by side with the male leadership of their movement, feminist groups' fear of co-optation left them quite isolated, as stated by Najat Razi, sociologist and president of the AMDF. Her group is known as openly secular and independent of all political allegiance or affiliation. She described the endeavor of the AMDF and its affiliated center FAMA to keep their autonomy in a conjuncture in which the "woman's question" has been at the center of political bargaining, claiming:

> For almost two decades, we have worked hard to build a reputation. We have gained recognition and respect from decision-makers and sponsors. They see us as holders of solutions and alternatives. They seek our expertise for the evaluation of their projects and include us into their committees. This was the result of our hard labor and personal sacrifice. However, now we have realized that our independence was highly priced. We started to fill in the gap left by the state and political parties alike for taking care of social problems and gender issues. In my opinion, political parties were no better than the state; they completely dropped the questions of gender equality from their agenda, shifting their responsibilities to us. We were seeking independence from political allegiances; we gained it, but we ended up alone in this struggle.

Another activist from the UAF outlined the type of questions that the feminist movement had to consider in a changed climate:

> After the Islamist march, we had to open new channels for communication with political parties. We needed to make them feel responsible; explain to them that what is at stake is not only women's rights but the survival of the democratic movement in Morocco. Islamist women work very closely with their party and have a strong voice within their movements. They are not scared of co-optation because they do not have any separate agenda from that of their male leadership. But we were so scared of co-optation that we preferred to do it alone. We found ourselves quite isolated.

In order to recreate those channels of communication with political parties, the Springtime of Equality established a yearlong calendar of meetings with all parties' leaders—with the exception of the Islamist al-'Adāla wa-l-tanmia—which was initiated by a meeting with the prime minister and a "memorandum" to the king, reiterating the expectations of feminist groups to see a codification that recognized "full equality of men and women in responsibilities and rights." Parallel to this mobilization, Springtime of Equality activated its membership in various political formations, with advocacy campaigns to grant women access to legislative and representative institutions in the forthcoming elections of 2002. This endeavor led these parties to adhere to a "code of honor" that granted 10 percent of seats in all representative bodies to women. The reform of the electoral code was another step toward encouraging the election of women, through the adoption of a system of lists instead of individual votes. This took the number of women sitting in the Parliament from two in 1997 to thirty-five in 2002, including six women from al-'Adāla wa-l-tanmia.

It is almost impossible to enumerate these breakthroughs without revisiting the impressive work done by the ADFM and its Center for Women's Leadership in Casablanca.[24] The center was created in 1997 as a feminist response to the conjuncture of political alternance. Since 1997 it has played an instrumental role in the instigation of women's candidacy, the training of candidates, and advocacy work on behalf of women who want to run for election. The policy of the center is to prepare women to enter the electoral process independently of their political affiliations, and training sessions were therefore open to women from conservative as well as leftist and Islamist affiliations. One of ADFM's sponsors is the American National Democratic Institute (NDI), which has assisted in the training of more than 120 potential candidates, including Islamist women from al-'Adāla wa-l-tanmia.[25] Ironically, in the municipal elections of September 2003 Rachida Tahiri, the national president of the ADFM who was also the key organizer of the center's activities, lost her election in favor of the Islamist candidate competing with her in the very district where the center is located.

It is also worth noting that Islamist women from al-'Adāla wa-l-tanmia, who opposed the feminist politics of quotas with a discourse of "merit," were the first to benefit from the "code of honor" that political parties endorsed before the 2002 election. Islamist women won six seats out of the forty-three gained by al-'Adāla wa-l-tanmia. An equivalent number of seats were won by socialist women from the USFP party, some of whom were active members of the feminist movement.

Approaching the Royal Council

Most feminist respondents described their appearance before the royal council as very challenging. Not only was the composition of the council a major source of concern, but also the attitude of its members was described as "distant" by some, and even as "hostile" by others. Similar reports about the tensions within the council and among its men's and women's components infiltrated the press to confirm the nature of the challenges facing feminist

groups as they prepared to address the council. There was a feeling shared by
the groups I visited, prior to appearing before the council, that they would
be maneuvering on unusual grounds. A leading member of the ESPOD association, which promotes women's micro-businesses, described the way she
broke the ice by taking an offensive, rather than a defensive, approach to the
council:

> When we entered that room, we were shocked by their reception. Some
> were turning their back to us. They did not respond to greetings, they did
> not look at us. This made me truly angry, but I think my anger helped me
> find the strength to talk in a more simple and direct way. I asked them, do
> you have anything against us? We are here because you invited us. We did
> not create the problems that women are facing in our country, yet we are
> the ones who have volunteered to help with solutions. We were invited by
> the king, and he listened to us; we expect the same thing from you.

Feminist groups had to strategize even at the level of the dress code, and
to decide who would make a "good impression" on the royal council among
their members. According to most feminist respondents, these sessions almost
turned into a trial of the feminist movement. Some of them described the
council as "a power technique used by the state to intimidate and discipline
the feminists." If this experience was "traumatic" for some respondents, to
others it only led to a "radicalization" of their demands.

Thus, in order to approach the council from a more legitimized place,
feminist groups used fragments of the king's public address to the council in
which he recommended a profound and a global reform of the *mudawwana*.
To feminist groups, this profound reform means respecting the full equality
of men and women within marriage, abolishing polygamy and repudiation,
and suppressing the notions of "obedience" and *qiwāma,* which defines the
man as the sovereign provider for the household. They also wanted to see a
recognition of women's inalienable rights for guardianship over children and
recognition of legal competency at the age of eighteen. These conditions were
considered the minimum base of revisions for any further negotiations with
the council. An activist from AMDF describes her group's approach to the
royal council:

> We did not change any of our habits; those of us who usually wear makeup
> or perfume just did. We dressed in our usual style [European]. We did not
> even change our discourse. It is true that we held meetings to get ready for
> these hearing sessions, but we decided to stick to the following statement:
> we are a women's rights organization, and therefore we have a legal approach

that we are ready to support through the presentation of concrete cases. We decided not to compete with the Islamists on their privileged terrain: the sharia. We made it clear to the council that since we are a women's rights organization, we refer to the international regulations that were also ratified by the Moroccan state; we made it clear to them that we work within *these,* not other, parameters.

Both Springtime of Equality and the National Coordinating Committee for Women's NGOs included the same vision in their separate memorandums. This vision is described as "a radicalization" of feminist demands because it restated even the points that the NPA did not cover, such as the eradication of polygamy. Feminists' "radical demands" were backed with religious arguments and buttressed with cases from feminist shelters and centers for legal assistance to women. To increase the pressure on the council, these two networks mounted several press conferences and addressed the king, the government, and the royal council with letters relating documented cases of violations of women's rights.[26] These strategies were denounced by the Islamist press as "subversive tactics" aimed to disturb the council and influence its decision in favor of the feminist claims.

Despite the feminists' frustrations with the royal council, the presence of three women on the council was a matter of satisfaction for most of them. Their appointment gratified the feminists' early endeavors to see women included in this type of decisional structure, and to see different areas of expertise represented in the decision-making process about women's rights. Though the women members of this council reportedly remained silent during the hearings, most of my respondents felt that their mere physical presence offered a tremendous source of support to feminist groups. In fact, and according to most media reports, although women represented a minor feminist voice within the council, they still managed to block the proposals that did not respond to the basic demands of feminist groups. To some, this explains why it took the council three years and two presidents before any consensual decision was reached. The resignation of Driss Dahak, the first council president, gave the public only a slight taste of the real challenges facing women sitting on the council, as well as its conservatives.

In response to the secrecy, under royal command, that characterized the deliberations of the council, the independent and leftist press opened its columns to feminist groups' questions, analyses, and commentaries about the importance of the reform for the conjuncture of democratization. Through this media coverage, feminist groups reiterated their right to know about the council's deliberations and requested open responses to their demands. Khadija

and their libraries missing audio- or videotape documentation. Thus, using various audiovisual supports as means of dissemination for feminist discourse was a novel strategy that enabled feminist groups to communicate with broader audiences.

While Springtime of Equality used the profiles to raise people's awareness about gender oppression, the National Coordinating Committee, led by the UAF and Jussūr, used the technique of mailing postcards to "overwhelm"—a term used by my respondent—the royal council with thousands of concrete pleas from flesh-and-blood women. The UAF's postcards contained a short questionnaire filled out by volunteers who surveyed women at the entrances of courts with regard to their cases. This was an effective feminist strategy to counter the isolation of the feminist movement and ground it all the more in women's standpoints and lived experience.

The questionnaire also identified problems related to women's access to the juridical system and to their struggle with this system. This strategy makes more sense in a context where the illiteracy rate among women is one of the highest in the Arab world, reaching up to 85 percent in certain rural areas. It was also an adequate response to the charge of elitism made by Islamist women aiming to dismiss feminist claims. According to Fatima Maghnaoui of the UAF, ten thousand postcards were sent to the royal council bearing the heading "*urido hala*" (I need a solution).

In addition to feminist activism in networks, individual NGOs also excelled in finding new ways to extend their reach to unprecedented spaces. Already viewed as a mass organization, the LDDF expanded its urban-focused activities into rural areas. The concept of "Caravans for Women's Rights" was used by the LDDF as a new strategy. The caravan, an LDDF member explained, alludes to the old Arabic tradition of long trips across the Arabian desert, which combines the concepts of travel and market exchange with cultural contact, leisure, and political alliances. The LDDF used the concept to invoke this legacy and meet with isolated and subaltern populations in villages, mountains, towns, and marginalized suburbs. On the agenda was a full week of social services, meetings, legal advice, and conferences, but also music and theater with themes focusing on women's rights. This new approach to activism helped the LDDF create interest in women's issues both directly, through legal assistance, and indirectly, through listening to women's needs and providing concrete structures of support.

The LDDF started its first caravan in the summer of 2000, after the "shock of the Islamist march," only to make it an annual event. Each summer hundreds of LDDF members, among them lawyers, teachers, physicians, artists, and militants, tour villages and provincial towns. They set up one or two big tents in which they offer medical services, legal assistance, and literacy initiations. The caravans provide a unique opportunity for the creation of flexible and movable structures in which women can feel at home. At the same time, they allow this group to create a synergy among the local populations, local volunteer groups, professionals based in the region, and agents of the local administration. All collaborate in the creation of the event, making women and their needs the central concern. It would appear that tackling the issues of women's rights and gender equality in very creative ways, including theater, music, discussion forums, and audiocassettes, helped the LDDF to diminish the level of resistance from both local populations and local administrations. The latter has an interest in building bridges with these populations, especially at a time in which the state is looking for new ways to communicate its new image. The LDDF could be the instigator of a new dynamics of inclusion of these populations, since its activities notably take place in both the Arabic and Amazigh languages. The caravans have allowed the LDDF to diagnose the populations' needs through the use of questionnaires, which are filled out by LDDF activists and local NGO partners and used as a means to advocate the reform of family law.

As a movement moment, the Islamist rally of 2000 highlighted the contradictory nature of political alternance and the tensions around projects of social change. This chapter has shown how these conflicts are played on the gender field and how disputes over political power and legitimacy take place around questions of women's rights and women's inclusion in the decision-making process. I have illustrated the disruptive effect of the Casablanca march on the process of the state's transition, reversing the Islamists' marginalization in the Parliament and absence from the government through a forceful presence in "civil society" and the street. For Islamist women, the rally offered the opportunity to be seen as a movement with identifiable groups and leaders. Their writings in the press and multiple television appearances, notably on the pan-Arabic al-Jazeera network, enabled them to integrate into a global discursive community based on women's rights through "cultural translations" (Bhabha 1994) of the United Nations' regime of rights. They did this by redefining "international law" as a product of historical contingencies in order to cancel out its universalist and value-neutral claim, subjecting it to pragmatic and selective uses in order to reclaim through it the right for a woman to veil, to not be discriminated in the workplace, and to be part of a more inclusive "democratic" process. This articulation of the discourse of rights is becoming inevitable in the context of a global market that is defining women's images and bodies as a means to determine their modes of inclusion or exclusion.

Through their unique location in the political landscape, these activists have also shaped the discourse and agendas of the feminist movement. I termed these changes the Islamization of feminist groups, referring this time to the ways feminism has been articulated within the framework of the sharia. Were these changes strategic? Did they affect the core value of the feminist movement?

In their theory of discourse, Laclau and Mouffe (1985) argue that the "articulation" of "separate elements into moments" (unities) leads to the transformation of the identity of what is articulated. In this chapter, I have shown that the changes occurring in feminist politics and practice were closely shaped by the contingencies of the Islamist march and the immediate responses it required. These changes have enlarged the scope of this movement from a focus on reforming the laws to a validation of feminist activism among various—notably subaltern—populations of women.

If perceived as strategic, these shifts nevertheless transformed the way feminist groups had previously related to such populations through a top-down approach to their rights, resulting in a more inclusive approach to the perspectives, resistance, and representations of all women. Similar to Islamist women's approach to activism, it is in the cultural field (Raka 1999) that feminist activism started to play out. Changing the state legal institutions and laws became contingent on changing "peoples' representations" of feminism, as an alien discourse that is hostile to Islam.

These "cultural translations" (Bhaba 1994) of feminist demands required what Najmadabi calls the "rewriting of an original text" (quoted in Abu-Lughod 1998, 20). In the case of feminist groups, this entails first validating the international framework through selective readings of the Islamic sharia, which was legitimized by the involvement of the 'ulama in the feminist struggle. Second, feminist translations required also changing "common-sense" notions about feminism in the "popular mind" by "simplifying" the discourse, translating it into the familiar "ways of seeing" (Berger 1972), feeling, and speaking by "subaltern" populations of men and women. This was occurring parallel to a rationalist approach to the state, through conducting case studies, compiling data, lobbying, and a devising a narrative of "state obligations" to the "international community."

This dualist approach was not pursued by all feminist groups. Few of them kept the state and its institutions as the focus of struggle, but all have understood the importance of adopting their discourses to various populations and engaging new pedagogies on top of providing training and legal advice and assistance to women. If these groups' references to the international framework could be considered the defining quality of their collective identities, and therefore as the core value of their movement, then it is important to understand how this definition was constructed in the relational realm of contentious politics. By this I refer to the context of struggles over legitimacy and power between feminist and Islamist women's movements. None of these movements have been presented as homogenous categories, but rather through their struggle to overcome or negotiate their divisions. However, as this chapter has shown, their divisions were also mediated by multiple players including the state, the media, political parties, and global regulatory regimes.

In the next chapter, I will pursue my analysis by showing how the War on Terror, as a global regulatory regime, once again shifted the terms of the debate, enabling new adjustments by feminists and Islamist women's movements. I will discuss the contradictions, ruptures, and continuities related to the third movement moment: the Casablanca attack of May 2003. How did feminist and Islamist women participate in shaping the war's rhetoric and its agenda? What was the effect of women's voices on domestic gender policy in this new conjuncture? What are the spaces opened by women through their appropriation and subversion of the war's rhetoric?

4

Feminism and Islamism Redefined: In Light of the 2003 Terror Attack on Casablanca

In May 2003, five simultaneous explosions shook the city of Casablanca, killing forty-five people, including the twelve men, all Moroccans, involved in the attacks. The targets were a Spanish cultural center hosting a restaurant, a Jewish community center, a Jewish cemetery, the Belgian consulate, and the Farah Hotel. The young men involved in the attack were identified as part of the radical web al-Salafiyya al-jihādiyya. On-the-ground local analysts and activists blamed the attack on social and economic deprivation after learning that the twelve perpetrators came from the shantytown of Sidi Moumen, and more precisely all from the same slum, Douar Toma, and most had very little education and no stable jobs.

Links were found between this attack and Osama bin Laden's videotape broadcast of February 2003, in which he denounced Morocco as one of the apostate states and pointed to American satellites in the region. Media reports about Morocco's collaboration with Washington and the CIA in their so-called War on Terror were also confirmed through the antennas of al-Jazeera by the Egyptian writer and political analyst Mohamed Hassanein Heikal,[1] who cited Rabat among four Arab capitals to which the United States allegedly off-shored the interrogation of its detainees after the invasion of Afghanistan.[2]

Other local and international analysts saw the Casablanca attack as the result of the government's "importation of Islamist ideology," notably the doctrine of the Muslim Brotherhood during the 1960s that fought against the secular and leftist discourse of pan-Arabism during the cold war (Darif 1999; Kepel 2000; Tozy 1999), and the Wahhabi doctrine of the 1980s that countered the dissident groups inspired by the Muslim Brotherhood. The press, especially the independent and socialist press, played a crucial role in this process by exposing these views to larger audiences. For example, Antoine Basbous, director of the Observatory of Arab Countries in Paris, and speaking for *Le Journal-Hebdo,* a prominent independent weekly newspaper, refers to "thirty years of infiltration, tolerance, and encouragement of the Wahhabi discourse by the Ministry of Islamic Affairs."[3]

The Muslim Brotherhood inspired the Islamists of al-ʿAdl wa-l-ihsāne and al-Tawhīd wa-l-islāh, who have gradually engaged with social institutions, banned violence, and emphasized self-discipline and education. The Wahhabi doctrine is thought to stand behind the webs of radicals who are allegedly part of al-Salafiyya al-jihādiyya, a group that gained public notoriety only after the Casablanca bombing. The security apparatus erected after the attack pointed to links between this group and the interpretations of Islam conveyed by independent preachers such as Mohamed al-Fizazi or the theologian Hassan al-Kettani, among others, all of whom were found guilty of "incitation to violence," and were arrested immediately after the attack.[4] Following the attack, a string of arrests spanning Morocco and Europe led more people to conjecture that al-Salafiyya al-jihādiyya may be part of a larger web with links to al-Qaeda and transnational Jihadist groups.

Deeply shocked by this attack, the Moroccan people shifted their gaze from the trauma of the war in Iraq and the Palestinian intifadah to the problems mushrooming in their own neighborhood. For decades, the official discourse had described Morocco as a land of tolerance and defined it as the place where "modernity" and "authenticity" meet and never clash. Tolerance was perceived through more than one thousand years of cohabitation between the Moroccan Muslim and Jewish communities, and by King Mohammed V's refusal to deliver the Moroccan Jews to the Vichy government during World War II.

Yet the Jewish community was the target of two of these attacks. According to Abdelhamid Amin, a long-standing human rights activist and president of the Moroccan Organization for Human Rights, "it is Morocco's alignment with the agenda of American imperialism that caused the attack."[5] The first reaction of the Moroccan government was to claim that the attack must have been perpetuated by "outsiders." Confronted with the fact that the persons involved were Moroccan nationals with no obvious connection to global terrorist networks, the pro-government press rushed to rephrase the attack as "an assault on democracy" and "modernity," both defined as inalienable "rights" and "choices" of the Moroccan people.

The independent press, such as *Al-Ayām, Al-Sahīfa, Le Journal Hebdo,* and *Tel-Quel,* to cite only the most prominent publications, questioned the connections between the five targets and the Palestinian struggle, as well as its disputed links to the American coalition in the war on Iraq (Roy 2003). In the case of the Farah Hotel, the rumor that a delegation of Americans was present at the time of the attack was the only way to understand the relevance of this target at the current international conjuncture.

Horrified and alarmed by the attack, political parties and nongovernmental organizations responded by organizing a rally at which everyone, except veiled women and bearded men, was welcome. The leadership of the two most important Islamist forces of the country, al-'Adl wa-l-ihsāne and al-Tawhīd wa-l-islāh, along with their affiliated party, al-'Adāla wa-l-tanmia, was denied access to the rally. It is worth noting, however, that no member of these two movements was found guilty in relation to the Casablanca bombing despite the arrest and interrogation of key members. The fact is that both movements have increased their legitimacy, due to their position regarding the NPA, under the anxious gaze of the socialist majority in the government, fearing that the Islamists could win the major cities in the upcoming communal elections.

Morocco between Osama bin Laden and George Bush

The videotape attributed to Osama bin Laden, in which he depicted the country as an American satellite, only confirmed the image of the Moroccan state among the larger Arab family. King Mohammed VI's declared pro-Palestinian policy apparently did not help to change the image of a country perceived as a pole of American influence in the Middle East.[6] Many factors contributed to the perception of Morocco as a Western ally during the cold war and as a major player in the new American "imperial episode" (Nederveen Pieterse 2004). Among these factors were Morocco's geostrategic location at the crossroads of Africa, the Middle East, and Europe, the liberal orientation of its monarchy, and the postcolonial distance it maintains from both communism and the anti-imperialist, secular, and leftist discourse of pan-Arabism.

Furthermore, regional struggles unique to the Maghreb are significant in understanding Morocco's alignment with the current policies of the United States in the Middle East. Neighboring Algeria harbors and supports a movement for independence in Western Sahara, considered a Moroccan territory by the Moroccan government, a claim disputed by the Polisario Front.[7] This struggle is a chief cause of the Moroccan government's pro-Americanism. The monarchy fears a solution such as a referendum for self-determination that would politically devastate the regime, not only because of the symbolic capital the Moroccan state has drawn from this "question" since the end of 1970s but also because of capital *tout court,* and the massive investments made by the state in the region. The United States also fears an armed conflict between Morocco and Algeria that would threaten the success of the U.S. War on Terror and the post-9/11 U.S. project the Middle East Partnership Initiative (MEPI). Morocco is a key player in both.

MEPI comprises a vision of reforming the Middle East as a means to enhance the U.S. security (Salime 2010). It is a politics of intervention through soft political reforms and economic programs that aims to manufacture consent with regard to American policies in the region, while enhancing the poor image of the United States since the invasion of Iraq, which has been confirmed by many polls and studies.[8] Morocco is actively involved in this project. As early as October 2000, a public relations campaign led by an important delegation of governmental agents, diplomats, and representatives of corporate unions, in a visit to the United States, attracted the interests of the American media and staked out three pages in the *New York Times* (October 9, 2000). Under the heading "U.S.-Moroccan Relations Built on Historical Foundations," Morocco was qualified as an "old" and "best" friend of the United States. Fathallah Oualalou, the socialist Minister of Finance and long-standing activist in student and academic leftist unions during the 1980s, explained how "we [Morocco and the United States] found ourselves together in the frontline in the fight for freedom during the Second World War."

Another heading celebrated: "New King Opens Doors to Liberal Economy." This section explained that, "though Morocco has traditionally maintained much closer economic ties with the European Union [which accounts for 60 percent of its foreign trade] than with the U.S., it seems to be striving toward a more balanced relationship with these two economic giants." In the columns of the same article, André Azoulay, the economic adviser of King Mohammed VI, introduced the country as "market-oriented, business-minded, and open to all its partners and investors." Azoulay, pursuing his advocacy, defined Morocco as "a key player with an important role in the Middle East–North Africa (MENA)." Nadia Hayat, the female president of the Professional Association of Stock Exchange Companies, speaks in the same supplement about Morocco's achievements in the stock exchange and its ranking by the *Financial Times* of London as the fifth-best performing financial industry in the world in 1998.

In a continuation of this move, Morocco signed the final draft of the Free Trade Agreement with the United States in April 2004.[9] In May 2004 the Moroccan government volunteered to host the Forum for the Future. This meeting was expected to bring together government agents and "civil society" from the United States, Europe, and the Middle East to discuss corporate-driven political reforms. Yet its first round failed to draw support from both the Islamists and most nongovernmental organizations, including the feminist and Islamist groups that are subjects of this study (Algerian Press Service 2004).

If the Forum for the Future did not send a strong enough signal about the endorsement of the Bush administration's big plans for "civil society," the bilateral Free Trade Agreement launched in January 2003 made the government's endorsement clear. Raymond Ahearn, speaking for the American trade division, defined Morocco as a "moderate state" and "a strong ally of the U.S. in its war against terrorism."[10] The negotiations with Morocco, explained Robert Zoellick, the U.S. Trade Representative, "send a powerful signal to the rest of the Muslim world that President Bush is committed to supporting the development of open, prosperous societies in all regions of the world."[11] Free trade agreements are also shaped by political concerns, as announced by this business roundtable discussion: "free trade with Middle Eastern nations such as Morocco is also strategically critical to the U.S. in the war against terror."[12]

As is clear from these statements, the War on Terror is delivered in a package of neoliberal reforms, such as those set forth in the MEPI, the Forum for the Future, and bilateral free trade agreements. These projects are interconnected. I have argued elsewhere that as an economic program, neoliberalism needs the War on Terror as a technique for discipline and control that works through stigma and racial profiling, but also through triggering internal divisions, as illustrated in Iraq (Salime 2007). This mix does not work without tensions, however. While neoliberalism requires a small government and an active civil society, one that can replace the state in the social sectors, the War on Terror needs a wide-ranging security apparatus and a docile civil society (Salime 2007). Yet both the War on Terror and its underlying neoliberal agenda require an inflated state security apparatus, reducing the state to its disciplinary dimensions. I will illustrate these arguments in the following discussion.

A Gender Reform

Gender became central once again to the positioning of the Moroccan state in the new conjuncture of the War on Terror. In fact, as the Moroccan state strived to position itself as a player in the U.S. war against terrorism, a new code of the family—one that recognized the equality of husband and wife before the law—started to make sense to the monarchy in a whole new way. It was through the reform of family law that the Moroccan monarchy truly recovered its image as a moderate regime, the Casablanca attack notwithstanding. The new family code was presented by the king in a broadcast speech to the Parliament in October 2003. In a gesture to appease the Islamists, who had actively opposed the reform for two decades, the king introduced the new family code as a reform that was inspired by the Islamic sharia. The new code was closely built on the liberal feminist proposals of women's rights and the rhetoric of gender equality.

In this reform, the family becomes the responsibility of both husband and wife, the age of marriage is raised to eighteen for both men and women, polygamy is restricted though not abolished, repudiation is no longer legal, both parties have equal access to the court to file for a divorce, the *wilāya* is abolished, and the requirement of a wife's obedience was eliminated from the new code, which also gave women unconditional rights to custody and alimony, among many other changes. The new code is no longer named the *mudawwana,* but simply the Code of the Family, as a statement of rupture with the past.

Positioning Morocco ahead of most Arab and Islamic countries, the reform obviously made international headlines, and King Mohammed VI was congratulated by the U.S. Secretary of State Colin Powell and praised by President George W. Bush for being on the right democratic path.[13] It is worth stating, however, that the reform of the *mudawwana,* though inspired by feminist demands, responded to the ways in which both feminist and Islamist women's movements had managed to bring gender back to center stage with the advent of the War on Terror.

Though introduced by the king to Parliament as an outcome of consensus and *ijtihād*—a pressing demand from both feminists and Islamists—it was clear that the reform was inspired more by feminist rhetoric and demands than by the Islamist's reservations. However, coming only a few months after the Casablanca attack, it was obvious that the feminists' articulation of their movement as a "fence against religious radicalism" and a "pledge of the state's espousal of the values of democracy and modernity" found their way to the decision makers. Another gain for feminist groups was seeing the project of reform brought to a vote in the Parliament. Morocco was also moving toward lifting its limitations on CEDAW, ratified in 1993. This announcement was made by the first woman Secretary of State in Charge of the Family, Childhood, and Disabled Persons, Yasmina Baddou, at the United Nations plenary session of the 49th Session on the Situation of Women in March 2005.

Completely silenced by the hostile climate of May 16, the Islamists of the party al-'Adāla wa-l-tanmia endorsed the reform of the *mudawwana,* welcoming the new Code of the Family. Nonetheless, while the reform of the *mudawwana* was received with a great deal of enthusiasm in Morocco and was welcomed by foreign leaders and the international press,[14] a different sort of appreciation was garnered for the state of human rights by local and inter-national human rights groups. The War on Terror produced major setbacks to some of the rights gained by Moroccans during the 1990s.

Feminist theory stresses the ways in which the women's movement has played a major role in the identification of how states are formed and organized around gender meanings and practices. For instance, Moghadam argues that women may become the sign or marker of political goals and of cultural identity, not only during processes of revolution and state building, but also when power is being contested or reproduced (2000, 44). She states that "representations about women assume political significance, and certain images of women define and demarcate political groups, cultural projects, or ethnic communities" (44).

Other studies have shown that some political transformation may increase the political space available to women's organizations, while still actively repressing other sectors of civil society (Alvarez 1990, 262; Jelin 1998). This argument is right to the point. In fact, the reform of the *mudawwana* came at the expense of greater setbacks in the arena of other rights and freedoms, including the right to information. The endorsement of the new Code of the Family by the king in the conjuncture of fighting terrorism makes my definition of gender as a marker of political shifts exceedingly relevant. The new code indeed came to mark Morocco's open participation in the global War on Terror, and enabled the state to portray itself as democratic even without implementing radical changes to the structure of power, still dominated by the king as the central player.

Morocco's Patriot Act

Nederveen Pieterse (2002) sees the new component of the American war on terrorism in the narrowing of the spectrum of American debate and the curtailment of domestic dissent. What else expresses this better than the Patriot Act? Consequently, if one defines globalization in terms of the blurring of national boundaries and erosion of the power of nation-states (Wallerstein 1999), then the consequences of this war would certainly have global implications. In Morocco, May 16 was seized as a strategic moment to legitimize the government's open alignment with the American definition of the spaces of freedom through its Patriot Act.

Only a few days after the Casablanca attack, the Moroccan Parliament rushed to pass the very controversial Antiterrorist Law. It had been proposed by the government after 9/11 but failed to draw enough support in the Parliament and was opposed by various human rights organizations in Morocco.

After May 16, however, the law was unanimously endorsed by the Parliament, including the Islamists who had actively rejected it before this date.[15]

Though Article 9 of the Moroccan constitution guarantees the freedom of speech, Article 19 of the Moroccan constitution almost nullifies it, since it defines the person of the king as existing outside of this freedom. With the Antiterrorist Law, the domain of sovereignty of the king and the nation became more intertwined. Hence, broader categories of citizens fell under the definition of terrorism. The immediate targets were journalists. During the first decades of Morocco's independence, the arrests of journalists and the closing of newspapers were not unusual. These actions were directed against the Islamists, leftists, and, in some cases, the nationalist opposition of the Istiqlal Party. This time, the censorship shifted to the independent press, the only remaining active opposition after the integration of the socialists and the silencing of the Islamists, notably after May 16.

The press was found guilty of diffusion of information, interviews, or discourses of some Islamist groups, such as the banned organization al-'Adl wa-l-ihsāne and some alleged members of al-Salafiyya al-jihādiyya. For instance, Mustafa Qasheni, the director of the Arabic newspaper *Al-Hayāt,* and Mustafa Alawi, the director of *Al-Usbou',* were arrested and charged under the Antiterrorist Law for "encouraging terrorism." Mohamed al-Hadr, the director of the newspaper *Al-Sharq,* was sentenced to four years in prison for promoting terrorism. Ali L'mrabet, director of the magazine *Demain,* was condemned to five years for publishing a caricature of the king. L'mrabet became an icon of the Moroccan independent press with his resilient will to counteract several bans on his newspapers by creating new ones. But for this particular trial, L'mrabet managed to attract a wave of international solidarity, notably when he began an unlimited hunger strike. Other types of harassment were directed toward female journalists, such as Maria Mkreim, a columnist with the weekly *Al-Ayām,* who received anonymous death threats after her interviews with a group of detainees allegedly connected to al-Salafiyya al-jihādiyya.

Blaming Democracy

Jerry Falwell, who made himself notorious along with Billy Graham for articulating the Christian fundamentalist version of the clash of civilizations, asserted that the 9/11 attack was caused by "Pagans, and the abortionists, and the feminists, and the Gays and the Lesbians [and] the American Civil Liberties Union" (quoted in Peters 2003, 152). A similar case was made by the Moroccan government, though with less of an impact on world politics. In a broadcast speech, the technocrat-appointed Prime Minister Driss Jettou blamed an "excess of democracy" for causing the attack. Driss Jettou held human rights organizations, "civil society," and the press accountable, and condemned their "misuse of democracy" and "irrational exploitation of political freedoms."[16] To the prime minister, it was these agents' advocacy of human rights, their criticism of the government, and their rejection of the Antiterrorist Law prior to the attack that encouraged the radicals to blow themselves up in Casablanca. It is worth noting that the king's appointment of Driss Jettou from outside the government's socialist majority after the election of 2002 caused widespread frustrations that were expressed by NGOs and intellectuals through the independent press.

Intimidating the Islamists

After May 16, screening the funds of Islamist organizations made sense. The Antiterrorist Law allowed banks to report any suspicious transactions. Accordingly, the government mandated an investigation directed against the al-Tawhīd wa-l-islāh movement, and targeted its funding campaign in support of the Palestinians during the April 2002 Israeli invasion of the Jenin refugee camp.[17] To Mohamed Darif, political scientist and local expert of Islamist movements, this campaign was to be understood in relation to Colin Powell's visit to Morocco and the American war declared on the financial sources of funding to terrorism, more precisely on the sources of support to the Palestinian resistance.[18]

To most analysts, these power techniques were meant to intimidate the Islamists and silence the most vocal activists among them. As far as al-'Adāla wa-l-tanmia is concerned, these tactics prepared the terrain for more concessions by the party in the forthcoming communal elections.[19] At first glance, the conjuncture described above would appear to be very helpful to feminist groups' positioning in the political field and their activism in reaction to the Islamists. It is interesting then to see how both movements articulated this conjuncture, and how Islamist women positioned themselves by co-opting the discourse of "moderation."

Clash of Civilizations?

I will open this section with two statements by leaders of feminist organizations. These statements show the level of anxiety raised by the Islamist mobilization as both feminists and Islamists were using the same means of transportation, the same train and bus stations, and the same rest areas when they were joining the two marches. In fact, there were two separate campaigns requesting free public transportation from regional city councils to enable more participants to join. These sites of encounter became charged with tensions and emotion as the supporters of both movements found themselves in a face-to-face situation, which led to the feelings described below by this feminist leader:

> When you see the Islamists as a group, you remember the military. The type of power exhibited by the Islamists is military; everything about them reminds you of the military, they have military structures, a military organizational style, a military attitude. Even the way they organize their rallies reminds you of the military. It was frightening to see them at that rest area between Meknes and Rabat; the level of hatred expressed on their faces when they saw us getting off the bus was frightening.
>
> We do not fight in similar ways. Men and women traveled together on the same bus. We did not have buses for men and others for women. We marched together. But to the Islamists, marching is already a form of jihad; it has to be in a certain way; it is also subject to a strict regulation. We are "cool," "relaxed."

Another activist talked about fear:

> I was scared. It was the first time I realized that the Islamists are here and that they are dangerous. I remember the confrontations that I had with them because of the NPA: It is disturbing. I remember their look—despising, spiteful, and insolent. It was absolutely depressing. To me there is before and after the NPA, and before and after the Islamist rally of 2000. The NPA changed the course of our history. For the first time, we had to draw a line between two antagonistic societal projects, two clashing visions of the world: a modernist one and one that is a traditional and conservative. The NPA was not only backed by women, but was cheerfully carried by all men and women who aspire to a modern and democratic society.

The modernist binaries expressed in these two statements formed the main framework of articulation of feminist responses to the Casablanca attack. Most feminist activists viewed the attack as the expression of two "clashing worldviews": a modernist one represented by the feminists and an archaic one promoted by the Islamists. There is then a similarity in the way the feminist respondents perceive the Islamists, as one block of evil, and the government's discourse, notably through its socialist press. All converged to discredit their major political opponents: the Islamists of the party al-'Adāla wa-l-tanmia. The latter were held responsible for "blocking the progress of Morocco" by opposing the NPA, and were found "guilty of encouraging and disseminating a discourse of hatred."

Empowered by May 16, feminist groups urged the state to adopt with no further delays their project of reform of the *mudawwana*. Not only did some leaders of these groups become more assertive about their feminism, but they also managed to rearticulate their definition of feminism as the fence against "religious extremism." Najat Razi, the former president of the AMDF, is now open about her feminist identity:

> Feminist groups used to have problems with the term "feminist." We wanted to avoid it. Personally, I am no longer concerned with this debate. Yes, I am a feminist. Feminism is an identity, a world vision, a project of social change and a political practice. Feminism enables us to define women as persons with rights; it proposes a project of change based on equality and respect of the autonomous will of women. It rejects discrimination based on sex, and motivates actions to fight against it. In these terms, I am a feminist. Our movement is a holder of change; it is modernist and a carrier of democratic alternatives.

Despite their disagreement with the U.S. war on Iraq, thought to be devastating for the cause of women, feminist groups co-opted the rhetoric of the War on Terror but redefined its terms and conditions. To them, espousing the values of "democracy" and "modernity" is the only path for any country to prevent potential American intervention and preserve its territorial and national sovereignty. Najia Zirari (ADFM/Casablanca) argues that eliminating the motives for an American intervention definitely depends on the state's handling of religious extremism and its enhancement of women's rights. However, she continues, eradicating the sources that feed religious extremism is contingent on encouragement by the state of other "democratic" players, notably feminist groups.

I have not discussed whether feminist groups have critically or even seriously questioned the notions of democracy and modernity, but it is obvious that the postmodern debate about both notions has yet to make its way into my respondents' articulations. Therefore, there are unresolved questions and tensions: first, between the feminists' activism and discourse on democracy and rights and their call for the eradication of the Islamist component of political life; second, between their claim for more spaces of individual and political freedoms that should benefit all and the desire to see a more interventionist state that cracks down on the "fundamentalists."

To these activists, there is only one women's movement. Najia Zirari defines this movement as "one that prioritizes the cause of women, fights for equality, and recognizes the international norms." This movement "carries the hopes and aspirations of women for a better world, for fair access to resources, and for equality before the law." Hence, this movement is "modernist in its approach, democratic in its goals," argues Leila Rhiwi (ADFM/Rabat). Accordingly, "Islamist women cannot be and are not part of it," states Fatima Maghnaoui (UAF). Saadia Wadah, a lawyer and founding member of the Center d'Ecoute in Casablanca, claimed that "the Islamist women's project is different; they do not work for the cause of women [*qadiat al-mar'a*], but for the cause of the Islamic state, and women are secondary in this project." Another activist maintained that while "the feminists are a force of change, Islamist women are a force of regression and stagnation." "We are a democratic force," said Khadija Rougani (FAMA Center), "they are a regressive force." "They are just the sisters, the wives, and daughters of the brothers," claims Bouchra Abdou (LDDF). In the best-case scenario, the differences between the Islamists and the feminists are expressed in Najat Razi's (AMDF) terms: "We are a civic force, they are political force."

To demarcate themselves as a "civic force," the feminists strove to respond to May 16 with new structures emphasizing their distinguished societal project. May 16 pushed the feminists to clearly locate themselves within the new trend, namely the marriage of modernity and democracy.[20]

The Network Modernity/Democracy was created in the aftermath of the Casablanca Islamist rally of March 2000, but it was the Casablanca attack that gave the network its impetus. This large network was formed by a broad range of urban elites who found themselves united against both the Islamist project and the government-sponsored setbacks in human rights and democratic freedoms. In this network, feminist groups were represented by Leila Rhiwi, a university professor of communication and president of ADFM/Rabat. The ADFM's leadership played a critical role in joining this group of intellectuals, professionals, and activists together and hosting their meetings in the ADFM center in Rabat.

My own participation in one of the first meetings of this network in the summer of 2003 was critical to my understanding of the dynamics of interactions between the feminists and the Islamist movement in the aftermath of the Casablanca attack. The memorandum of the Network Democracy/Modernity, presented by Leila Rhiwi at this meeting, attempted to capture these dynamics. It was a three-page statement that detailed specific demands and goals. The introductory statement gives an idea of the centrality of the themes of democracy and modernity in this project:

> We, the persons signing this communiqué, state our adherence to the enlightened values of modernity. We believe that the democratic project is based on respect of freedoms, the right to difference, and the values of

solidarity, equality, and tolerance, and is the only path to grant Morocco's full membership in the contemporary human civilization, and ensure its contribution to its universals. . . . We are convinced that these universals are a common heritage to humanity, and that in turn they enrich our particularism. We are also confident that multiple sources of inspiration from our culture have a lot to contribute toward the advancement and evolution of these universals. (ADFM 2004)

The Network Modernity/Democracy was formed after many attempts by feminist groups to attract the state's attention to the violations of human rights that were taking place in marginal suburbs, as well as in the streets of big cities, in the name of religion. As women's rights advocates, the feminists were particularly subject to defamation by preachers during their religious sermons and through audiotapes sold at the entrances of mosques. The LDDF multiplied the calls in the press to attract the government's attention to these excesses.[21] Its Observatory for Women's Rights held an Islamist Watch in order to document and report on acts of violence, hate speech, and crimes committed on persons found guilty of inappropriate behavior or "nonobservance of Islamic morals," according to radicals in their communities.

The Observatory for Women's Rights was created by the LDDF after the Islamist March of 2000. Its goal was to assist women who were victims of domestic violence as well as women suffering from other types of violations of rights, such as sexual harassment in the workplace. The center maintains a library on women and gender and compiles data on violations of individual freedoms of both men and women. Activists at the center confirmed that various cases of violence were reported by young women assaulted in the street for nonobservance of the veil. This was very intimidating, especially in the marginal suburbs where some radical groups flourished in the absence of any effective presence of the state, putting themselves in charge of deciding the rules, "taxes," and modes of punishment. In this context, many working-class women were compelled to wear the veil in order to become invisible to these groups.[22] It is natural then that the feminists' articulations of the Casablanca attack were again expressed in legal terms to claim the "rule of law" and the intervention of the state, viewed as a warrant for the safeguard of the values of democracy, freedom, and modernity.

Once again, the feminists and the leftist majority of the government found themselves united in their fight against their major political opponents, the Islamists of the party al-'Adāla wa-l-tanmia. The implications of this party and its press in systematic campaigns of defamation that targeted these two groups were clear. After the Casablanca attack, both groups accused the party's press of being a podium for campaigns of defamation against feminists and leftists. It is also a fact that no member of this party or its mother organization, al-Tawhīd wa-l-islāh, was found guilty of violent acts, and none of them was found guilty in relation to the Casablanca bombing attack. Nevertheless, the public condemnation of this party made the headlines of the media, notably through the Arabic socialist newspaper *Al-Ahdāth al-maghribiyya,* which labeled the party members "religious traffickers" and multiplied the calls for the eradication of the party from the political field. The Islamists of al-'Adl wa-l-ihsāne were less affected by these calls, since they had not been participating in the electoral process.

In this highly tense and hostile environment, Islamist women had to organize their responses by positioning themselves in the new platform of "tolerance, respect of difference, and moderation." This change in the tone of the Islamists and shift in their discourse was noticeable to my feminist interviewees. As one feminist activist expressed it, "Now the Islamists want to *flirt* with us; after appalling us, they are trying to seduce us."

Islamists: Low Profile

The immediate reaction of the Islamists was to adopt a low profile. Also noteworthy was the way in which women's voices almost disappeared from the Islamist press. The waves of arrests, harassment of Islamist groups, and systematic calls to close down their organizations were partly responsible for the fading of Islamist women's voices in the aftermath of the Casablanca attack. One might wonder if, now that serious issues were at stake, men would reassume control. There was also a paternalist and protectionist reaction that has been common among Islamist groups, limiting their female membership in periods of crisis. In fact, one can speak of a web of families forming the Islamist organizations, husbands and wives, brothers and sisters, as well as the younger generations of children. Therefore, the patriarchal, or rather neopatriarchal (Sharabi 1988), characteristic of these webs is always at work, and is more active during periods of crisis.

With the exception of very few women, such as Nadia Yassine from al-'Adl wa-l-ihsāne, who gave several interviews to the press, or Fouzia Hajbi from al-'Adāla wa-l-tanmia, who maintained her column in the weekly newspaper *Al-'Asr,* Islamist women did not comment on the attack in the media. Thus, the views expressed in this chapter are based mainly on my own interpretations of personal interviews with the Islamist women's leadership, which I conducted in the summers of 2003 and 2004.

Islamist women articulated that the attack distanced their politics from radical Islamist groups. They define themselves as the *wassat* (median). This is a Qur'anic term, invoked to describe the Muslims as the *wassat*, which signifies a median location and a moderate position at the same time. Therefore, when Islamist women define their politics as *wassat* they locate themselves in reference to the "extremists of the left," called "eradicators," and the extremists speaking in the name of Islam, called the Wahhabi by women of al-'Adl wa-l-ihsāne. Both "extremes" are thought to mirror, attract, and feed each other. Islamist women claim that representing the *wassat* allows them to ask for *more*, not *less*, space to maneuver.

Subverting Motherhood

To this end, they brought to the forefront their definitions of womanhood and motherhood. Womanhood is understood as a set of natural qualities and psychological dispositions that prepare women for their role as mother. If womanhood is viewed in essentialized terms, motherhood is defined as a social location, a *wassat*. To Nadia Yassine, motherhood does not have to be connected to maternity and procreation. It bears a broader meaning. Motherhood is "the factor of humanization of the social." To Suad al-Amari, one of the few women elected to one of the city councils of Casablanca and a member of al-Tawhīd wa-l-islāh, motherhood is distinctly an "intersecting location," a *wassat*, because it is "the point where the social and the individual meet and overlap."

Since they exist at the intersection of the social and the personal, women develop qualities and skills to deal with these connections; they are conflict managers, peacemakers, and moderators. "Women carry life, give and maintain life"; this is why they are "predisposed to protect life," said Ghislane al-Bahrawi, the president of the women's section of al-'Adl wa-l-ihsāne. These meanings were not constructed with reference to a certain feminist theory. They were the outcome of women's interpretations and readings of the sources and "sacred history" of Islam, to borrow Zubaida's (1987) wording.

Nevertheless, it is among women of al-'Adl wa-l-ihsāne, and more precisely the small group of leaders working around Nadia Yassine, that the limits of these interpretations are pushed in extremely fascinating ways. For instance, Nadia Yassine claims that men "have hijacked Islam since the early time of the revelation, making it this patriarchal and sexist religion." The Wahhabi, she claims, "have excelled in their focus on the women's body, have become obsessed with this body, and have gotten entrenched in outdated views, interpretations, and practices." Now she argues: "It is up to women to take Islam back."

In order to prove women's exceptionalism, Ghislane al-Bahrawi maintained that of all the reciters of the *hadīth*s (prophet's sayings), it was a woman,

Aisha, the youngest spouse of the prophet, whose version was never contested by the *muhaddithūn* (reciters). It was also Aisha who had the exclusive ability to transmit all the *hadīth*s about compassion, love, and tolerance to generations of Muslims. Aisha is therefore viewed as a moderate voice that had even corrected distortions in the way some *hadīth*s were reported by male companions of the prophet.

These activists push their views about women's exceptionalism even further. In a tone reminiscent of Lacan's notion of "lack," al-Bahrawi claims that Adam, god's first human creation, was created from earth and the soul came as a second step. This is why "men are not complete and feel a constant lack and desire to be completed." Women do not feel the same way. When women were created, "the body was not waiting for the soul, both were already connected."

Women's median location gives them another privilege over men: their appreciation of the whole picture. "Men have a superficial view of things, a truncated view. They do not perceive the whole picture," said al-Bahrawi. "They need the woman's gaze. It is a more in-depth view and more encompassing that perceives at the same time the details without omitting the whole picture." It is no wonder that Nadia Yassine and her group were declared apostate by the radicals of al-Salafiyya al-jihādiyya, a fact confirmed by Yassine during our meetings.

New Spaces

No matter how seriously one takes these interpretations about men's and women's qualities, they are to be understood within the goals of these leaders to "help women recover their self-esteem." According to Hoda, an activist working with women in some of the marginal suburbs in the city of Fez:

> Respect is lacking from the way society treats women in general, and poor women in particular. We do not work with the elites, hence the problems we encounter are not known by the elites. The women we work with have a poor image of the self, they have been told they are worth nothing; we work with women who have been treated as purely sexual objects by husbands [speaking about Islamist radicalism], we work with women who have been asked to give up their femininity and hide themselves behind dark cloths and closed doors. These women need another image of the self. This is our starting point.

To reach this goal, this leadership created learning structures and pedagogies that enabled them to educate women from different social and economic backgrounds. One of these structures is called Madrasat al-sahabiyyat (the School of Women Companions of the Prophet).[23] It is a monthly meeting facilitated by the women's section of al-'Adl wa-l-ihsāne in various places across the country that aims at connecting women with the Islamic legacy as it was understood, transmitted, and practiced by women known to be close friends and companions of the prophet.

Opening a learning space that carries the name of "al-sahabiyyat" and is inspired by their stories is a very powerful symbol. Most oral and written histories known to the Muslims reiterate the lives and role modeling of *al-sahāba* (male companions of the prophet). Looking at Islamic heritage through the lens of women's questions, practices, and contributions brings back women's voices as a viable source for learning about the Islamic faith and an important source to legitimize Islamist women's own interpretations and aspirations.

In the summer of 2004, I took part in one of these meetings, held at one of the old Moorish houses in the Medina of Fez. The house was donated by a member, I was told. It hosts a few offices and a library on the second floor, and leaves its first floor available for meetings and religious retreats. The meeting started at 3:00 P.M. and was led by Mouna Khlifi, a high school teacher and the president of the woman's umbrella organization Insaf. I was joined by sixty women representing a wide range of ages, education levels, and social backgrounds. Everybody was sitting on a floor covered by Moroccan carpets and prayer mats in the open patio of the house. The art and mosaics decorating the floors and walls did not divert these women's attention from what Mouna Khlifi was there to say. Mouna was talking about aspects of the personalities of the women *sahabiyyat* (companions of the prophet). After introducing me as a sister, a researcher, and *dā'iyya* in charge of changing the views about Islam and Muslims in the West, Khlifi reminded the audience of the three founding principles of the movement al-'Adl wa-l-ihsāne: "No to secrecy, no to foreign funds or allegiance, and no to violence."

Mouna introduced the women to me as "active participants" in their learning process. She made sure at the opening of the meeting to congratulate those who had passed their university exams, along with those who finished their literacy programs and those who had accomplished the difficult task of memorizing the entire Qur'an. She did not neglect to remind the participants of their duties as Muslims, to come in aid of those who had lost jobs or loved ones or even to pay visits to the members who had given birth or gotten married. Prayers were made for those absent because of sickness or deaths in their families. Other prayers went also to Nadia Yassine and Sheikh Abdessalam Yassine for their encouragement of these kinds of initiatives. After this ritual, the meeting ensued with comments by the assistants about the previous meetings, questions about the next assignments, and short presentations of research on respective subjects.

As a facilitator of the debate and a group leader, Mouna Khlifi, who had traveled from the city of Meknes, stressed that she considered a woman who expresses her feelings or opinions as valuable as the one who makes a presentation and writes a text. Therefore, she encouraged everybody to share how they had felt since the last meeting, whether they had seen a change in their perspectives and perception of self, and whether this kind of learning helped them solve some of their daily problems or improve their relations with their children and husbands. Reading the texts becomes a requirement only after the women who are not able to read have become comfortable with this practice after being involved in the mandatory literacy programs established by volunteers across Morocco. It is worth noting that the most recent media accounts state that this movement is on its way to becoming the major representative force of Morocco's Islamism in Western Europe, and is also expanding in the United States.

Expressing feelings becomes an inclusive mode of participation for women who otherwise could not speak on the same scholarly grounds as the educated members of the group. It is clear that this type of exchange is grounded in a pedagogy of praxis. Sharing is part of this pedagogy. Coming to the meeting with a question, sharing information or a prayer is also considered active participation. "Every woman gives according to her capabilities and receives according to her needs," said Khlifi. The meeting was interrupted in order to allow women's call to prayer to be performed collectively, also uncommon in non-Islamist circles, in which a collective prayer is always led by a man.

This practice of collective empowerment is not the only occasion for women to build a more positive self-image. For the growing membership of al-'Adl wa-l-ihsāne among the Moroccan diaspora in Europe and the United States, weekly conferences and chat rooms are organized via the Internet.[24] In addition, meetings take place in women's homes designed around their particular needs in education, budget management, conflict resolution, and employment. This program is not exclusively about religion, said Aisha, one of the designers of its activities in Fez city.

The curriculum deals with labor rights and unionization for working-class women, self-help organizations, structures for women living in slums, strategies for survival in academia for students, solidarity, respect for neighbors' rights, and conflict management in crowded urban areas and within extended families. Women's sexual lives, their "femininity," benefits from a major interest by the women's leadership of al-'Adl wa-l-ihsāne. Audiocassettes used by women in the intimacy of their homes complete and support the group discussions about women's sexual life, love, and intimate relationships between husbands and wives.[25] All these activities, questions, examples, and solutions are built within the same Islamic sources of reference to these groups: the Qur'an and the sunna.

Another strength of al-'Adl wa-l-ihsāne stems from the way the leadership is elected among the most active participants. The membership's growth imposes a multiplicity of spaces and requires the rise and involvement of many leaders. The Supreme Guide and Council of Guidance require groups to create new units once the number of participants reaches ten. Each unit of ten is called a family (al-usra) and has to organize its own schedules and programs to accommodate its members' needs. The leadership also has its own training program during which a unified vision is developed. Leaders find support in the writings of remarkable figures in the history of Islamic spirituality and scholarship, thought to have espoused an advanced vision of women's rights, status, and role in Islam. The writings of the prominent Sufi scholars Muhyiddin Ibn 'Arabi (Islamic Spain, 1165–1240), Ibn Hazm al-Andalusi (Islamic Spain, 994–1063), and the fifteenth-century Moroccan judge and 'alim Ibn Ardoun, are held in high esteem by this leadership. These scholars are viewed as the best example of how Muslim scholars and men should represent their relationship to Muslim women. They illustrate the way "Muslim men held women in a high esteem throughout their lives and writings," explained al-Bahrawi.

Women's engagement with the most positive "feminist" writing in Islam was fundamental to engendering the field of Islamic studies in Moroccan universities. Most leaders I spoke to, from both al-'Adl wa-l-ihsāne and al-Tawhīd wa-l-islāh, were affiliated with an academic program to get a degree in Islamic studies or the sharia, in addition to their original fields of expertise in hard sciences, humanities, and social sciences. Receiving a degree is more than a need; it is the path for legitimizing what women have already learned through independent reading and research, supporting their claims to religious leadership and to the sphere of da'wa.

As I discussed earlier, women's median position as mothers and their "instinctive" qualities as "moderators" and "peacemakers" are activated, put at the forefront, and defined as the best protection for the young generations against "extremisms of all kinds." As mothers, "women carry, give, and sustain life through their daily activities, strategies, and practice," asserted Suad al-Amari from al-Tawhīd wa-l-islāh. Therefore, they are "prepared to protect life," as many of my Islamist respondents said. Through the less threatening "private" sphere of motherhood, Islamist women started claiming their right to practice *da'wa* in times of crisis. One may see some overlap among these views and Western versions of difference feminism, grounding feminist politics in women's fundamental differences with men. Few Arab feminists have countered these essentialized differences by showing that women are as poorly equipped as men when it comes to seeking power and keeping it (see Mernissi 1993). However, the point that Islamist women wanted to make by stressing women's fundamental differences lies elsewhere.

By emphasizing women's exceptionalism, this leadership aims at helping women "recover their self-esteem and reconcile with themselves," as most of them have stated. This discourse creates its own hegemonic space within the male-dominated Islamist organizations and movements. May 16 did not change the grounding of such discourse in the emerging culture of gratification of womanhood and celebration of political motherhood. Rather, it provided Islamist women with the opportunity to hear an echo to their long-standing demands for preaching in mosques, and for official recognition of their religious expertise and responsibilities as *dā'iyyat.*

The fragmentation and hybridization of the religious field that resulted from the emergence of the Islamist movements in the 1970s and the 1980s, symbolized by the self-appointed 'ulama, independent preachers, and private mosques, opened tremendous opportunities for women's entrance into positions of religious leadership. During the 1990s women began to open spaces for discussion and learning in their neighborhood mosques, but they faced many restrictions; their efforts were subjected to the good will of the men responsible for the mosques and to state surveillance. Naima Benyaich, a teacher in her thirties and the one woman elected to the executive committee of al-Tawhīd wa-l-islāh based in Tangier, traveled around the nation for *da'wa.* I met Benyaich in Rabat during one of her trips for *da'wa* and then in her northern city of Tangier. Once in Tangier, Benyaich introduced me to a large group of activists who kindly hosted me in their homes. I had the chance to get a good sense of the struggles that these women faced while trying to get the state to hear their requests, or merely their voices. Naima Benyaich described her own struggle to get women officially recognized as *dā'iyyat* by the Ministry of Islamic Affairs and to see spaces and times formally designated to women's lectures in the mosque. She said:

> I had been writing to the Ministry of Islamic Affairs since 1994. I asked for its recognition of women's expertise in religion and involvement in *da'wa.* I never received any response. At that time, I did not have any degree in Islamic studies; I pursued this goal later. In 1997, when the minister was visiting Tangier city, I went to the meeting and walked to the podium to

talk to him. I asked him to give me the Islamic arguments preventing women from exercising *da'wa* in mosques. I asked him to think whether he expected women to be good educators, mothers, and wives if they were not themselves educated in the true ethics of Islam and were not fully knowledgeable of the Islamic doctrine. He asked me if I were ready to take an exam in the sciences of the Qur'an, the *hadīth, fiqh* [Islamic jurisprudence], and the history of Islam. I said yes. A few days later, I was invited by the local delegate of this ministry to set a date for my exam before the 'ulama's council of the city. It was not easy. I was answering the questions of the most notorious 'ulama of the Northern region of Morocco. I passed my exam and set a precedent for other women.

In fact, Naima Benyaich paved the way for a movement by Islamist women "to take the mosques back," using Nadia Yassine's phrasing. In the year 2000, women received official appointment from the Ministry of Islamic Affairs to give lectures in local mosques. According to Fatema Nejjar, one of the women *dā'iyyat* from al-Tawhīd wa-l-islāh, the Ministry of Islamic Affairs nominated about two hundred women as *dā'iyyat* in mosques within the city of Casablanca alone, while others were appointed to various mosques around the country. On November 5, 2003, Rajaa Naji Mekkaoui, a university professor of law, became the first woman to deliver a religious sermon in the royal presence. Her sermon opened the series of conferences organized by the palace to commemorate the holy month of Ramadan in the palace's mosque. Since this speaker's series was instituted by King Hassan in the 1980s, male scholars from all over the Islamic world have been invited to speak before a select audience of 'ulama, diplomats, government members, and international guests in the presence of the Commander of the Faithful. These sermons are broadcast on radio and television, making it possible for a wide audience to follow them live.

Yet Mekkaoui's religious sermon was only the first step toward recognition of women's expertise in religion. A second, more important, step was reached when, in an unprecedented move, the king appointed thirty women to the 'ulama's councils in May 2004, one of whom was Fatima al-Kabbaj who was appointed to the Supreme Council of the 'ulama. Though the politics of these *'alimat* (female theologians) are not very well known to the general public, some were already known, such as Fouzia Hajbi, political scientist and columnist in the Islamist newspaper *Al 'asr* and an active member of the Islamist organization al-Tawhīd wa-l-islāh. Hajbi gained notice as one of the main opponents of feminist groups and feminism, devoting her eloquent Arabic style of writing to opposing the NPA and commenting on hot-button issues, such as the ban on the veil in France, the war on Iraq, and the Palestinian intifadah.

I met Fouzia Hajbi a few years after her appointment to the 'ulama's council in Casablanca in June 2007. She explained how women were changing the dynamics in these councils by introducing a gender lens on the activities of the councils, thereby opening those councils to a women's audience. I was more interested in what she had to say about the War on Terror and feminism, and so she invited me to attend her lecture at a local mosque that was going to close its yearly calendar of lectures by women. More than one hundred women were sitting on carpets in the upper level of the mosque, some praying, others talking while their children jumped around and ate candies offered by other women. In this familial atmosphere, Fouzia Hajbi introduced her lecture by citing verses of the Qur'an and recalling sections from the royal speeches. After stressing that Islam is a moderate religion and does not endorse terrorism, she spoke about the meaning of "responsible citizenship" for women. She related the latter to issues ranging from the preservation of the environment to the education of children and the rights of neighbors. Fouzia also devoted time to explaining why it is important for Muslims to "respect other people's faiths," supporting her claim with verses of the Qur'an and the prophet's sunna, and by referring to the Moroccan good traditions of "tolerance" and "hospitality." In relation to terrorism, Fouzia stressed once again the role of women and mothers as educators of generations of tolerant Moroccans, aligning her discourse with the official line. In the end, Fouzia answered the audience's questions and made herself available to the women willing to talk to her privately. How to understand the shift in this activist discourse? As I have argued elsewhere, my purpose was not to claim that the war was good or bad for women (Salime 1997). Instead, I wanted to explore how the feminist and the Islamist women's movements responded to the War on Terror as a discursive regime through specific discourses, strategies, and structures.

As a movement moment, the Casablanca attack is a good place to start an investigation of the War on Terror as an economic rationale and a political culture. I have located the Casablanca attack in the global conjuncture of the War on Terror and the new American interests and policies in North Africa and the Middle East. I have emphasized the contradictions related to Morocco's alignment with the American agenda of reforming the Middle East by showing the major setbacks in human rights and democratic freedoms legitimized by what I call the global Patriot Act, while at the same time showing the significant advances in women's rights made possible by the new Code of the Family, passed into law by the government in February 2004. I have argued that this reform helped the Moroccan government to position itself as "democratic" and "modern" without making any significant changes to the structure of political power in which the king remains the central player. Stressed here are the contradictions inherent to the framing of international relations in terms of a War on Terror in the name of women's rights, and the losses experienced in the arenas of individual and collective freedoms.

Second, this chapter has stressed women's use of the war as a discursive site to create new spaces, which have contributed to redefining this global rhetoric through a gender lens while simultaneously co-opting and challenging the agenda of the war to gain more space in the decision-making about women's rights. The Casablanca attack provided the feminist movement with tremendous opportunities for negotiating a privileged position as representatives of the forces of "modernity" and "democracy" in contrast to the "obscurant" and "archaic" Islamist groups. In this context, feminism gained a normative value and was defined as a "fence against Islamic radicalism." Accordingly, feminist groups wanted a big government, a paternalistic state that would crack down on the fundamentalists (al-usūiyūn), in order to protect the feminists.

Third, this chapter has shown how Islamist women have positioned themselves through a discourse that defines Islamist women as the agents of moderation in relation to both "secular" feminists and the "religious extremists," to use these activists' own terminology. They have done this by articulating motherhood as a median location, a *wassat*. Redefining motherhood as a political site was meant to demarcate Islamist women from both "extremisms," those of certain Islamist radicals and those of the forces called the eradicators (al-isti' sāliūn). This is a term coined by the Islamist press to denounce the calls made by socialists and feminists for the eradication of the Islamists from the political spectrum. Both are said to attract each other. Nadia Yassine expressed this view during her first conference at the University of California–Berkeley in April 2005, when she compared Osama bin Laden and George Bush, arguing that the two men attract and mirror each other.[26] Despite a politics of fear induced by the political climate of the Casablanca attack, Islamist women responded by claiming *more* space to maneuver, and pursued their long-standing demands to be officially recognized as educators of the masses. Previously, this demand was directed inward to the male leadership of the movement; it was now directed to the state.

Last but not least, this chapter has emphasized how both the feminist and Islamist women's leadership mobilized gender to create hegemonic spaces and discourses. With the Casablanca attack, both liberal feminists and "moderate" Islamists had to articulate their demands in a conjuncture where women's issues were not priorities on the agenda. By appropriating the discursive tropes of democracy, modernity, and moderation, these groups have certainly engendered the agenda of the war but also reproduced some of its most oppressive aspects.

Despite their different approaches to social change—through legal reform for liberal feminists and hegemony in civil society for the Islamists—both have responded by adopting the war policy of the state as a valid framework for action. Both positioned themselves as the appropriate agents for the era of fighting terrorism. By articulating their claims within the framework of the war and keeping its modernist discourse unchecked, both groups, with no major differences, have contributed in making the "war" agendas hegemonic.

5

Subversive Veiling: Beyond the Binary of the Secular and the Religious

The terms "feminism" and "Islamism" have genealogies rooted in colonial representations about Islam and postcolonial identifications with modernity. Gender lies at the center of these representations. The question of women's oppression in Islam was crucial to legitimizing not only the colonial enterprise (Ahmed 1992; Haddad and Smith 1996; Zayzafoon 2005), but also the nationalist resistance couching the project of postcolonial modernity in women's emancipation, their participation in public life, and, more importantly, their unveiling (al-Fassi 1953; Chraibi 1954).

Since the 1980s, the veiling of a young generation of educated and professional women has complicated the binary of modernity versus tradition, which was articulated by intellectuals and political elites in Morocco (Chraibi 1954; Laroui 1976; see also Pandolfo 2000). Epitomized by the resurgence of the veil and intensified by the 9/11 attacks, these binaries have formed a lens through which mainstream feminist literature (see Sabbagh 1996; Lazreg 1994; Mernissi 2001), represented Islam as incommensurate with modernity (see Hippler and Lueg 1995; Huntington 1996; Lewis 2002; Said 1978).

The past decade, however, brought about important scholarship on the Middle East that questioned these orientalist representations of a monolithic, ahistorical Islam, as opposed to a normative Western modernity (Abu-Lughod 1998; Asad 2003; Mitchell 2000; Moallem 2005). This literature has shifted the lens to the encounters of Islam and modernity in the colonial and postcolonial (dis)junctures. As the growing field of sociology of religion began to consider modernity as the framework for understanding the resurgence of religion "as a public force" (Hefner 1998, 98) in modern times, the entanglement of the Islamist movements with secular modernity came to be understood in a new light (Emerson and Hartman 2006; Hefner 1998).

In the Middle East, these movements are viewed as a reaction to processes of secularization (Tibi 1998, 2000), "failed" development projects (G. Amin 1997; Tibi 1995; Ibrahim 1998), and related aspects of individualization and privatization of religion in postcolonial state formations. But the most important contribution to this debate came from the feminist scholarship on the Middle East, notably from postcolonial and postmodern critics of the secularist, developmentalist, and liberal underpinnings of Western feminism (Abu-Lughod 1998; Bodman and Tohidi 1998; Cooke 2001; Lazreg 1986, 2002; Mahmood 2005; Mir-Hosseini 1999; Moalem 2005; Tohidi 1991; Treacher and Shukrallah 2001). These studies have shown how women's political identities are located at the encounters of modernity and Islam, and how articulations of "feminisms" (Karam 1998), "modernness" (Deeb 2006) agency (Mahmood 2005), and rights (Afkhami and Friedl 1997) are shaped by global discourses and regulatory regimes, as well as women's identifications within Islam and feminism, in these junctures. In what follows, I pursue this debate by showing how feminist and Islamist politics have overlapped in Morocco through the narratives of activists in both movements. I depict five areas in which these encounters have been most visible.

The Veil

In the past two decades, young women's veiling practices have generated enormous passions in public opinion and rich academic debates (El Guindi 2007; Macleod 1991; Slymovics 1996). The veil has surely been the most potent signifier of women's identity politics, demarcating the boundaries of secularism and Islamism in its original stages of emergence. However, in the past decade, the hijab became the means for blurring these boundaries and bridging gaps between women from various economic backgrounds and political sensibilities. While a politics of identity is still a principal definer of educated women's mode of veiling, the veil itself no longer demarcates women's political affiliation and sensibilities, neither does it demarcate the geographical boundaries of secular and religious territories. The widespread adoption of the veil at the end of the 1990s challenges any understanding of the veil within these fixed terms. For instance, it is no longer surprising to see members of leftist parties attending their party meetings wearing the hijab. During the 2007 legislative elections, very few unveiled women ran for the Islamist party's municipal seats, while many veiled women ran on behalf of the socialist party. Hence, the ethics of Islamic modesty are no longer synonymous

with militant Islam. In fact, there has been a blurring of the differences between women's identities as Muslims, which is stressed by the observance of
the hijab as coupled with women's political convictions as leftists and feminists.

This was already visible during both rallies over the NPA. In the feminist rally, hundreds of women who marched in support of feminist organizations were veiled. Few unveiled women marched with the Islamists.

After every trip back to Morocco, I see more friends and family members adopting the veil. Mostly professional and middle class, my own friends
and family members see the veil as a symbol of adherence to Islamic morals
and ethics. However, some of them acknowledge having made that decision
only after a personal tragedy such the death of a young relative, a major illness, and so on and so forth. Some even started veiling against the will of a
husband or a father. However, it came as a surprise to hear women make a
connection between their veiling and what they called "traumatic events,"
such as the Israeli invasion of the Jenin refugee camp in 2002, and the U.S.
invasion of Iraq in 2003. They all noted a significant increase in the numbers of veiled women in the streets.

During the Israeli invasion of Jenin, schoolchildren and teens were the
most active agents in daily demonstrations and strikes protesting the images
brought home by satellite dishes. Veiled Palestinian mothers, widows, and
orphans who resisted the invasion by staying in what was left of their homes
became the role models for this new generation, rather than "wives of the
prophet." For schoolchildren, wearing the hijab was definitely not a symbol
of adherence to Islamist politics, but rather a sign of awareness and solidarity in reaction to the scope of oppression and destruction shown on television screens. In this context, some of my friends claimed, it was difficult for
them to walk in the streets unveiled next to their young daughters who wore
the veil as a sign of solidarity and protest. This was politicization working
the other way around, from young daughters to their mothers.

When I asked women if they had been able to notice any change in the
practices of veiling after the Casablanca attack, their accounts were different.
According to them, there was a decrease in the number of veiled women in
the streets. They all knew of women who abandoned the veil and uncovered
their hair. If this was true, it may have been animated by women's awareness of
the risks involved, but also catalyzed by women's decision to demarcate themselves from political Islam, so often confused now with Islamic "extremism."

My own observations during the same period of time point to another
conclusion. May 16 did not diminish the presence of the veil in the streets,
but rather encouraged a new form of veiling that I call the "subversive veil."
The latter does not conform to either the strict Islamist veiling (loose, long

dress and hair cover) or the European fashion, but looks like a hybrid style, an in-between version of both, carefully adopted by new categories of veiled women. Headscarves were loosely tied around the neck, keeping part of the hair uncovered, and worn in association with tight jeans and fashionable sweaters. The hybridity of this new dress code became more pronounced with a touch of make-up, previously unheard of in the more "orthodox" version of Moroccan veiling. These overlaps were already visible during the 2000 feminist rally in support of the NPA, in which the crowd chanted, "We are all Muslims and we support the NPA." It bears repeating that during the Islamist march, few unveiled women were among the marchers.

Feminism

Despite their self-proclaimed differences, these groups' relationship to feminism remains unsettled and subject to negotiations, yet it contains major overlaps. The problem of identification with feminism relates less to concerns about the label itself than about marking boundaries, especially when these boundaries have been constantly shifting and even vanishing. By rejecting the label of "feminism," Islamist activists wish to stress their differences with feminist groups who, presumably, have left the colonial, secular, and individualistic grounds of the term unchecked. To them, feminism sets men and women against one another by placing too much emphasis on conflicts and asymmetries. Their alternative is a discourse that stresses men's and women's equality before god. For instance, women of Al-'adl wa-l-ihsāne use the image of a pyramid in which men and women occupy both ends of the base and are both connected to the top of the pyramid, god. In this perception, men's and women's relationships are not "horizontal," I was told, but "triangular." Both occupy the bottom of the pyramid and both report to the highest level, god. They are tied together through their mutual responsibilities toward each other and their mutual obligations to honor their commitments vis-à-vis god. Thus, neither women nor men have rights in abstract terms. Women's "rights" are their husbands' obligations before god and vice versa. Accordingly, Ghislane al-Bahrawi, the president of the Women's Section of al-'Adl wa-l-ihsāne, rejects feminism because it stresses women's rights independently from their obligations, and because it eliminates the mediating dimension of the divine. She thinks that feminist discourse creates a truncated view, in which rights become detached from any notion of moral obligation and accountability to god.

If feminism is not acceptable to this leadership, it is also because it subsumes all social, political, and economic problems under gender divisions, while leaving out questions of economic exploitation, (neo)colonialism, and political despotism. Instead of engaging in these struggles, I was told repeatedly, feminist groups shift the focus to men, setting them as the enemies within.

The term "gender" is subject to similar doubts. Besides its presumably Western origin, a gender narrative goes as far as erasing the natural differences between men and women while paving the way for alternative sexual identities, orientations, and families. Naima Benyaich, the only woman member of the executive committee of al-Tawhīd wa-l-islāh, defines her "femininity" in relation to her "humanity." To her, thinking within gender categories is very reductive. She contends: "As a woman, my rights are an integral part of my human rights and my rights as a member of a community. Yes, we do have problems as women, but the focus should be on our rights as humans living within a community of people. My individual rights cannot be dissociated from my people's rights. Feminism is alien because the priorities set by Western feminism are not ours."

Curiously enough, similar views about feminism are expressed by the leaders of feminist organizations. Many of them objected to my use of the term "feminism" to refer to their activism. But while Islamist activists are unanimous in their rejection of the term, feminists' positions could be described as existing along a spectrum of voices ranging from open feminism, which is a minor trend, to a more nuanced engagement with or total rejection of the term. I introduce through the voices of these activists three types of negotiations around the meanings of feminism.

Assertive Feminism

As I showed earlier, this is the position that some activists adopted in the aftermath of the Casablanca attack. Leaders of feminist groups reaffirmed their identity politics as feminists and defined the term as almost interchangeable with "democracy" and "modernity." Najat Razi, the president of the AMDF, and Leila Rhiwi, the president of the ADFM/Rabat, represent the minor trend. Razi articulated her identification with the term as a process of negotiation, appropriation, and self-naming as follows: "I used to have problems with the term feminism because of its Western connotations. I am no longer concerned with this debate. Yes, I am a feminist. Feminism is an identity, a world vision, and a politics. Feminism defines women as persons with rights, rejects discrimination based on gender, and motivates actions to fight against it. It does not condone injustice and oppression directed toward women. In these terms, I am a feminist."

Difference Feminism

Other leaders of feminist organizations choose an intermediary location by articulating the discourse of equality and that of difference in terms of "shared responsibilities" and "complementary roles." Najia Zirari, a long-standing activist in ADFM, expressed this view as follows: "I believe in equality between men and women as long as it does not erase their differences. We are different yet equal. To me, equality implies true partnership, shared responsibilities, and complementary roles. It does not mean blurring natural differences between men and women, because in this case there will be no meaning for a feminist identity or a feminist struggle. We need rights that respect our particular needs as women and our differences with men."

Khadija Amiti, a founding member of the UAF, expressed her doubts about feminism along similar binaries of East and West characteristic of the discourse of Islamist activists. She also claims that her adoption of feminism as an identity politics is contingent on recognition of men's and women's differences on the one hand, and the inclusion of men in the struggle for women's rights on the other: "To me, feminism should not be a call for erasing the natural differences of men and women, but an endeavor to acknowledge those differences and work within them. As a movement, feminism should not be based on gender wars. This is a Western understanding of feminism that alienates men. We do not want to alienate men. We have them in our movement, and they are as much committed as we are in the struggle for women's rights. If feminism means to consider men as the enemies, then I am not a feminist."

Khadija expressed a dominant trend in feminist organizations: to implicate men in various women's groups and centers. Whether as individuals or as activists, from a wide spectrum of nongovernmental organizations and political parties, men are responding to these centers' needs for more doctors, lawyers, journalists, students, and academics. During the feminist rally of March 2000, there were thousands of men among the protestors, representing a wide range of ages and educational and social categories. This explains why these activists want to stress the inclusiveness of feminism as a category for both men and women.

Distant Feminism

The third position on feminism is expressed by activists in the feminist movement who reject feminism as a term, yet adopt it as a politics. For instance, Leila (from Jussūr) rejects the term "feminism" at the same time as she holds both men and women responsible for sustaining conditions of gender oppression. Objecting to my use of the term, she states: "No, I am not a feminist. I do not have problems with men but with patriarchy and machismo, and to be honest, I consider women to be equally responsible [as men] for sustaining their seeds through a sexist socialization of generations of children. We managed to reform the *mudawwana,* but we realized that changing the law is only the starting point. We have to act on mentalities, we have to reform education, and we have to work on reeducating the masses. This is our priority now in Jussūr."

Bouchra, an LDDF member, expressed her rejection of feminism on similar grounds: "We are not feminists. We are *feminine* militants. This means that we do not prioritize men in our struggle, but we do not consider them as enemies. We have men in our movement; they are as committed as we are to women's rights. We do not fight against men; our fight is directed toward the state, the law, and the system, not men. Men can also be mobilized for our cause. We should not alienate them."

Halima Benawi, the director of one of the LDDF centers for legal assistance and literacy in Rabat, rejects feminism for the same reasons: "I reject feminism because it pushes women to position themselves against men in order to get rights. We do not think that men are to blame, but the patriarchal society and the way it has shaped mentalities."

These activists' rejection of feminism should be seen in conjunction with the Islamist discourse about feminism as a Western assault upon the cohesion of the Muslim (heterosexual) family. This position was legitimized through an anti-imperialist rhetoric that emphasizes ideological divides between the Muslim *self* and the feminist *other,* connecting the latter to concrete acts of military aggression, occupation, and invasion witnessed across the Middle East.

It is worth nothing that the leftist background of feminist activists prepared them to respond positively to the anticolonial rhetoric of Islamist groups. In fact, both feminists and Islamists have been involved in rallies, sit-ins, and petitions in protest of what was perceived by *both* camps as the devastating policies of the United States in the Middle East.[1] Feminist activists who stated their Islamic religious identity also expressed their fear of being labeled "feminist" as long as the term was not freed from its Western legacy of secularism, colonialism, and gender wars.

As we have seen in the previous chapters, the feminist articulation of women's rights became problematic when faced with the Islamist rhetoric of "family rights," meaning the rights of all family members. Thus, to the feminist "gender-lens" methodology, Islamist women responded with the "family-centered" approach that, according to many respondents, better respects the "balance of power" within the family and the needs and interests of all its members.

This family-centered approach was appropriated by feminist groups to lobby the royal council on the NPA. Halima, an LDDF member, argued that "the struggle for women's rights is in fact a struggle for the entire family." She claimed that the LDDF is not fighting only for women, but for "the whole family," and therefore "the law change will benefit all family members." It is interesting to see how these interactions among the feminist and Islamist movements on the battlefield of gender also worked the other way around, shaping Islamist women's perception of men's power, patriarchy, and oppression of women. I explore these overlaps in the following section.

Leadership

Despite Islamist women's claim that they operating in an open field with males within Islamist organizations; emerging voices among women are discrediting this claim. For instance, in one of her interviews with al-Jazeera, Khadija Mufid, an active member in al-Tawhīd wa-l-islāh, denounced women's marginalization in the Islamist movements and held the male leadership responsible for preventing women from reaching positions of power in these movements:

> Women have actively participated in building Islamist thought and the Islamist movements. This endeavor is not reflected in the positions they have occupied. The Islamist movements confined women to marginal committees, dubbed the "committee for the family" or the "committee for women." Women could not reach any of the decisional levels that they deserve in Islamist movements. In fact, anything that men did not want to do was given to women. Even within the Islamist movements, men are not ready to give up their social privileges, knowing that these were not gained but given, and are not necessarily based on any individual merit, but rather on an unequal access to power. And no matter how unfair these privileges have been to women, men would still hold onto them. The most dangerous discourse men use to justify women's marginalization is [gender] "particularism." Under this pretext, women are excluded because of their assumed natural differences with men. Yet this rhetoric is only used when men have to deal with questions of power-sharing with women. Every time they see a woman claiming her right to reach a decisional level, they give you a speech, a theory about particularism. When women are expected to go out, reach out to the public, mobilize and organize the people, work for the party, bring votes, then they are "equal" and no mention is made

of their particularism. When they mobilize the masses for the party, they are no different from men and the "particularism" narrative disappears. Yet if the same woman shows her ambition to reach positions of power, then the discourse about particularism surfaces. . . . One must also say that some women are ready to give up their rights and give men the lead. By taking a passive position, this category of women undermines the efforts of those who are trying so hard to reverse women's submission to the might of men and their dependence on male decisional power.[2]

The question of women's access to the decisional levels in the Islamist movements is therefore central to feminist debate in both feminist and Islamist organizations. In both cases, women are also aware of the importance of setting the ground for a new generation of leaders through training and by providing role models. Islamists and feminists are opening centers and setting training programs for women to facilitate their entry into formal political institutions. A case in point is ORWA's Center for Training Women Leaders, created in 2003. In contrast to the 1997 ADFM Center for Women's Leadership, created by the ADFM to support women's candidacy for the legislative elections, ORWA's center is open to teens and high school students.

In al-'Adl wa-l-ihsāne women have even a longer history of struggle and face even more constraints for reaching the highest decisional level such the Council of Guidance. They are still not formally represented in that council, though they are informally consulted, especially thanks to the leadership of Nadia Yassine. The female leadership of al-'Adl wa-l-ihsāne recalls the struggle of Nadia Yassine, during the 1980s, when she began organizing women around notions of self-esteem, rights, and public engagement. One of the most challenging tasks for women has been that of "changing the brothers," I was repeatedly told.

Nadia Yassine has been implementing programs for women since the late 1980s, but most of these programs fell under men's supervision until very recently. It took her almost an entire decade to identify and train a larger group of community leaders who helped undertake the difficult task of changing the sisters, and more important, changing the brothers. Even when men endorsed the creation of the Women's Section in 1998, its independence remained a contentious topic, and women are still working on it. They are still missing from *majlis al-irshād* (the council of guidance), and although they are now consulted, they have only been admitted informally because of a widespread belief that the "base" is still not ready for it, as I was told. Although it took women almost two decades from the birth of the movement in 1974 to gain control over their own structures, some of this new female leadership reassured me "more changes are to come; it is just a question of time." I understood this claim, as women soon came to be represented in *majlis al-irshād*.

Education

Education has been the terrain of predilection for Islamist women in their struggle against secularism. Whether we think about state educational institutions infiltrated by Islamist teachers and activists, or we look at the various training programs and spaces opened for youth education and cultural activities in Islamist organizations, a pedagogy of praxis exists at the heart of the Islamist project. Both al-'Adl wa-l-ihsāne and al-Tawhīd wa-l-islāh have built support structures for schoolchildren, that is, awards, scholarships, cultural and art competitions, summer camps, and dissemination and publication of work produced by students, as well as numerous projects in which education has been the entry point for creating a counter-hegemony to a perceived secularization of everyday life.

Education is becoming a priority for feminist groups too. The turning point, as many of them confirmed, was the Islamist march. This "show of force" pushed feminist groups to consider establishing new programs for youth and targeting other community members such as teachers, judges, police officers, and state agents, in order to sensitize them to gender issues. Beside the annual caravans and their mobile literacy courses, feminist groups established new programs that focus on training and consciousness-raising with students and teenagers. The ADFM, LDDF, UAF, and Jussūr are now implementing these programs through their organizations.

The ADFM was the first group to get involved in 1997, when they joined a project of rewriting secondary school textbooks through a gender lens, sponsored by the communist-affiliated Minister of Education, Ismail Al-Alawi. Currently, the ADFM is implementing a project to support the education of rural girls. The project was initially funded by USAID (United States Agency for International Development), until alternative funds were secured through the European Union and other sponsors. The Education of the Rural Young Girl project also provides many training programs for a younger generation of leaders of NGOs working with rural populations on promoting girls' education. The ADFM provides workshops on gender issues and human rights, as part of their training. Both the ADFM Center of Women's Leadership in Casablanca, and the Center for the Education of the Rural Girl housed in the ADFM offices in Rabat are involved in such programs. These educational activities for young NGO leaders take place alongside older programs and training for women, including what the ADFM calls "legal literacy," which started in the of the 1980.

The LDDF created its own literacy textbook for women. In this book, the subjects, activities, pictures, and questions center on women, their lives, their contributions, their rights, and their voices. In addition, the LDDF has invented new pedagogies and methods to attract schoolchildren, opening a library to support their research activities and organize focus groups on citizenship, human rights, and "religious extremism." The LDDF also started offering support and guidance to students with their research and commenced its first summer camps after the 2000 Islamist march.

The feminist group Jussūr offers programs for children alongside the literacy programs for mothers. Their center for literacy, located in a poor area of Rabat-Medina, offers a kindergarten for children and a day care, all for free, as well as a staff to oversee babies while their mothers are taking literacy courses. During my visit to Jussūr's center centers, I learned that some of the beneficiaries alternate between Jussūr and one of the Islamist centers for literacy open in the same neighborhood. Three of these women explained to me their choice in a very pragmatic way: "Here we learn about our rights, there we learn about our religion."

Foreign Funds and the Charge of Westernization

Islamist activists have articulated their discourse of authenticity in opposition to the presumed feminist allegiance to Western agendas and funds. As a matter of fact, most feminist centers and programs are supported by European partners and funds. Nonetheless, these groups are also very cautious about choosing "partners" who do not conflict with their perceived "national interests and the Arab cause." Leila Rhiwi, the president of ADFM/Rabat, calls these partners "the family of the democrats." By this she means the European Union—with the exception of Britain because of its pro-American policy after the invasion of Iraq—the United Nations, and European NGOs. Though some of these leaders confirmed that they have started to accept funds "even from the Americans," they all stated their preference for "the family of the democrats," especially in the context of the American invasion of Iraq.

The AMDF and LDDF receive European funds, and, as a "political choice," they receive "no American money," I was told by the leadership. British funds are treated in the same way as American funds, because of the British support to the Iraq War. This makes sense, since all these groups have shown a great deal of concern about American policies in the Middle East, which they view as devastating to the cause of women. In addition, they have all been organizing rallies, sit-ins, and demonstrations to contest these policies during the past decade. They, along with Islamist groups, boycotted the American-led regional meeting of the Forum for the Future held in Morocco in April 2004.

By contrast, Islamist women leaders are shifting toward a more flexible position regarding international funds. Mouna Khlifi confirmed that some sponsors, such as the European Union, are requiring Islamist organizations to take part in governmental projects that are also supported through their funds. She was personally invited to one of these meetings but did not get support because of the government's sanctions against any organization working within the lines of Al-'adl wa-l-ihsāne.

There are other signs of Islamist groups' openness on Western circles of influence and funds. One case in point is the intervention of American diplomacy in favor of the case of Nadia Yassine in 2005. Nadia Yassine was charged by the Moroccan government for defamation of the monarchy in a statement to a journalist during her first conference at the University of California–Berkeley in April 2005. In this interview, Nadia Yassine expressed her opinion about monarchic rule in Morocco and stated her preference for a republican political system. The court of Rabat took immediate action against her and against the Moroccan journalist who published the interview. In response to these proceedings, the U.S. State Department made the following statement to the independent weekly magazine *Le Journal Hebdo:* "This case in which the government has altered freedom of speech is a considerable source of concern to us. It is a decision that goes against the multiple advances made by Morocco in the field of human rights. We consider that freedom of speech is necessary to the consolidation of democracy. Therefore, we encourage the Moroccan government to promote laws that recognize and protect the freedom of expression and speech" (Jamaï et al. 2007).

The intervention of the State Department was effective, since the charges against Nadia Yassine were not pursued, although they remained in the court files, and her trial was suspended. American government's decision to intervene is more likely to be understood in the context of its shifting strategies toward normalization with "moderate" Islamist groups in the Arab world. Represented by a woman, al-'Adl wa-l-ihsāne offers the best case for the American government, despite the monarchy's perception of it as a dissident group. When I asked leaders of feminist organizations to comment on this act of intervention, they all agreed that the move to support Nadia Yassine was not animated by a genuine concern for freedom of speech or democracy. Both were defied by the realities in Guantanamo and Abu Ghraib. Instead, they believe that the United States has embarked on a new mission—that of instrumentalizing "moderate" Islamists who present themselves with a "modern outlook."

I will conclude this discussion by establishing a few points. First, I would stress the mediating factors shaping the divisions among the feminist and Islamist women's movements. These divisions are discursively based, historically contingent, and mediated through various players and institutions, including the law, the media, religious, political parties, and global regimes of rights. During my conversations with women, I was surprised to see how little Islamist and feminist groups knew about each other's actual thoughts, positions, and writings, beyond the issue of family law reform. The press, domestic and international, played a tremendous role in the way these divisions were constructed and packaged for public consumption, notably after the 2000 rallies. For example, the BBC chose the title *Moroccan Women's Misery* to introduce the British public to the controversy, bringing it down to the usual categories of feminist/antifeminist and illustrating the latter through the voice and image of Nadia Yassine.

Not only did these disputes over women's rights put Islamist women on the itineraries of international reporters, but they also enabled these women to reverse their marginalization in the UN's hegemonic process and to shape the agenda of liberal feminism. Islamist women's mobilization of cultural relativism was in fact their means to participate in a global discursive community about women's rights. Thus, family law was not only the site where feminists and Islamists played out their antagonisms, but also the arena for the articulation of their overlapping societal projects.

Second, this study has shown that the boundaries of both feminism and Islamism have been negotiated at the intersections of feminism, Islam, and the global regulatory regime of neocolonial capitalist modernity. The labels of "feminism" and "Islamism," Abou-Bakr (2001) argues, indicate more of a conceptual territory about women's groups. Women's divisions are shaped by concrete struggles for power and legitimacy; they are also constructed and maintained through conceptualizations that create and consolidate these divisions. Feminist theory has mostly placed the debate on such boundaries in the broader framework of Third World and First World feminisms. Grounding these debates in their local contexts enables us to see how these local struggles to define women's rights mirror and shape global feminist debates and agendas.

Furthermore, social movement scholars consider boundaries as essential to the formation of politicized identities. Some have claimed that boundaries work to "mark off" the cultural counters of a group (Ferree and Roth 1998; Melucci 1995; Taylor and Whittier 1995). While acknowledging the importance of boundaries for the formation of collective identities, my intention is to show how these boundaries have been redefined and displaced as these movements have constructed their discourse.

Last and not least, focusing on the exchanges among Islamists and feminists enables us to see how these interactions have changed the state and its gender policy. However, the state's instrumentalization of gender and its cooptation of women's rights discourse have decreased the spaces of independent organizing by feminist and Islamist women's groups alike. It has enabled the Moroccan monarchy to monitor the discourse and activism of women's groups, and to create local allies among both women's movements while assuming the role of "neutral" mediator (Salime 2007).

This mediation found more legitimacy with the War on Terror, having been constructed based on the modernist category of "enlightened" Islam. The state's intervention to reform family law, a key feminist demand, has definitely increased rather than decreased internal divisions and tensions between the Islamist and feminist women's movements in Morocco.

The scope of this study and my own perceptions of the interactions between women's movements were limited by the context of the struggles over the reform of the *mudawwana*. To investigate the intersections of Islamist and feminist activism is to open new perspectives for further research on the dialectics of movements, and to problematize the conceptual boundaries of feminist and Islamist politics. The popular appraising in North Africa is providing hope for the rise of movements that mobilize for issues of social justice across ideological divides. The women's movement has been a major force in opening these debates two decades ago, in North Africa and the Middle East.

Notes

Introduction

1. Both rallies were held on March 12, 2000. Participation counts vary considerably; according to various sources, estimates range from six hundred thousand to a million for the Islamists and forty thousand to five hundred thousand for the feminists. See, for example, *Financial Times,* March 13, 2000; *New York Times,* March 13, 2000.

2. The most common translation used for Jamā'at al-'adl wa-l-ihsāne is Justice and Charity. The group's leadership uses Justice and Spirituality. The term "spirituality" expresses better the Sufi orientation of this organization, and therefore is preferred to the term "charity" by the members.

3. Louna al-Shabel's interactive weekly show *Li-al-nisā' Faqat* (Only for Women) opened the Moroccan debate to pan-Arabic al-Jazeera audiences through several interviews of leading feminist and Islamist activists between 2000 and 2004.

4. Definitions of feminism have been part of all studies of the women's movements. Feminism has been defined as both a political consciousness about women's oppression and the mobilization to challenge this oppression (Badran and Cooke 1990; Karam 1998).

5. Building alliances among state actors and women's groups was also one of the recommendations of the UNDP Human Development Report of 1990 (see UNDP 1990).

6. See, for example, Sisters in Islam (http://www.sistersinislam.org.my), the Web site of the leading Malaysian feminist organization in which the Moroccan reform is cited as the guiding example.

1. Gender and the Nation State

1. Spain withdrew from Western Sahara in 1976. On the northern Mediterranean coast, the cities of Ceuta and Melila are still under Spanish rule.

2. The Moroccan state grounds its Islamic identity in the *māliki fiqh* (Islamic jurisprudence) as its predominant doctrine. The *māliki fiqh* has been the main source for designing the code of *mu'āmalāt* (social transactions) and *'ibādāt* (religious observances) in Morocco.

3. During the 1980s, in the context of the struggle that opposed the democratic *kutla* (Istiqlal, USFP, and OADP) to the monarchy, and in the face of mounting Islamist challenges, the Minister of Religious Affairs, alongside three other ministries (Interior, Foreign Affairs, and Justice) was granted the title of Minister of Sovereignty; this simply indicates the king's authority to bypass the government while appointing or dismissing these ministers.

4. They are also called the "'ulama of the power" or "official 'ulama."

5. Al-Shabība al-Islāmiyya was formed in 1969, only two years after the Arab defeat in the Six-Day War with Israel. These activists perceived the defeat as a failure of Pan-Arabism as an ideology informing Nasserist and Ba'athist regimes. They posit the Islamic *umma,* a unity based on faith as an alternative to secular pan-Arabism. The Muslim Brotherhood was founded in Egypt in 1928 by Hassan al-Banna.

6. The monarchy was targeted by two failed military coups in 1971 and 1972, causing even more hardship to the opposition, comprising leftists and Islamists alike.

7. See the organization's Web site at http://www.aljamaa.net.

8. See Abdellah Hammoudi's (1997) study, *Master and Disciple,* for an analysis of the type of political authority that emerges from the spiritual connection grounded in Islamic mysticism.

9. Mariam al-Tigyi, "US-Sponsored Forum Addresses Muslim Reforms," available at http://IslamOnline.net (accessed August 5, 2005).

10. On the impact of these policies upon women, see the official studies by the Ministry of Employment (1995) and by the Secretary of State in Charge of Social Protection, the Family, and Childhood (Rabat: Sociodemographics and Socioeconomics, 1998).

11. Up to the end of the 1970s, the political left was tremendously successful in infiltrating universities, students' unions, and youth clubs. It was within these types of organizations that most women's rights groups and human rights organizations in Morocco took shape.

12. I refer to my own observations as a professor at École Normale Supérieure in Fez, and as a supervisor of teaching sessions by my students in high schools, for the Department of Islamic Studies between 1985 and 1995.

13. Small businesses were created to respond to veiled women's needs for privacy.

In the 1980s, women started offering small services for weddings and other cere-
monies, such as catering, photography, and music troupes.

14. In the 1990s, women formed 30.1 percent of high school teachers and 23.4
percent of university professors (see Ministry of Economic Prevision and Planning
1998). They comprised 44 percent of practicing physicians and 95 percent of dentists
(Ministry of Employment 1995, 43). In magisterial functions, even though women
were still precluded from certain legal positions such as the Higher Magistracy Council during the 1980s, they formed 12 percent of magistrates (107).

15. The opposition was represented by four parties: the nationalist and conservative IP; and three parties from the left: the USFP, the PPS, and the OADP.
These parties formed al-Kutla al-wataniyya (National Coalition) in 1992, after organizing against government censorship in 1990. In their campaign, the *kutla* focused
on the issues of free speech, transparent elections, democracy, and human rights (see
Brand 1998).

16. This position was filled by Omar Azziman, a founding member of the Organization Marocaine des Droits de l'Homme (Moroccan Organization for Human
Rights, or OMDH), active since 1987.

17. This alliance was one of the recommendations of the United Nations Development Program Human Development Report of 1990 (see UNDP 1990).

18. See McMichael 2000, for examples of the use of the WID discourse by
United Nations programs during the post-development era.

19. A governmental report published in 1997 counted seventy-six women's organizations operating under the title "Integrating Women into Development." The report showed that 78.5 percent of these organizations were created in the mid-1980s
(Ministry of Foreign Affairs and Cooperation 1997).

2. Feminization of the Islamist Movements

1. Brochure, *Le Collectif 95: Maghreb Egalite,* accessed through my own participation in the ADFM activities and meetings between the years 2000 and 2004.

2. This contrasts with the way the UAF was perceived then, as highly influenced and even funded by the OADP, a fact that has always been denied by UAF's
founding members.

3. I refer to my own involvement in some of these workshops and training
sessions between 1994 and 1999 in the cities of Fez, Rabat, Casablanca, and Marrakech. Some of these activities were also funded through the United Nations Population Funds, UNIFEM, the Washington-based National Endowment for Democracy,
and other transnational funds.

4. I focus here on the groups organized under the movement al-Islāh wa-l-
tajdīd because of their overwhelming presence during this controversy. Al-'Adl wa-
l-ihsāne was still involved in an open struggle for state recognition. This does not

mean that members of al-'Adl wa-l-ihsāne did not join the Islamist mobilization against the petition. It simply means that these activists were not as visible as those organized under the al-Islāh wa-l-tajdīd at this time.

5. See *Al-Rāya,* July 22, 1992, 4.

6. Adrit Suad, reader comment in *Al Forkāne,* no. 6 (1985): 59.

7. Reader comment in *Al Forkāne,* no. 6 (1985): 59.

8. See the interviews published in *Al-Rāya* under the title "Hawla qadāya al-mar'a: Muqāraba islāmiyya," March 9, 1992, 16.

9. See the interviews in *Al-Rāya,* March 9, 1992, 16–17. These were followed by a petition published in the same newspaper on July 6, 1992, 8–10.

10. A full report on the meeting is published in *Al-Rāya,* April 6, 1992, 15.

11. These quotations are selected from an article by Oum Yassir 1992.

3. Reversing the Feminist Gains

1. For example, the ADFM members were involved in a project for the Ministry of Education (1997–2000) to rewrite the school textbooks from a gender lens, and in another project to introduce "a culture of human rights" into the school programs and books.

2. In these elections the former opposition, notably the socialist (USFP) and Istiqlal parties, gain a slight advantage on the traditional majority, which was composed of royalist parties. Observers speak rather of "a controlled alternance" (Daoud and Ouchelh 1997; Leveau 1998, 2000), since King Hassan maintained the major decision-making power, including that of choosing his "Ministers of Sovereignty," appointed to the posts of Justice, Interior, Endowments and Islamic Affairs, and Foreign Affairs.

3. The latter organized under the royalist party, the Mouvement Populaire Constitutionel et Démocratique (MPCD), headed by the physician Dr. Ahmed Khatīb, who is perceived as a close ally to the palace. This party eventually changed its name to the current al-'Adāla wa-l-tanmia.

4. Zoulikha Nasri was one of the four women appointed by King Hassan in 1997 to the government of transition before serving as the new King's Counselor.

5. See the newspaper report on the disputes between Mdaghri and two feminist scholars, journalist Hinde Taarji and sociologist Fatima Mernissi, over their writings on women: "La bravure du Ministre des Affairs Islamic," *Liberation,* December 25, 1997, 1.

6. The al-Sahwa al-Islāmiyya conference was launched concomitantly with the rise of feminist calls for reforming the *mudawwana* in 1991. It was largely open to the participation of Islamist scholars and theologians from all over the Islamic world, and was instrumental in monitoring the discourse of Moroccan Islamists (Tozy 1999).

7. See the World Bank's 1994 report, "Morocco: Poverty, Adjustment and

Growth," available at http://web.worldbank.org/WBSITE/EXTERNAL/TOPICS/
EXTPOVERTY/EXTPA/0,,contentMDK:20208621~isCURL:Y~menuPK:435375
~pagePK:148956~piPK:216618~theSitePK:430367~isCURL:Y,00.html.

8. Notably, the royalist party, Union Constitutionelle (UC), which had been
a part of the government majority prior to political alternance, and the Mouvement
Populaire (MP), an Amazigh-oriented royalist party.

9. See Louna Chebel's interview of Nezha Chekrouni, a leading Moroccan feminist activist and Minister of the Family, on the same program from April 22, 2002;
and of Khadija Moufid from the Islamist organization al-Tawhīd wa-l-islāh on April
26, 2004. See also al-Qaradawi's comments on al-Jazeera regarding the Moroccan
project of reform, published by the newspaper *Al-Tajdīd*, March 8, 2000, 15.

10. Al-'Adl wa-l-ihsāne works through elected bodies in which women hold, I
was told, one-third of the seats. However, no woman is formally represented in *majlis
al-irshād*, the council of guidance, composed of nine men. In the past few years women
have been consulted by the *majlis*, namely Nadia Yassine, Ghislane al-Bahrawi, and
Mouna Khlifi, but only informally,

11. The program's name is *Tant qu'il y aura des Femmes* (As long as they are
women) and is hosted by Sylvie Koffi, Radio France Internationale.

12. Al-Badīl al-hadāri was created in 1995 as an elitist Islamist organization
comprising academics and professional men and women who embrace the sharia as
a way of life, but without rejecting secularism or political pluralism at the level of
the state. It was also the only Islamist organization engaged in teamwork with some
factions of the political left. It was authorized as a political party in June 2005, then
outlawed and its two leaders, Iamine Reggala and Mohamed Moatasime, were detained in February 2008, on accusations of "terrorism."

13. Espace Associatif is a nationwide network of NGOs active in the areas of
development, rights, education and literacy, and the environment. This network has
been the initiator and organizer of the yearly Moroccan Social Forum held in tan-
dem with the World Social Forum.

14. Khadija Marouazi's presentation at the ADFM's conference Assessment of
the Women's Movement in the Arab World, July 2000 in Casablanca.

15. Nadia Yassine, being the daughter of the Supreme Guide, played a major role
in opening the way for women's voices in the *majlis al-irshād*, the highest decisional
committee in al-'Adl wa-l-ihsāne and from which women have always been excluded.

16. Document distributed during the Spring of Equaliy Press Conference at
Farah Hotel on July 1, 2004.

17. *Maqāsid al-sharia*, or "purposes of the sharia," refers to the foundational principles of Islamic law. They comprise the notions of justice, equity, and equality, among
others. Stressing the "purposes" of Islam was a strategy that allowed feminist groups to
counter literal interpretations of the Qur'an by contrasting them with these general goals.

18. The LDDF has been active in the arena of women's rights since the early 1990s. Some of its founding members have well-known ties with the small leftist political party al-Talia.

19. Known as *rashidūn* (rightly guided), the four caliphs are viewed by the Islamists as role models that should be admired and emulated.

20. For examples of publications by these scholars on the question of women's rights, see Hamadi 2001 and al-Khamlishi 2004.

21. The Salafi school of political thought first emerged in the Middle East at the end of the nineteenth century with a call by reformists, led by Jamal al-Din al-Afghani and his student, the Egyptian thinker Muhammad Abdu, to modernize Arab society and enhance the status of women. Called liberal reformists by Joseph (2000) or modernists by Stowasser (1993), the Salafi are described by Stowasser as "proponents of back-to-the-Koran and onward-to-modernity" (1993, 8). Stowasser states that their theoretical breakthrough was that they separated—in both the Qur'an and sharia—the *'ibādāt* (religious observances) from the *mu'āmalāt* (social transactions) of which family law is a major part. She explains that the purpose of making this distinction was "to establish that while 'ibādāt do not admit interpretative change, the *mu'āmalāt* allow for considerable interpretation and adaptation by each generation of Muslims in light of the practical needs of their age" (1993, 8).

22. The conference was organized in July 2000 and included the participation of major international organizations such as Human Rights Watch, various European funding programs, and the United Nations Development Fund for Women, the United Nations Development Programme, and the United Nations Population Fund. Other transnational funding programs such as Oxfam and the Canadian ACDI were also involved. The major funds for the conference came from the German foundation Friedrich Ebert Stiftung.

23. The March 8, 2002, event attracted the bilingual and very popular radio station Medi 1 and the public television TVM, which opened their airtime to members of Springtime of Equality to express their concerns about the royal council.

24. It was sponsored by the European Union's Euro-Mediterranean Partnership program, MEDA.

25. The training program focused on developing communication skills in women running for election, and raising consciousness about women's needs and rights among these candidates. According to the NDI, one-third of women holding seats in the Parliament participated in this training program (see http://www.ndi.org/worldwide/mena/morocco/morocco.asp).

26. See the LDDF Report of Activity (2000) and the Springtime of Equality press conference (June 27, 2003, Casablanca, Farah Hotel).

27. See http://www.aljamaa.com.

4. Feminism and Islamism Redefined

1. See Stephen Grey and Ian Cobain, "Suspect's Tale of Travel and Torture," *The Guardian,* August 2, 2005, http://www.guardian.co.uk.

2. This information was reiterated on al-Jazeera by Mohamed Hassanein Haikel, the distinguished Egyptian writer, political commentator, and former diplomat. See the aljazeera.net series of talks, *Ma a'Haikel.*

3. Interview of Antoine Basbous, director of the Observatory of Arab Countries in Paris, in *Le Journal Hebdomadaire,* July 12–18, 2003, 8–9.

4. Al-Fizazi gave an interview to Islamonline.com (August 25, 2002) in which he explained his position about "the poles of atheism in Morocco," notably the USFP and the feminists. He accused al-'Adl wa-l-ihsāne, among other Islamist groups, of apostasy because of its alleged "sympathy" for the Iranian model and "hostility" toward al-Qaeda and the Taliban regime. Al-Fizazi also rejected the label of "al-Salafiyya al-jihādiyya" as an empty signifier created by the *makhzen.* After May 16, al-Fizazi was, for the first time, held accountable and sentenced to thirty years' imprisonment.

5. Abdelhamid Amin, *Al-'Asr,* May 30, 2003, 8.

6. For instance, after the Israeli invasion of Jenin in April 2002, King Mohammed VI closed down the Bureau of Liaison with Israel that his father, King Hassan, had opened in Rabat in September 1994.

7. Western Sahara is the land located in the southwest of Morocco on the Atlantic Ocean. It was under Spanish occupation until 1976 when King Hassan II organized the Green March to integrate the region into the Moroccan territory. In 2003 the report of James Baker, the United Nations delegate for the region, requested a period of autonomy and the organization of a referendum for self-determination within five years. This solution was considered unacceptable by the Moroccan government and was dismissed by George W. Bush's administration in support of their Moroccan ally.

8. I refer to the Pew Research Center's study published by *Le Journal-Hebdo* in February 2004, James Zoghby's Arab-American Institute study in March and April 2002, and Mark Tessler's article, "Do Islamic Orientations Influence Attitudes toward Democracy in the Arab World? Evidence from Egypt, Jordan, Morocco, and Algeria," published in the *International Journal of Comparative Sociology* (Spring 2003).

9. The creation of the Free Trade Zone took place in extreme secrecy. The project was never discussed by the government or in the Parliament. The period of negotiations was fraught with sit-ins and demonstrations by NGOs, human rights activists, and unions. These demonstrations were violently oppressed. See "Government Spokesman Deplores False Ideas about Free-Trade Agreement with the USA," January 30, 2004, http://www.bilaterals.org.

10. See http://www.fpc.state.gov/documents/organization/47084.pdf.

11. "Zoellick Joins Launching of Morocco FTA Congressional Caucus," *World Trade Magazine,* September 1, 2003, http://www.worldtrademag.com.

12. BBC, "Morocco Gets US Free Trade Deal," July 23, 2004, available at http://www.bilaterals.org/spip.php?article300.

13. See *Al-Ayām* no. 111, December 2003. See also Reuters, "Powell Praises Morocco's Anti-terror Cooperation," December 3, 2003, http://www.alertnet.org.

14. See "Réforme de la moudawana au Maroc: Revue de press," March 2003–November 2004, available at http://www.abhatoo.net.ma/index.php/Maalama-Tex tuelle/D%C3%A9veloppement-%C3%A9conomique-et-social/D%C3%A9velop pement-social/Soci%C3%A9t%C3%A9/Genre/R%C3%89FORME-DE-LA-MOUDAWANA-AU-MAROC-Revue-de-Presse-mars-2003-novembre-2004.

15. The law broadly defines terrorism as an act intended to create fear and threaten society's safety and unity. Under this law, administrative detention increased from forty-eight to ninety-six hours, with two additional ninety-six-hour extensions allowed at the prosecutor's discretion. According to human rights activists and local attorneys, this initial period was in some cases extended to weeks. The government estimates that several thousand persons were detained under this law, and local activists and attorneys estimate the number of detainees to be more than four thousand.

16. *Le Journal Hebdomadaire,* May 31, 2003, 19.

17. This pro-Palestinian campaign was launched through the al-Jazeera channel by the Qatari-based Egyptian religious scholar Sheikh Yusuf al-Qaradawi, and was carried out by Itilaf al-hhair (Coalition of Good), a transnational web of organizations given that name for the occasion. Al-Tawhīd wa-l-islāh was the Moroccan local representative of this network.

18. Mohamed Darif, *Al-Sahīfa* 140, December 12, 2003, 8.

19. The party agreed to cover only 19 percent of the seats reserved for the communal elections. See *Al-Ayām,* September 10, 2003, 13. Despite these restrictions, the party came in second for the number of people winning in the districts through an electoral list. It won the third position in Casablanca, the theater of the attack, despite the fact that it limited its participation to 50 percent of its districts. See *Al-Sahīfa,* September 19, 2003.

20. This information is from a memorandum of the Network Modernity/Democracy, formed as a response to the attack by various representatives of feminists, human rights groups, and NGOs working on different arenas of development, health, and environment. Among the leading figures of this network were Leila Rhiwi, president of ADFM/Rabat and coordinator of Springtime of Equality; Nordine Aouch, businessman and founder of Zakoura, an organization that provides micro-credit; as well as a group of academics, such as Mohamed al-Ayadi.

21. Copies of the calls have been made available by LDDF's Observatory for Women's Rights in Casablanca.

22. See the pioneering study of the Moroccan journalist Hinde Taarji, *Les Voilées de l'Islam* (1993), for an enumeration of the different factors behind women's veiling in five Islamic countries, including Morocco. This comparative study shows that among the prominent causes of women's decision to veil are economic factors, self-protection from sexual harassment in the crowded buses of Cairo, refraining from unnecessary consumption of cosmetics and fashion in the most impoverished capitals of the Middle East, or a desire to be able to go unnoticed in crowded slums.

23. Some of these interpretations and public talks are hosted by the Web site of al-'adl wa-l-ihsāne, http://www.aljamaa.com, under the entry *minbar al-mūmināt*.

24. See *minbar al-mūmināt* (http://www.aljamaa.com).

25. Parts of these audiotapes are available at http://www.aljamaa.com.

26. Presentation at the conference of Democracy and Global Islam, University of California–Berkeley, April 22, 2005, http://webcast.berkeley.edu.

5. Subversive Veiling

1. For instance, the LDDF was part of a delegation of women's NGOs that organized a visit to the Palestinian refugee camps in Lebanon during the Israeli invasion of the Jenin in 2002. The ADFM was a main opponent to the Forum for the Future and rejected an invitation to join the meeting in Rabat.

2. "'Maouqi' al-Nisa' fi al-Haraka al-Islamiya," al-Jazeera, interview given on April 4, 2004, available at http://www.aljazeera.net.

Glossary, Abbreviations, and Organizations

Arabic Terms

al-'ayn al-nissāiyya: the woman's gaze

al-dāira al-siyyāsiyya: political circle (for al-'Adl wa-l-ihsāne; see below, under
Islamist Organizations)

'alim: theologianal-isti'sāliūn: eradicators

al-jam'iyya al-'āma: general assembly

al-kutla al-wataniyya: national block

al-majlis al-thanfidi: executive council (for al-'Adl wa-l-ihsāne; see below, under
Islamist Organizations)

al-qādiriyya: a Sufi congregation

al-qitā'e al-nisai: the Women's Section (for al-'Adl wa-l-ihsāne; see below, under
Islamist Organizations)

al-sīra: prophet's example or behavior

al-usra: family

al-usūliyūn: fundamentalists

Amir al-Mu'minin: Commander of the Faithful

dā'iyya, dā'iyyat: woman or women practicing da'wa

da'wa: call or invitation of others to Islam

fatwa: a religious statement

fiqh: Islamic jurisprudence

fuqaha: scholars of Islamic jurisprudence

hadīth: prophet's saying

hijāb: veil

hudud: Islamic sanctions

'ibādāt: religious observances

imām: person who leads the prayer

ijtihād: renewed interpretation of the sharia

istikhlāf: perpetuation of the divine order

Jāmi'at al-sahwa al-islamiyya: University of the Islamic Revival

khatīb: preacher

kutla: the political coalition formed by opposition parties in the Moroccan
    Parliament in the 1980s

majlis al-irshād: the council of guidance (for al-'Adl wa-l-ihsāne; see below, under
    Islamist Organizations)

majlis al-shūrā: consultative council

makhzen: central government power in Morocco, the state

mālikī fiqh: one of the four schools of interpretation of the sharia followed in the
    Maghreb

maqāsid al-sharia: the objectives or essence of the sharia, defined as a quest for
    justice and search for virtue

mawadda: affection

mu'amalāt: social transactions

mudawwana: family code

muhaddithūn: reciters of the prophet's sayings

murāja'āt: revision

mut'a: alimony rights for women after divorce

mutabarrija: nonveiled, on display

qadiyyat al-mar'a: the woman's question

qiwāma: men as the providers

rahma: compassion

rashidūn: rightly guided

rūh: spirit

sahāba: male companions of the prophet

sahābiyyat: female companions of the prophet

Salafi: a twentieth-century school of thought

shaqāiq: equal before the law

sharia: corpus of interpretation of the Islamic holy sources by religious scholars

shūra: Qur'anic concept requiring consultation of the base during the decision-
    making process, used in Islamist literature as an alternative to the term
    "democracy"

sunna: prophet tradition, words and deeds

tahrīr: liberation

taqlīd: imitation

'ulama: theologians and legal scholars of Islam

umma: community of faith

'urf: custom

wālī: male guardian

wassat: middle way

wilāya: marital guardianship

Abbreviations

ACDI	Canadian Agency for Development
ADFM	Association Démocratique des Femmes du Maroc (Moroccan Women's Democratic Association)
AMDF	Association Marocaine pour les Droits des Femmes (Moroccan Association for Women's Rights)
CEDAW	United Nations Convention for the Elimination of All Forms of Discrimination against Women, also called the Copenhagen Convention
CERED	Demographic Center for Studies and Research on Population
ESPOD	Espace Point de Départ
FES	Friedrich Ebert Stiftung
IFD	Office for the Integration of Women in Development
IP	Istiqlal Party
ISESCO	Islamic Educational, Scientific, and Cultural Organization
KAS	Konrad Adenauer Stiftung
LDDF	La Ligue Démocratique des Droits des Femmes (Democratic League for Women's Rights)
MPCD	Mouvement Populaire Constitutionnel et Démocratique
MEPI	Middle East Partnership Initiative
NDI	National Democratic Institute
NPA	National Plan of Action for Integrating Women in Development
OADP	Organisation de l'Action Démocratique Populaire (Organization for Democratic Popular Action)
OMDH	Organisation Marocaine des Droits de l'Homme (Moroccan Organization for Human Rights)
ORWA	Organization for the Renewal of Women's Awareness
PPS	Partie du Progrès et du Socialisme (Party of Progress and Socialism)
UAF	Union de l'Action Feminine (Union of Women's Action)
UC	Union Constitutionelle
UNDP	United Nations Development Program
UNIFEM	United Nations Development Fund for Women
USFP	Union Socialiste des Forces Populaires
WID	Women in Development
WLUML	Women Living under Muslim Laws

Women's Organizations

Akhawāt al-safā: Sisters of Transparency

Amal

Association Démocratique des Femmes du Maroc: Moroccan Women's
    Democratic Association

Association Marocaine pour les Droits des Femmes: Moroccan Association for
    Women's Rights

Collectif 95 Maghreb Egalité

Ennakhīl

Espace Associatif

Espace Point de Départ

Jussūr: Bridges

La Ligue Démocratique des Droits des Femmes: Democratic League for
    Women's Rights

Printemps de l'Égalité: Springtime of Equality

Solidarité Féminine: Women's Solidarity

Union de l'Action Feminine: Union of Women's Action

Islamist Organizations

al-ʿAdl wa-l-ihsāne or Jamāʿat al-ʿadl wa-l-ihsāne: Justice and Spirituality

al-Hidn

al-Islāh wa-l-tajdīd: Movement for Reform and Renewal; combined with
    al-Mustaqbal al-islami to form al-Tawhīd wa-l-islāh

al-Mustaqbal al-islami: the Islamic Future; combined with al-Islāh wa-l-tajdīd
    to form al-Tawhīd wa-l-islāh

al-Qitāʿe al-nissaī: Women's Section of al-ʿAdl wa-l-ihsāne

al-Salafiyya al-jihādiyya: Salafi Jihadist

al-Shabība al-islāmiyya: the Islamic Youth

al-Tawhīd wa-l-islāh or Harakat al-tawhīd wa-l-islāh: Movement of Unification
    and Reform; fusion of al-Mustaqbal al-islami and al-Islāh wa-l-tajdīd

al-Thaqāfa al-bāniyya: Constructive Culture

Organization for the Renewal of Women's Awareness

Political Parties

al-ʿAdāla wa-l-tanmia: Justice and Development Party

al-Badīl al-hadāri: The Civilizational Alternative

al-Shūra wa-l-istiqlal: a nationalist party

Istiqlal Party: Party of Independence

kutla: 1980s oppositional coalition

Mouvement Populaire Constitutionnel et Démocratique

Organisation de l'Action Démocratique Populaire: Organization for Democratic Popular Action

Partie du Progrès et du Socialisme: Party of Progress and Socialism, formerly the Communist Party

Union Constitutionnelle

Union Socialiste des Forces Populaires

Newspapers and Magazines Cited

Al-Ahdāth al-maghribiyya: socialist daily newspaper; Casablanca

Al-'Asr: Islamist newspaper; the daily newspaper of the Islamist party Justice and Development; Rabat

Al-Ayām: independent weekly newspaper; Casablanca

Al-Sahīfa: independent newspaper; suspended in 2007

Al-Usbou'assahafi: independent weekly newspaper; Oujda

Bayāne al-Yaoum: communist daily newspaper; Rabat

Demain: independent magazine; suspended in 2000

Al Forkāne: Islamist magazine launched in 1984; Rabat

Le Journal-Hebdo: weekly magazine created in 1997; Casablanca

Al-Rāya: Moroccan Islamist newspaper

Al-Sahwa: magazine published by the Minister of Habous and Islamic Affairs

Al-Sharq: independent newspaper; Oujda

Al-Tajdīd: Islamist newspaper published by the Renewal and Reform Movement; Rabat

Tel-Quel: independent monthly magazine; Casablanca (http://www.telquel-online .com/318/couverture_318.shtml)

Thamānia Mars: feminist magazine launched in 1983

Bibliography

Abbot, Andrew. 2001. *Time Matters: On Theory and Method.* Chicago: University of Chicago Press.

Abou-Bakr, Omaima. 2001. "Islamic Feminism? What's in a Name? Preliminary Reflections." *Journal for Middle East Women's Studies* 25, no. 4, and 26, no. 1, http://www.amews.org.

Abu al-Saad, Mustafa. 1984. "Adoua'e 'ala al-'Amal al-Nisai al-Islami." *Al Forkāne* 11:36–39.

Abu-Lughod, Lila. 1998. Introduction to *Remaking Women,* edited by Lila Abu-Lughod, 1–12. Princeton: Princeton University Press.

———. 2002. "Do Muslim Women Really Need Saving? Anthropological Reflections on Cultural Relativism and Its Others." *American Anthropologist* 104(3): 783–90.

ADFM (Association Démocratique des Femmes du Maroc). 2004. Memorandum of Democracy/Modernity. Rabat, July.

Afkhami, Mahnaz, and Erika Friedl, eds. 1997. *Muslim Women and the Politics of Participation: Implementing the Beijing Platform.* Syracuse: Syracuse University Press.

Afshar, Halef. 1985. "Women, State, and Ideology in Iran." *Third World Quarterly* 7(2): 256–78.

———. 1999. *Islam and Feminisms: An Iranian Case Study.* London: Palgrave Macmillan.

Ahmed, Leila. 1992. *Women and Gender in Islam: Historical Roots of a Modern Debate.* New Haven: Yale University Press.

Akesbi, Najib. 1991. "L'economie marocaine: Des desequilibres inquietants." In *L'état du Maghreb,* edited by Yves Lacoste, 443–47. Casablanca: Le Fennec.

Akhter, Farida. 2003. "Huntington's 'Clash of Civilizations' Thesis and Population Control." In *After Shock: September 11, 2001: Global Feminist Perspectives,* edited by Susan Hawthorne and Bronwyn Winter, 328–32. Berkeley, Calif.: Raincoast Books.

al-Ahnaf, Mohamed. 1994. "Le code du statut personnel." *Maghreb Machrek* 145:3–26.

al-Ali, Najde. 2000. *Secularism, Gender, and the State in the Middle East: The Egyptian Women's Movement.* Cambridge: Cambridge University Press.

Alami, Houria. 2002. *Genre et politique au maroc: Les enjeux de l'egalité hommes-femmes entre Islamism et Modernism.* Paris: L'Harmattan.

al-Azmeh, Aziz. 1996. *Islam and Modernities.* London: Verso.

Alexander, Jacqui, and Chandra T. Mohanty, eds. 1997. *Feminist Genealogies, Colonial Legacies, Democratic Futures.* New York: Routledge.

al-Fassi, Allal. 1979. *Al-Naqd al-Thati.* 5th ed. Rabat: Imprimerie al-Rissala. Orig. pub. 1953.

Algerian Press Service. 2004. "Des ONG marocaines contre l'accord de libre-échange." October 23, http://www.yabiladi.com/forum/marocaines-contre-accord-libre-echange-2-367384.html.

al-Khamlishi, Ahmed. 2004. *Limatha la Narbit baina al-Tanthir wal-Mumarassa? Manshurat al-Zaman.* Casablanca: Matba't al-Najah al-Jadida.

al-Sareh, Rabia. 1984. "Al-Makiaj wa Tashi' al-Mar'a." *Al Forkāne* 14:34–35.

Alvarez, Sonia. 1990. *Engendering Democracy in Brazil: Women's Movements in Transition Politics.* Princeton: Princeton University Press.

Amin, Galal. 1997. "Economic Change, Social Structure, and Religious Fanaticism." In *Arab Society,* edited by Nicholas Hopkins and Saad Eddin Ibrahim, 575–83. Cairo: American University.

Amin, Qasim. 1992. *The Liberation of Women and the New Woman.* Translated by Samiha Sidhom Peterson. Cairo: American University in Cairo Press.

Aminzade, Ronald. 1992. "Historical Sociology and Time." *Sociological Methods and Research* 20(4): 456–80.

Anderson, Benedict. 1991. *Imagined Communities.* London: Verso.

Andrews, Kenneth. 2002. "Movement-Countermovement Dynamics and the Emergence of New Institutions: The Case of 'White Flight' Schools in Mississippi." *Social Forces* 80(3): 911–36.

An-Na'im, Abdullahi. 1992. Introduction to *Human Rights in Cross-Cultural Perspectives: A Quest for Consensus,* edited by Abdullahi An-Na'im, 1–15. Philadelphia: University of Philadelphia.

———. 2002. "Sharia and Islamic Family Law: Transition and Transformation." In *Islamic Family Law in a Changing World: A Global Resource Book,* edited by A. An-Na'im, 1–22. New York: Zed Books.

Anzaldua, Gloria. 1987. *Borderlands/La Frontera.* San Francisco: Spinsters/Aunt Lute Press.

Asad, Talal. 2003. *Formation of the Secular: Christianity, Islam, Modernity.* Stanford: Stanford University Press.

Badran, Margot. 1994. "Gender Activism: Feminisms and Islamisms in Egypt." In *Identity Politics and Women: Cultural Reassertions and Feminisms in International Perspective,* edited by Valentine Moghadam, 202–27. Boulder, Colo.: Westview Press.

————. 1995. *Feminists, Islam, and Nation.* Princeton: Princeton University Press.

Badran, Margot, and Miriam Cooke, eds. 1990. *Opening the Gates: A Century of Arab Feminist Writing.* Bloomington: Indiana University Press.

Baina, Abdelkader. 1981. *Le systeme de l'enseignement au Maroc: Les instruments ideologiques.* Casablanca: Les Editions Maghrebines.

Basu, Amrita, ed. 1995. *The Challenge of Local Feminisms: Women's Movements in Global Perspective.* Boulder, Colo.: Westview Press.

Bayes, Jane, and Nayereh Tohidi. 2001. Introduction to *Globalization, Gender and Religion: The Politics of Women's Rights in Catholic and Muslim Contexts,* edited by Jane Bayes and Nayereh Tohidi, 1–15. New York: Palgrave.

Beck, Ulrich. 2000. *What Is Globalization?* Malden, Mass.: Blackwell.

Belarbi, Aisha. 1997. "Le mouvement associatif au Maroc." *Prologue* 9:28–33.

Benchekroun, Mohamed. 1992. *Introduction et évolution de l'enseignment au Maroc: Des origines jusqu'a 1956.* Rabat: Imprimerie Arrisala.

Benhabib, Seyla. 1991. "Feminism and the Question of Postmodernism." In *The New Social Theory Reader: Contemporary Debates,* edited by Steven Seidman and Jeffrey Alexander, 11–39. New York: Routledge.

Benkirane, Abdelilah. 1993. "Bayan haoula taghir moudanat al-ahwal al-shakhcia." *Al-Rāya,* April 21, 17.

Berger, John. 1972. *Ways of Seeing.* London: Penguin.

Bhabha, Homi K. 1994. *The Location of Culture.* London: Routledge.

Bishara, Azmy. 1995. "Islam and Politics in the Middle East." In *The Next Threat: Western Perceptions of Islam,* edited by Jochen Hippler, Andrea Lueg, and Laila Friese, 82–115. Boulder, Colo.: Pluto Press with Transnational Institute.

Blanchard, Eric M. 2003. "Gender, International Relations, and the Development of Feminist Security Theory." *Signs: Journal of Women and Culture in Society* 28(4): 1289–312.

Bocock, Robert. 1986. *Hegemony.* London: Tavostock Publications/Ellis Horwood Limited.

Bodman, Herbert, and Nayereh Tohidi, eds. 1998. *Women in Muslim Societies: Diversity Within.* Bolder, Colo.: Lynne Rienner.

Bowman, Paul. 2002. "Ernesto Laclau, Chantal Mouffe, and Post-Marxism." In *The*

Edinburgh Encyclopaedia of Modern Criticism and Theory, edited by Julian Wolfreys, 799–808. Edinburgh: Edinburgh University Press.

Brand, Laurie A. 1998. *Women, the State, and Political Liberalization: Middle Eastern and North African Experiences.* New York: Columbia University Press.

Calhoun, Craig. 1992. Introduction to *Habermas and the Public Sphere,* edited by Craig Calhoun, 1–48. Cambridge, Mass.: MIT Press.

Carnoy, Martin. 1980. *The State and Political Theory.* Princeton: Princeton University Press.

Chafetz, Janet Saltzman, and Anthony Gary Dworkin. 1987. "In Face of Threat: Organized Antifeminism in Comparative Perspective." *Gender and Society* 1:33–60.

Charles, Nickie. 2000. *Feminism, the State, and Social Policy.* New York: St. Martin's Press.

Charrad, Mounira. 1997. "Policy Shifts: State, Islam, and Gender in Tunisia, 1930s–1990s." *Social Politics* 4(2): 285–319.

———. 1998. "Cultural Diversity within Islam: Veils and Laws in Tunisia." In *Women in Muslim Societies: Diversity within Unity,* edited by H. L. Bodman and N. Tohidi, 63–79. Boulder, Colo.: Lynne Rienner.

———. 2001. *States and Women's Rights: The Making of Colonial Tunisia, Algeria, and Morocco.* Berkeley: University of California Press.

Chatty, Dawn, and Annika Rabo. 1997. Introduction to *Organizing Women: Formal and Informal Women's Groups in the Middle East,* edited by Dawn Chatty and Annika Rabo, 1–22. New York: Berg.

Chraibi, Driss. 1954. *Le passé simple.* Paris: Editions Gallimard.

Clement, Jean-Francois. 1992. "Les tensions urbaines au Maroc." In *Le Maroc actuel: Une modernisation au miroir de la tradition,* edited by Jean-Claude Santucci, 393–407. Paris: CNRS.

Cohen, Shana. 2005. *Searching for a Different Future: The Rise of a Global Middle Class in Morocco.* Durham: Duke University Press.

Collectif 95. Maghreb Egalité. 1995. *One Hundred Measures and Provisions: For a Maghrebian Egalitarian Codification of the Personal Statute and Family Law.* Rabat: Friedrich Ebert Stiftung.

Collins, Patricia H. 2000. *Black Feminist Thought.* New York: Routledge.

Cooke Miriam. 2001. *Women Claim Islam: Creating Islamic Feminism through Literature.* New York: Routledge.

Daoud, Zakya. 1993. *Feminisme et politique au Maghreb: Soixante ans de lutte.* Casablanca: Eddif.

Daoud, Zakya, and Brahim Ouchelh. 1997. "A Peaceful Transition? Morocco Prepares for Political Change." *Le Monde Diplomatique,* June, http://www.hartford-hwp.com/archives/32/098.html.

Darif, Mohamed. 1999. *Al-Islamiyoun al-Maghariba*. Casablanca: Manshūrat al-Majala al-Maghribia li 'ilm al-ijtima'a al-Siyyassi.

Deeb, Lara. 2006. *An Enchanted Modern: Gender and Public Piety in Shi'i Lebanon*. Princeton: Princeton University Press.

Delphy, Christine. 2003. "A War for Afghan Women?" In *After Shock: September 11, 2001: Global Feminist Perspectives,* edited by Susan Hawthorne and Bronwyn Winter, 328–47. Berkeley, Calif.: Raincoast Books.

Denoeux, Guillaume, and L. Gateau. 1995. "L'essor des associations au Maroc: A la recherche de la citoyenneté." *Magreb-Machrek* 150: 19–39.

Dubois, W. E. B. 1903. *The Souls of Black Folk*. Chicago: A. C. McClurg and Co.

Eisenstein, Hester. 2005. "A Dangerous Liaison? Feminism and Corporate Globalization." *Science and Society* 69(3): 487–518.

El Guindi, Fadwa. 1999. *Veil: Modesty, Privacy, and Resistance*. New York: Berg.

———. 2007. "What Is 'Private' in the Middle East?" *International Journal of Middle Eastern Studies* 39:172–73.

El Haddad, Tahar. 1930. *Notre femme dans la charia et la société*. Tunis: Maison tunisienne de l'édition.

El Mossadeq, Rkia. 1995. *Consensus ou jeu de consensus? Pour le réajustement de la pratique politique au Maroc*. Casablanca: Imprimerie Najah El Jadida.

Elyachar, Julia. 2002. "Empowerment Money: The World Bank, Non-Governmental Organizations, and the Value of Culture in Egypt." *Public Culture* 14:493–513.

Emerson, Michael, and David Hartman. 2006. "The Rise of Religious Fundamentalism." *Annual Review of Sociology* 32:127–44.

Enloe, Cynthia. 2004. *The Curious Feminist: Searching for Women in a New Age of Empire*. Berkeley: University of California Press.

Eschle, Catherine. 2001. "Globalizing Civil Society? Social Movements and the Challenge of Global Politics from Below." In *Globalization and Social Movements,* edited by Pierre Hamel, Jan Nederveen Pieterse, and Sasha Roseneil, 61–85. New York: Palgrave.

Escobar, Arturo. 1994. *Encountering Development: The Making and Unmaking of the Third World*. Princeton: Princeton University Press.

Ferree, Myra Marx. 1992. "The Political Context of Rationality, Rational Choice, and Resource Mobilization." In *Frontiers in Social Movement Theory,* edited by M. Aldon and C. McClurg Mueller, 29–52. New Haven: Yale University Press.

Ferree, Myra Marx, and Patricia Y. Martin. 1995. *Feminist Organizations: Harvest of the New Women's Movement*. Philadelphia: Temple University Press.

Ferree, Myra Marx, and David Merrill. 2000. "Hot Movements, Cold Cognition: Thinking about Social Movements in Gendered Frames." *Contemporary Sociology* 29:1454–62.

Ferree, Myra Marx, and Silke Roth. 1998. "Gender, Class, and the Interaction between

Social Movements: A Strike of West Berlin Day Care Workers." *Gender and Society* 12:626–48.

Fetner, Tina. 2008. *How the Religious Right Shaped Lesbian and Gay Activism.* Minneapolis: University of Minnesota Press.

Foucault, Michel. 1978. *The History of Sexuality.* New York: Vintage.

———. 1980. *Power/Knowledge: Selected Interviews and Other Writings, 1972–1977,* edited by Colin Gordon. Brighton: Harvester Press.

———. 1990. "Sexual Discourse and Power." In *Culture and Society: Contemporary Debates,* edited by Jeffrey C. Alexander and Steven Seidman, 199–204. Cambridge: Cambridge University Press.

Frazer, Nancy. 1995. "Politics, Culture, and the Public Sphere: Toward a Postmodern Conception." In *Social Postmodernism: Beyond Identity Politics,* edited by L. Nicholson and S. Seidman, 287–312. Cambridge: Cambridge University Press.

Freeman, Amy. 2004. "Re-locating Moroccan Women's Identities in a Transnational World: The 'Woman Question' in Question." *Gender, Place, and Culture* 11(1): 17–41.

Freeman, Carla. 2001. "Is Local: Global as Feminine: Masculine? Rethinking the Gender of Globalization." *Signs: Journal of Women and Culture in Society* 26(4): 1007–37.

Gale, Richard P. 1986. "Social Movements and the State: The Environmental Movement, Countermovement, and Government Agencies." *Sociological Perspectives* 29(2): 202–40.

Gamson, William A. 1992. "The Social Psychology of Collective Action." In *Frontiers in Social Movements Theory,* edited by Aldon Morris and Carol McClurg Mueller, 53–76. New Haven: Yale University Press.

Gibbon, Peter. 1997. "Civil Society, Politics, and Developmentalist States." In *Social Movements in Development,* edited by Staffan Lindberg and Arni Sverrison, 78–98. New York: St. Martin's Press.

Gilliam, Angela. 1991. "Women's Equality and National Liberation." In *Third World Women and the Politics of Feminism,* edited by Chandra Talpade Mohanty, Ann Russo, and Lourdes Torres, 215–36. Bloomington: Indiana University Press.

Glenn, Evelyn N. 2000. "The Social Construction and Institutionalization of Gender and Race." In *Revisioning Gender,* edited by Myra Marx Ferree, Judith Lorber, and Beth Hess, 3–43. New York: Rowman and Littlefield Publishers.

Goldman, Michael. 2005. *Imperial Nature: The World Bank and Struggles for Social Justice in the Age of Globalization.* New Haven: Yale University Press.

Gordon, Colin. 1991. "Governmental Rationality: An Introduction." In *The Foucault Effect: Studies in Governmentality,* edited by G. Burchell, C. Gordon, and P. Miller, 1–51. Chicago: University of Chicago Press.

Grossberg, Lawrence. 2006. "Does Cultural Studies Have Futures? Should It? (Or What's the Matter with New York?)." *Cultural Studies* 20(1): 1–32.

A Group of Muslim Women. 1992. *Al-Rāya,* April 19, 11.

Guessous, Nezha. 2004. "Masar ciyarhat mudawanat al-usra: Hacila wa-Afaq." In *Thawra hadia: Min Mudawanat al-Ahwal al-Chakhciya ila Mudawanat al-Usra,* edited by Manshūrat al-Zaman, 91–103. Casablanca: Matba't al-Najah al-Jadida.

Guidry, John, Michael Kennedy, and Mayer Zald. 2000. "Globalizations and Social Movements." In *Globalizations and Social Movements: Culture, Power and the Transnational Public Sphere,* edited by John Guidry, Michael Kennedy, and Mayer Zald, 1–53. Ann Arbor: University of Michigan Press.

Haas, Tanni. 2004. "The Public Sphere as a Sphere of Publics: Rethinking Habermas' Theory of the Public Sphere." *Journal of Communication* 54(1): 178–84.

Habermas, Jurgen. 1985. *The Theory of Communicative Action.* Vol. 2, *Lifeworld and System: A Critique of Functionalist Reason.* Translated by Thomas McCarthy. New York: Beacon Press.

Haddad, Yvonne, and Jane Smith. 1996. "Women in Islam: The Mother of All Battles." In *Arab Women: Between Defiance and Restraint,* edited by Suha Sabbagh, 137–50. New York: Olive Branch Press.

Hale, Sondra. 1997. *Gender and Politics in Sudan: Islamism, Socialism, and the State.* Boulder, Colo.: Westview Press.

Hall, Stuart. 1996. "On Postmodernism and Articulation." In *Critical Dialogues in Cultural Studies,* edited by Dave Morley, 131–50. New York: Routledge.

Hamadi, Driss. 2001. *Afaq tahrīr al-Mar'a fi al-Shariaal-Islamiya.* Rabat: Dar Abi Raqraq.

Hammoudi, Abdellah. 1997. *The Master and the Disciple: The Cultural Foundations of Moroccan Authoritarianism.* Chicago: University of Chicago Press.

Hardt, Michael, and Antonio Negri. 2000. *Empire.* Cambridge, Mass.: Harvard University Press.

Hatem, Mervet. 1996. "Economic and Political Liberalization in Egypt and the Demise of State Feminism." In *Arab Women: Between Defiance and Restraint,* edited by Suha Sabbagh, 171–93. New York: Olive Branch Press.

Hawthorne, Susan, and Bronwyn Winter. 2003. Introduction to *After Shock: September 11, 2001: Global Feminist Perspectives,* edited by Susan Hawthorne and Bronwyn Winter, 11–22. Berkeley, Calif.: Raincoast Books.

Hefner, Robert. 1998. "Multiple Modernities: Christianity, Islam, and Hinduism in a Globalization Age." *Annual Review of Anthropology* 27:83–104.

Hippler, Jochen, and Andrea Lueg, eds. 1995. *The Next Threat: Western Perceptions of Islam.* Boulder, Colo.: Pluto Press with Transnational Institute.

hooks, bell. 2003. "Feminism as a Transformational Politics." In *Feminist Theory*

Reader: Local and Global Perspectives, edited by Carole R. McCann and Seung-Kyung Kim, 464–69. New York: Routledge.

Huntington, Samuel. 1996. *The Clash of Civilizations and the Remaking of World Order.* New York: Simon and Schuster.

Ibrahim, Saad Eddine. 1998. "Religion and Democracy: The Case of Islam, Civil Society and Democracy." In *The Changing Nature of Democracy,* edited by Takashi Inoguchi, Edward Newman, and John Keane, 213–27. Tokyo: United Nations University Press.

Jahan, Roushan. 1995. "Men in Seclusion, Women in Public: Rokeya's Dream and Women's Struggles in Bangladesh." In *The Challenge of Local Feminisms: Women's Movements in Global Perspective,* edited by Amrita Basu, 87–109. Oxford: Westview Press.

Jamaï, A., F. Iraqi, H. Houdaïfa, and A. Rhanime. 2007. "La fille du Cheick et le 'Grand Satan.'" *Le Journal-Hebbo,* May 10, http://web.archive.org/web/2007 0510091811/www.lejournal-hebdo.com/article.php3?id_article=4312.

Jeffery, Patricia, and Amrita Basu, eds. 1998. *Appropriating Gender: Women's Activism and Politicized Religion in South Asia.* New York: Routledge.

Jelin, Elisabeth. 1998. "Toward a Culture of Participation and Citizenship: Challenges for a More Equitable World." In *Cultures of Politics, Politics of Cultures: Re-visioning Latin American Social Movements,* edited by Sonia Alvarez, Evelyn Dagnino, and Arturo Escobar, 405–14. Boulder, Colo.: Westview Press.

Jenkins, Richard. 1992. *Pierre Bourdieu.* New York: Routledge.

Joseph, Suad, ed. 2000. *Gender and Citizenship in the Middle East.* Syracuse: Syracuse University Press.

Kamat, Sangeeta. 2004. "The Privatization of Public Interest: Theorizing NGO Discourse in a Neoliberal Era." *Review of International Political Economy* 11(1): 155–76.

Kandiyoti, Deniz. 1998. "Bargaining with Patriarchy." *Gender and Society* 2(3): 274–89.

Karam, Azza. 1997. "Women, Islamisms, and State: Dynamics of Power and Contemporary Feminisms in Egypt." In *Muslim Women and the Politics of Participation: Implementing the Beijing Platform,* edited by Mahnaz Afkhami and Erika Friedl, 18–28. Syracuse: Syracuse University Press.

———. 1998. *Women, Islamisms, and the State.* New York: St. Martin's Press.

Katzenstein, Mary. 1995. "Discursive Politics and Feminist Activism." In *Feminist Organizations: Harvest of the New Women's Movement,* edited by Myra Marx Ferree and Patricia Yancey Martin, 35–52. Philadelphia: Temple University Press.

Keck, Margaret E., and Kathryn Sikkink. 1998. "Transnational Advocacy Movement Society." In *The Social Movement Society: Contentious Politics for a New Century,* edited by David Meyer and Sidney Tarrow, 217–38. Lanham, Md.: Rowman and Littlefield.

Kepel, Gilles. 1997. *Allah in the West: Islamic Movements in America and Europe.* Stanford: Stanford University Press.

———. 2000. *Jihad: Expansion et déclin de l'islamisme.* Paris: Editions Gallimard.

Khalil, Fatema (Oum Naoufal). 1991. "Bitaqat Ta'rif." *Al Forkāne* 21:8–12.

Klandermans, Bert. 1992. "The Social Construction of Protest and Multiorganizational Fields." In *Frontiers in Social Movement Theory,* edited by Aldon Morris and Carol McClurg Mueller, 77–103. New Haven: Yale University Press.

Klatch, Rebecca. 1987. *Women of the New Right.* Philadelphia: Temple University Press.

———. 1999. *A Generation Divided: The New Left, the New Right, and the 1960s.* Berkeley: University of California Press.

———. 2001. "The Formation of Feminist Consciousness among Left- and Right-Wing Activists of the 1960s." *Gender and Society* 15:791–815.

Kumar, Radha. 1995. "From Chipko to Sati: The Contemporary Indian Women's Movement." In *The Challenge of Local Feminisms: Women's Movements in Global Perspective,* edited by Amrita Basu, 58–81. Oxford: Westview Press.

Laclau, Ernesto, and Chantal Mouffe. 1985. *Hegemony and Socialist Strategy.* London: Verso.

Lacoste, Yves. 1991. *L'état du Maghreb.* Casablanca: Le Fennec.

Lamrabet, Asma. 2002. *Musulmane tout simplement.* Lyon: Imprimerie Tawhid.

Laroui, Abdellah. 1976. *La crise des intellectuels arabes: Traditionalisme ou historicisme?* Paris: La Decouverte.

———. 1993. *Les origines sociales et culturelles du nationalisme marocain (1830–1912).* Casablanca: Centre Culturelle Arabe.

Lazreg, Marnia. 1986. "Feminism and Difference: The Perils of Writing as a Woman on Women in Algeria." *Feminist Studies* 1:81–107.

———. 1994. *The Eloquence of Silence: Algerian Women in Question.* New York: Routledge.

———. 2002. "Development: Feminist Theory's Cul-de-Sac." In *Feminist Post-Development Thought,* edited by Kriemild Saunders, 123–45. New York: Zed Books.

LDDF (La Ligue Démocratique des Droits des Femmes). 2001. *Hukuk al-mar'a wa mudawanat al ahwal al-shakhcia.* Casablanca: Ifriquia al-Shark.

Leveau, Remy. 1998. "The Monarchy as Central Actor: A Democratic Transition in Morocco?" *Le Monde Diplomatique,* December, http://www.icnrd.org/researches_details.php?id=214.

———. 2000. "The Moroccan Monarchy: A Political System in Quest of a New Equilibrium." In *Middle East Monarchies: The Challenges of Modernity,* edited by J. Kostiner, 117–30. Boulder, Colo.: Lynne Rienner Publishers.

Lewis, Barnard. 2002. *What Went Wrong? The Clash between Islam and Modernity in the Middle East.* Oxford: Oxford University Press.

Lo, Clarence Y. H. 1982. "Countermovements and Conservative Movements in the Contemporary U.S." *Annual Review of Sociology* 8:107–34.

Maadi, Zineb. 1992. *Al-Mar'a baina al-thaqafi w-al qudsi.* Casablanca: Le Fennec.

———. 1997. "Le statut de la femme marocaine dans l'institution familial." In *Droits de Citoyenneté des Femmes au Maghreb,* 210–23. Casablanca: Le Fennec.

Macleod, Arlene. 1991. *Accommodating Protest: Working Class Women, the New Veiling, and Change in Cairo.* New York: Columbia University Press.

Maddy-Weitzman, Bruce. 2003. "Islamism, Moroccan-Style: The Ideas of Sheikh Yassine." *Middle East Quarterly* (Winter), http://www.meforum.org.

Maghraoui, Abdeslam. 2001. "Political Authority in Crisis: Mohammed VI's Morocco." *Middle East Report* 28:12–17.

Mahmood, Saba. 2005. *Politics of Piety: The Islamic and the Feminist Subject.* Princeton: Princeton University Press.

Mamdani, Mahmood. 1996. *Citizens and Subjects: Contemporary Africa and the Legacy of Late Colonialism.* Princeton: Princeton University Press.

———. 2000. Introduction to *Beyond Rights Talk and Culture Talk,* edited by Mahmood Mamdani, 1–13. New York: St. Martin's Press.

Mansbridge, Jane. 1995. "What Is the Feminist Movement?" In *Feminist Organizations: Harvest of the New Women's Movement,* edited by Myra Marx Ferree and Patricia Yancey Martin, 27–34. Philadelphia: Temple University Press.

Margolis, Diane R. 1993. "Women's Movements around the World: Cross Cultural Comparisons." *Gender and Society* 7(3): 379–99.

Marks, Gary, and Doug McAdam. 1999. "On the Relation of Political Opportunities to the Form of the Collective Action: The Case of the European Union." In *Social Movements in a Globalizing World,* edited by Donatella della Porta, Hanspeter Kriesi, and Dieter Rucht, 97–111. New York: St. Martin's Press.

Marshall, Suzan E., and Anthony M. Orum. 1986. "Opposition Then and Now: Countering Feminism in the Twentieth Century." *Research in Politics and Society* 2:13–33.

Martin, Patricia Yancey, and David L. Collinson. 2000. "Gender and Sexuality in Organizations." In *Revisioning Gender,* edited by Myra Marx Ferree, Judith Lorber, and Beth Hess, 285–310. New York: Rowman and Littlefield Publishers.

McAdam, Doug. 1982. "The Political Process Model." In *Social Movements: Perspectives and Issues,* edited by Steven Buechler and F. Jurt Cylke, 172–92. New York: McGraw-Hill.

McCarthy, John, and Meyer Zald. 1977. "Resource Mobilization and Social Movements: A Partial Theory." *American Journal of Sociology* 82:1221–41.

McGlen, Nancy E., and Karen O'Connor. 1988. "Toward a Theoretical Model of Countermovement and Constitutional Change: A Case Study of the Era." *Women and Politics* 8:45–69.

McMichael, Philip. 2004. *Development and Social Change: A Global Perspective.* 3rd ed. Thousand Oaks, Calif.: Pine Forge Press.

McRobbie, Angela. 2004. "Post-Feminism and Popular Culture." *Feminist Media Studies* 4(3): 255–64.

Mdaghri, Abdelkabir al-Alawi. 1999. *Al-Mar'a baina Ahkami al-Fikh w-al da 'wa ila a-taghr'ir.* Mohamedia: Matba'at Fdala.

Melucci, Alberto. 1995. "The Process of Collective Identity." In *Social Movements and Culture,* edited by Hank Johnston and Bert Klandermans, 41–63. Minneapolis: University of Minnesota Press.

———. 1998. "Third World or Planetary Conflict?" In *Cultures of Politics, Politics of Cultures: Re-visioning Latin American Social Movement,* edited by Sonia E. Alvarez, Evelina Dagnino, and Arturo Escobar, 422–29. Boulder, Colo.: Westview Press.

Mercer, Claire. 2002. "NGOs, Civil Society and Democratization: A Critical Review of the Literature." *Progress in Development Studies* 2(1): 5–22.

Mernissi, Fatima. 1987. "Professional Women in the Arab World: The Example of Morocco." *Feminist Issues* 7(1): 47–65.

———. 1988. *Doing Daily Battle: Interviews with Moroccan Women.* Translated by Mary Jo Lakeland. New Brunswick: Rutgers University Press.

———. 1993. *The Forgotten Queens of Islam.* Translated Mary Jo Lakeland. Minneapolis: University of Minnesota Press.

———. 2001. *Sheherazade Goes West: Different Cultures, Different Harems.* New York: Washington Square Press.

Meyer, David, and Suzanne Staggenborg. 1996. "Movements, Counter Movements, and the Structure of Political Opportunity." *American Journal of Sociology* 101:1628–60.

Meyer, David S., and Sydney Tarrow. 1998. *The Social Movement Society: Contentious Politics for a New Century.* New York: Rowman and Littlefield.

Mies, Maria. 1986. *Patriarchy and Accumulation on a World Scale: Women in the International Division of Labor.* 2nd ed. New York: St. Martin's Press.

Ministry of Economic Prevision and Planning. 1998. *Genre et Developement: Aspects Soci-Demographiques et Culturels de la Differenciation Sexuelle.* Rabat: CERED.

Ministry of Employment. 1995. *Research for the Setting Up of a Female Development Action Strategy.* Kingdom of Morocco, Direction of Social Affairs. Rabat: EDESA.

Ministry of Foreign Affairs and Cooperation. 1997. *Répertoire des Départements Ministériels et ONG Oeuvrant dans le domaine de l'integration de la Femme au Développement.* Directon de la Coopération Mulilatérale.

Mir-Hosseini, Ziba. 1996. "Stretching the Limits: A Feminist Reading of the Shari-ain Post-Khomeini Iran." In *Feminism and Islam: Legal and Literary Perspectives,* edited by Mai Yamani, 285–319. New York: New York University Press.

———. 1999. *Islam and Gender: The Religious Debate in Contemporary Iran.* Princeton: Princeton University Press.

Mitchell, Timothy. 1988. *Colonizing Egypt.* Cambridge: Cambridge University Press.

———. 2000. *Questions of Modernity.* Minneapolis: University of Minnesota Press.

Moallem, Minoo. 2005. *Between Warrior Brother and Veiled Sister: Islamic Fundamentalism and the Politics of Patriarchy in Iran.* Berkeley: University of California Press.

Moghadam, Valentine. 2000. "Gender, National Identity, and Citizenship: Reflection on the Middle East and North Africa." *Hagar International Social Science Review* 1:41–70.

———. 2001. "Transnational Feminist Networks: Collective Action in an Era of Globalization." In *Globalization and Social Movements,* edited by Pierre Hamel, Jan Nederveen Pieterse, and Sasha Roseneil, 111–39. New York: Palgrave.

———. 2002. "Islamic Feminism and Its Discontents: Toward a Resolution of the Debate." *Signs: Journal of Women and Culture in Society* 27(4): 1135–71.

———. 2005. *Globalizing Women: Transnational Feminist Networks.* Baltimore: Johns Hopkins University Press.

Moghissi, Haideh. 1999. *Feminism and Islamic Fundamentalism: The Limits of Postmodern Analysis.* New York: Zed Books.

———. 2004. "September 11 and Middle Eastern Women: Shrinking Space for Critical Thinking and Oppositional Politics." *Signs: Journal of Women and Culture in Society* 29(2): 594–95.

Mohanty, Chandra Talpade. 2003. *Feminism without Borders: Decolonizing Theory, Practicing Solidarity.* Durham: Duke University Press.

Molyneux, Maxime. 1985. "Mobilization without Emancipation? Women's Interests, the State, and Revolution in Nicaragua." *Feminist Studies* 11(2): 227–54.

Molyneux, Maxime, and Shahra Razavi. 2002. Introduction to *Gender Justice, Development, and Rights,* edited by Maxime Molyneux and Shahra Razavi, 1–42. Oxford: Oxford University Press.

Morris, Aldon. 2000. "Reflections on Social Movement Theory: Criticism and Proposals." *Contemporary Sociology* 29:445–54.

Mottl, Tahi L. 1980. "The Analysis of Social Movements." *Social Problems* 27:620–35.

Mouffe, Chantal. 1995. "Feminism, Citizenship, and Radical Democratic Politics." In *Social Postmodernism: Beyond Identity Politics,* edited by Linda Nicholson and Steven Seidman, 315–31. Cambridge: Cambridge University Press.

Moulay R'chid, Abderrazak. 1991. *La femme et la loi au Maroc.* Casablanca: Le Fennec.

Narayan, Uma. 1997. *Dislocating Cultures: Identities, Traditions, and Third-World Feminism.* New York: Routledge.

Nassef, Fatema. 1999. *Droits et devoirs de la femme en Islam a la lumière du Coran et de la Sunna*. Lyon: Editions Tawhid.

Nayyar, Javed. 1994. "Gender Identity and Muslim Women: Tool of Oppression Turned into Empowerment." *Convergence* 27:58–68.

Nederveen Pieterse, Jan. 1989. *Empire and Emancipation: Power and Liberation on a World Scale*. NewYork: Praeger Publishers.

———. 2001. "Globalization and Collective Action." In *Globalization and Social Movements*, edited by P. Hamel, H. Lustiger-Thaler, J. Nederveen Pieterse, and S. Roseneil, 1–40. New York: Palgrave.

———. 2002. "Globalization at War: War on Terrorism." *International Journal of Peace Studies* 7(2): 75–93.

———. 2004. *Globalization or Empire*. New York: Routledge.

Noonan, Rita K. 1997. "Women against the State: Political Opportunities and Collective Action Frames in Chile's Transition to Democracy." In *Social Movements: Readings on Their Emergence, Mobilization, and Dynamics*, edited by Doug McAdam and David Snow, 252–67. Los Angeles: Roxbury.

ORWA (Organization for the Renewal of Women's Awareness). 1995. "Concept and Pacte. Manshourāt al- wa'e al-nissāī." Casablanca: Matbaa't al-Najāh al Jadīda.

Oum Yassir, Zoubida. 1992. "Al-Islamiūn w-al-mar'a: Ru'ya mina al-dākhil." *Al Forkāne* 28:51–55.

Paidar, Parvin. 2002. "Encounters between Feminism, Democracy, and Reformism in Contemporary Iran." In *Gender Justice, Development, and Rights*, edited by Maxime Molyneux and Shahra Razavi, 240–76. Oxford: Oxford University Press.

Pandolfo, Stefania. 2000. "The Thin Line of Modernity: Some Moroccan Debates on Subjectivity." *Questions of Modernity*, edited by Timothy Mitchell, 115–47. Minneapolis: University of Minnesota Press.

Paoli, Maria Celia, and Vera Da Silva Telles. 1998. "Social Rights: Conflicts and Negotiations in Contemporary Brazil." In *Cultures of Politics, Politics of Cultures: Revisioning Latin American Social Movements*, edited by Sonia E. Alvarez, Evelina Dagnino, and Arturo Escobar, 64–92. Oxford: Westview Press.

Paris, Mirelle. 1989. "Mouvement de femmes et feminism au Maghreb." *Annuaire de l'Afrique Du Nord* 28:430–44.

Paye, Lucien. 1992. *Introduction et evolution de l'enseignement moderne au Maroc: Des origines jusqu'a 1956*. Edited by Mohamed Benchekroun. Rabat: Imprimerie Rissala.

Peters, Cynthia. 2003. "What Does Feminism Have to Say?" In *After Shock: September 11, 2001: Global Feminist Perspectives*, edited by Susan Hawthorne and Bronwyn Winter, 149–55. Berkeley, Calif.: Raincoast Books.

Pierson, Paul. 2004. *Politics in Time: History, Institutions, and Social Analysis*. Princeton: Princeton University Press.

Poster, Winifred, and Zakia Salime. 2002. "The Limits of Micro-Credit: Transnational Feminism and USAID Activities in the United States and Morocco." In *Women's Activism and Globalization: Linking Local Struggles and Transnational Politics,* edited by Nancy A. Naples and Manisha Desai, 191–219. New York: Routledge.

Pratt, Mary Louise. 1998. "New Social Movements: Where To? What Next?" In *Cultures of Politics, Politics of Cultures: Re-visioning Latin American Social Movement,* edited by Sonia E. Alvarez, Evelina Dagnino, and Arturo Escobar, 430–36. Boulder, Colo.: Westview Press.

Raka, Ray. 1999. *Fields of Protest: Women's Movements in India.* Minneapolis: University of Minnesota Press.

Rao, Arati. 1995. "The Politics of Gender and Culture in International Human Rights Discourse." In *Women's Rights, Human Rights: International Feminist Perspectives,* edited by Julie Stone Peters and Andrea Wolper, 167–75. New York: Routledge.

Ray, R., and A. C. Korteweg. 1999. "Women's Movements in the Third World: Identity, Mobilization, and Autonomy." *Annual Review of Sociology* 25:47–71.

Robnett, Belinda. 1997. *How Long? How Long? African-American Women in the Struggle for Civil Rights.* New York: Oxford University Press.

Roy, Olivier. 2003. Interview in *Le Journal Hebdomadaire,* July 12–18, 8.

Ryan, Barbara. 1992. *Feminism and the Women's Movement: Dynamics of Change in Social Movement Ideology and Activism.* New York: Routledge.

Ruby, Jennie. 2003. "Is This a Feminist War?" In *After Shock: September 11, 2001: Global Feminist Perspectives,* edited by Susan Hawthorne and Bronwyn Winter, 177–79. Berkeley, Calif.: Raincoast Books.

Saadi, Said Mohamed. 2004. "Ithmaj al-Mar'a fi al-Tanmia." In *Thaoura Hadia: Min Mudawanat al-Ahwal al-Sakhcia ila Mudawanat al-Usra,* edited by Mamnshūrat al-Zaman, 31–46. Casablanca: Matba't al-Najah al-Jadida.

Saadi, Said Mohamed, and Abdelkader Berrada. 1992. "Le grand capital privé marocain." In *Le Maroc actuel: Une modernisation au miroir de la tradition?,* edited by Jean-Claude Santucci, 325–92. Paris: CNRS.

Sabbagh, Suha. 1996. Introduction to *Arab Women: Between Defiance and Restraint,* edited by Suha Sabbagh, xi–xxvi. New York: Olive Branch Press.

Said, Edward W. 1978. *Orientalism.* New York: Pantheon Books.

Saldbury, Julia. 1998. *"Other Kinds of Dreams": Black Women's Organizations and the Politics of Transformation.* New York: Routledge.

Salime, Zakia. 1997. "L'entreprise féminine à Fès, une tradition." In *Initiatives féminines,* edited by A. Belarbi, 31–46. Casablanca: Le Fennec.

———. 2000. "Femmes-politique, alliance difficile: Parole de jeunes." In *Femmes et democratie: La grande question,* edited by Aicha Belarbi, 37–66. Casablanca: Le Fennec.

———. 2007. "The 'War on Terrorism': Appropriation and Subversion by Moroccan Women." *Signs: Journal of Women and Culture in Society* 33(1): 1–24.

———. 2010. "Securing the Market, Pacifying Civil Society, Empowering Women: The Middle Partnership Initiative." *Sociological Forum* 25 (4): 725–45.

Schild, Veronica. 1998. "New Subjects of Rights? Women's Movements and the Construction of Citizenship in the 'New Democracies.'" In *Cultures of Politics, Politics of Cultures: Re-visioning Latin American Social Movements,* edited by Sonia E. Alvarez, Evelina Dagnino, and Arturo Escobar, 93–117. Boulder, Colo.: Westview Press.

Scott, Joan Wallash. 2002. "Feminist Reverberations." *differences: A Journal of Feminist Cultural Studies* 13(3): 1–23.

Sered, Suzan Starr. 2000. "'Women' as Symbol and Women as Agents: Gendered Religious Discourses and Practices." In *Revisioning Gender,* edited by Myra Marx Ferree, Judith Lorber, and Beth Hess, 193–221. New York: Rowman and Littlefield.

Sharabi, Hassan. 1988. *Neopatriarchy: A Theory of Distorted Change in Arab Society.* Oxford: Oxford University Press.

Sharama, Kalpana, and Ammu Jospeh, eds. 2003. *Terror, Counter Terror: Women Speak Out.* London: Zed Books.

Skali, Loubna. 2006. *Through a Local Prism: Gender, Globalization, and Identity in Moroccan Women's Magazines.* Lexington, Mass.: Lexington Books.

Slyomovics, Suzan. 1996. "Hassiba Ben Bouali, If You Could See Our Algeria: Women and Public Space in Algeria." In *Arab Women: Between Defiance and Restraint,* edited by Suha Sabbagh, 211–20. New York: Olive Branch Press.

Snow, David A., and Robert Benford. 1992. "Master Frames and Cycles of Protest." In *Social Movements: Perspectives and Issues,* edited by Steven Buechler and F. Kurt Cylke, 456–72. New York: McGraw-Hill.

Springtime of Equality. 2002. *Equal to Equal.* Rabat: El Maarif al-Jadida.

Staggenborg, Suzanne. 1995. "Can Feminist Organizations Be Effective?" In *Feminist Organizations: Harvest of the New Women's Movement,* edited by Myra Marx Ferree and Patricia Yancey Martin, 339–55. Philadelphia: Temple University Press.

Stamatopoulou, Elissavet. 1995. "Women's Rights and the United Nations." In *Women's Rights, Human Rights: International Feminist Perspectives,* edited by Julie Stone Peters and Andrea Wolper, 36–48. New York: Routledge.

Stowasser, Barbara F. 1993. "Women's Issues in Modern Islamic Thought." In *Arab Women Old Boundaries, New Frontiers,* edited by Judith E. Tucker, 3–28. Bloomington: Indiana University Press.

Strassberg, Barbara Ann. 2004. "A Pandemic of Terror and Terror of a Pandemic: American Cultural Responses to HIV/AIDS and Bioterrorism." *Zygon* 39(2): 435–63.

Swidler, Ann. 1995. "Cultural Power and Social Movements." In *Social Movements and Culture,* edited by Hank Johnston and Bert Klandermans, 25–37. Minneapolis: University of Minnesota Press.

Taarji, Hinde. 1992. *Les voilées de l'Islam.* Casablanca: EDIF.

Tarrow, Sydney, 1989. *Struggle, Politics, and Reform: Collective Action, Social Movements, and Cycles of Protest.* Ithaca: Cornell University. Center for International Studies.

———. 1994. *Power in Movement: Social Movements, Collective Action, and Politics.* Cambridge: Cambridge University Press.

Taylor, Verta, and Nancy Whittier. 1992. "Collective Identity in Social Movement Communities: Lesbian Feminist Mobilization." In *Frontiers in Social Movement Theory,* edited by Aldon D. Morris and Carol McClurg Mueller, 104–29. New Haven: Yale University Press.

———. 1995. "Analytical Approaches to Social Movement Culture: The Culture of the Women's Movement." In *Social Movements and Culture,* edited by Hank Johnston and Bert Klandermans, 163–86. Minneapolis: University of Minnesota Press.

Thamānia Mars Collective. 1993. "Journals for an Emerging Women's Movement (Morocco)." In *Alternative Media: Linking Global and Local,* edited by Peter Lewis, 61–72. Report on Media and Mass Communication. New York: UNESCO Publishing.

Tibi, Bassam. 1995. *The Crisis of Modern Islam: A Preindustrial Culture in the Scientific-Technological Age.* Ann Arbor, Mich.: UMI.

———. 1998. *The Challenge of Fundamentalism.* Berkeley: University of California Press.

———. 2001. *Islam between Culture and Politics.* New York: Palgrave.

Tohidi, Nayereh. 1991. "Gender and Islamic Fundamentalism: Feminist Politics in Iran." In *Third World Women and the Politics of Feminism,* edited by Chandra Talpade Mohanty, Ann Russo, and Lourdes Torres, 251–67. Bloomington: Indiana University Press.

Tozy, Mohamed. 1999. *Al-Malakya wal-Islam al-Siyassi.* Casablanca: Le Fennec.

Treacher, Amal, and Shukrallah Hala. 2001. "Preface to the Realm of the Possible: Middle Eastern Women in Political and Social Spaces." *Feminist Review* 69:1–12.

Trimbur, John. 1993. "Articulation Theory and the Problem of Determination: A Reading of 'Lives on the Boundary.'" *JAC* 13(1): 33–50.

Tucker, Judith E., ed. 1993. *Arab Women: Old Boundaries, New Frontiers.* Bloomington: Indian University Press.

UNDP (United Nations Development Program). 1990. *Human Development Report.* New York: Oxford University Press.

Wadud, Amina. 1999. *Quran and Women: Rereading the Sacred Texts from a Women's Perspective.* Oxford: Oxford University Press.

Walker, Alice. 1983. *In Search of Our Mothers' Gardens: Womanist Prose.* New York: Harvest Books.

Wallerstein, Emmanuel. 1999. "States? Sovereignty? The Dilemmas of Capitalists in an Age of Transition." In *States and Sovereignty in the Global Economy,* edited by David A. Smith, Dorothy J. Solinger, and Steven C. Topik, 20–33. New York: Routledge.

Waltz, Suzan. 1995. *Human Rights and Reform: Changing the Face of North African Politics.* Berkeley: University of California Press.

Warren, Kay. 1998. "Indigenous Movements as a Challenge to the Unified Social Movement Paradigm for Guatemala." In *Cultures of Politics, Politics of Culture: Re-visioning Latin American Social Movements,* edited by Sonia E. Alvarez, Evelina Dagnino, and Arturo Escobar, 165–95. Boulder, Colo.: Westview Press.

Waterbury, John. 1970. *The Commander of the Faithful: The Moroccan Political Elite.* New York: Columbia University Press.

Willis, Michael. 1999. "Between Alternance and Makhzen: Al-Tawhid wa al-Islah's Entry into Moroccan Politics." *Journal of North African Studies* 4(3): 45–80.

Yamani, Mai. 1996. Introduction to *Feminism and Islam: Legal and Literary Perspectives,* edited by M. Yamani, 11–27. New York: New York University Press.

Yassine, Abdessalam. 1998. *Islamiser la modernité.* Rabat: Al Ofok.

Yassine, Nadia. 2003. *Toutes voiles dehors.* Casablanca: Le Fennec.

Young, Marion. 2003. "The Logic of Masculinist Protection: Reflections on the Current Security State." *Signs: Journal of Women in Culture and Society* 29(1): 1–25.

Yudice, George. 1998. "The Globalization of Culture and the New Civil Society." In *Cultures of Politics, Politics of Cultures: Re-visioning Latin American Social Movements,* edited by Sonia E. Alvarez, Evelina Dagnino, and Arturo Escobar, 353–97. Boulder, Colo.: Westview Press.

Zayzafoon, Lamia Ben Youssef. 2005. *The Production of the Muslim Woman.* Lanham, Md.: Lexington Books.

Zeghal, Malika. 2005. *Les islamistes marocains: Le défi à la monarchie.* Casablanca: Le Fennec.

Zeleza, Paul. 1997. "Gender Biases in African Historiography." In *Engendering African Social Sciences,* edited by Ayesha M. Imam, Amina Mama, and Fatou Sow, 81–115. Dakar: Codesria.

Zerai, Assata, and Zakia Salime. 2005. "A Black Feminist Analysis of Responses to War, Racism, and Repression." *Critical Sociology* 32(2–3): 503–26.

Zubaida, Sami. 1987. "The Quest for the Islamic State: Islamic Fundamentalism in Egypt and Iran." In *Studies in Religious Fundamentalism,* edited by Lionel Caplan, 25–50. London: Macmillan.

———. 2004. "Islam and Nationalism: Continuities and Contradictions." *Nations and Nationalism* 10(4): 407–20.

Index

Yassine, Abdessalam, 17, 126; decision-
making powers of, 9; memorandum
from, 7–8
Yassine, Nadia, xvii, 8, 17, 18, 79, 123,
130, 132, 142, 146, 153nn10
15; charges against, 125, 145; on
femininity/feminism, 20; march

and, 19, 80; motherhood and,
124; on *mudawwana,* 19; prayers
for, 126

Zirari, Najia, 84–85, 120, 139
Zoellick, Robert, 114
Zohra, Fatima, 65

ZAKIA SALIME is assistant professor of sociology and women's and gender studies at Rutgers University.

(continued from page ii)

DATE DUE